A.T.Q. STEWART was born in Belfast, where he was educated at the Royal Belfast Academical Institution and Queen's University. After some years in teaching, he returned to Queen's as a lecturer, and was appointed Reader in Irish History in 1975. He took early retirement in 1990 to devote more time to writing, and he is a frequent broadcaster on radio and television. He was consultant to both BBC Television's *The History of Ireland* and Thames Televisions's *The Troubles* and was a presenter for the Channel 4 series *The Divided Kingdom*. Since 1970 he has contributed to many encyclopedias and works of reference and written articles for newspapers and journals, including the *Spectator*, the *Irish Arts Review*, *History Ireland*, the *Irish Times*, *Irish Independent*, *Sunday Tribune* and the *Belfast Telegraph*. In 1977 he was a joint winner of the first Christopher Ewart-Biggs Memorial Prize for *The Narrow Ground*. He is married with two sons and lives in Belfast.

# A
# DEEPER
# SILENCE

The
Hidden Origins
of the
United Irishmen

A.T.Q. STEWART

THE
BLACKSTAFF
PRESS

BELFAST

First published in hardback in 1993 by
Faber and Faber Limited
This Blackstaff Press edition is a photolithographic facsimile
of the first edition printed by Clays Limited

First published in paperback in 1998 by
The Blackstaff Press Limited
3 Galway Park, Dundonald, Belfast BT16 2AN, Northern Ireland

A.T.Q. Stewart has asserted his right under the
Copyright, Designs and Patents Act 1988 to be identified as
the author of this work.

Printed in Ireland by ColourBooks Limited

A CIP catalogue record for this book
is available from the British Library

ISBN 0-85640-642-2

*In memoriam patris*

*vires ultra sortemque senectae*

But this was not all. The Volunteers of Belfast, of the first or green company, were pleased . . . to elect me an honorary member of their corps, a favour which they were very delicate in bestowing . . .

> Theobald Wolfe Tone, 1791


And in the eighteenth century the pauses are still longer and the silences yet deeper.

> C. Litton Falkiner, 1909

# Contents

# CONTENTS

# Acknowledgements

My thanks are expressed to Dr Anthony Malcomson, Deputy Keeper of the Records of Northern Ireland, for permission to quote from documents in his charge, including the Bruce papers, donated by the late Michael Bruce, and the Caldwell papers, donated by the late Miss Grace Crosby. Mr Michael Duffin has kindly allowed me to quote extensively from the correspondence of his ancestor, Dr William Drennan. A catalogue of books belonging to Alexander Stewart, and some of his business letters in the Londonderry papers, are cited by permission of the Lady Mairi Bury. For similar privileges I wish to thank the Librarians of Edinburgh University Library (Black MSS), the Queen's University of Belfast (microfilm of Hutcheson letters) and the Linen Hall Library (Joy MSS).

Some writers of a scientific turn of mind make life difficult for their fellow scribes. Thus William Poundstone in *Labyrinths of Reason* (p. 135) observes: 'We have all seen those overly-effacing prefaces in which the author (after thanking spouse and typist) takes responsibility for the "inevitable" errors.' From such innocent disclaimers logicians have constructed what they call 'the paradox of the preface' which can be used to demonstrate that no such thing as non-fiction exists. I will not therefore attempt to categorize this book, or speculate on the possibility of errors. I merely record that in the course of writing it I have incurred many obligations. The first, as always, is to Professor J.C. Beckett. Many others are indicated in the Notes and Bibliography, but I owe a special debt, for assistance in my research, to John Killen of the Linen Hall Library, Bill Maguire of the Ulster Museum and Gerry Slater of the Public Record Office of Northern Ireland. Louis Lord must take the blame for persuading me to return to the Age of Enlightenment, but he has made amends by reading many drafts of the manuscript, and it owes much to his vigilant eye.

Finally, I will not be deterred by the speculations of philosophers from thanking John and Valerie Burnside for their skills at the word-processor, or my wife and sons for their affectionate and constant, but never uncritical, support.

A. T. Q. STEWART, *Belfast, June* 1992

# Proem

The American came in just as dawn was breaking over the Copelands, a toy ship etched against the eastern sky. As the light strengthened, and the waters of the lough turned from pewter to silver, she was revealed as a square-rigged sloop of war, with royals and top-gallants and a purposeful set of studding-sails. Her bows were raked for speed, and a bright yellow stripe ran the whole length of her topworks. In mid-morning she stood in towards Kilroot Point, and her commander trained his glass on His Majesty's warship *Drake* lying in the Carrickfergus Roads.

In the course of the preceding week he had carried out a series of exploits that created a legend in naval history, and made immortal his assumed name, which was John Paul Jones. The British regarded him as a privateer, preying on merchant shipping along the northern coasts, and he is still so described in school textbooks. In transatlantic eyes he was one of the first naval officers commissioned by the country which was soon to call itself the United States of America, and his sloop *Ranger* was one of its first warships. His real name was plain John Paul, and he was a Scot, 'the son of Mr Craik's gardener' at Arbigland in Galloway.[1] He knew these waters like the back of his hand. On this bitterly cold morning in April 1778, when snow lay 'in three kingdoms',[2] he was at the entrance to Belfast Lough and he was persuading his half-mutinous crew that he could capture the *Drake*.

Captain Burden, the *Drake*'s commander, a superannuated officer who was not in the best of health, had been warned that an American privateer was in the offing, and he lost no time in investigating the stranger. Despite her stylish raking and undercut stern, he could not be certain that she was not an innocent trader. A boat was put off, in the charge of a lieutenant. Jones kept his crew below decks and his stern to the gig, so that the lieutenant could not see his gun-ports. When the British sailors went on board they were politely told that they were prisoners of the American Navy.

The *Drake*'s signals were not answered. Gradually she was lured out to the mouth of the lough where Jones considered that he had more room to manoeuvre. The cat-and-mouse game went on for most of the afternoon, and the sun was already beginning to decline when Jones decided that the time had come for action. Abruptly he brought the *Ranger* athwart the *Drake*'s bows and raked her decks with grapeshot. The fight was 'warm, close and obstinate',[3] as Jones later reported, and lasted for an hour and five minutes, at which point Captain Burden was killed by a musket-shot in the head, and the *Drake* struck her colours and was boarded. Among those mortally wounded in the encounter was a young naval officer, Lieutenant Dobbs of Dobbs Castle, a member of a prominent local family, who had gone aboard the *Drake* just before the action began.[4] Jones paid every respect to the fallen officers. 'I buryed them in a spacious grave', he later wrote to Lady Selkirk, 'with the Honours due to the memory of the brave.'[5]

At sunset the gentlemen of Donaghadee watched the *Ranger* tow her prize through the still sound between the Great Copeland and Orlock Head, and the following day both ships were hove-to off Ballywater. On that day Jones achieved two other feats of incidental significance. He gave his name to a dance in which you capture a new partner when the music stops. And he changed the course of Irish history.

# I
# THE GREEN COMPANY

# I

# The Day Approaching

Or so, at least, some history books would have us believe. In time Jones's incursion came to be associated in the popular mind with the origins of the Irish Volunteer movement, which had such momentous consequences for Ireland during the next two decades. The government did nothing to discourage the impression that the patriotic citizens of Belfast had been galvanized into martial ardour by his impudent raid. It was true that the battle had been followed with keen interest on the coast,[1] and signal fires had been lit on both shores of Belfast Lough, but for reasons of contemporary politics the sympathies of the watchers were divided. The people of Antrim and Down, overwhelmingly Presbyterian, had particular incentives to identify with the American cause, being irked by civil disabilities which led them to compare their situation to that of the colonists. A contemporary ballad which relates the story of the encounter made no bones about these divided loyalties:

> Now while we cheer our own brave crew
> We'll give one for the Yankee, O!
> In honour bright both ships did fight,
> That day off Carrickfergus, O![2]

The prospect of an invasion by the French was quite a different matter. In the autumn of 1778 the mayor of Belfast, Stewart Banks (his official name was the 'sovereign'), was sufficiently alarmed by the activities of French and Spanish privateers on the coast to apply to Dublin Castle for military assistance to defend the town. The answer he is supposed to have received became a popular legend. The Chief Secretary, Sir Richard Heron, regretted that he could afford no other assistance than 'half a troop of dismounted horse and half a company of invalides'. The phrase was long savoured. 'Abandoned by Government in the hour of danger', wrote Lord Charlemont, the Lord Lieutenant of Co. Armagh, 'the inhabitants of Belfast were left to their own

defence, and boldly and instantly undertook it; associations were
formed, arms were purchased; uniforms were provided; officers were
chosen; parades were appointed and every diligence exerted towards
the necessary acquirement of military skill and discipline.'[3]

The truth, as usual, was more untidy. Popular memory elided the
dates and foreshortened a complex train of events. The date on the
original muster-roll of the Belfast First Volunteer Company stands
uncompromisingly as 17 March 1778, a whole month before John
Paul Jones's raid, and five months before Banks made his appeal to
the government.[4] In that request he specifically refers to the exertions
which the citizens had already made on their own behalf. Thirteen
years were still to elapse before the company would adopt patriot
colours and call itself 'the Green Company'. To begin with, it was not
green but red. In smart new uniforms of scarlet turned up with black
velvet, black hats, white waistcoats and breeches, its members paraded
to church on a Sunday late in June, and listened to 'a very sensible and
polite' sermon commending the spirit which had led to the company's
formation.[5]

A second company was raised in April, on the eve of Jones's raid.
Scorning to be called second, it styled itself simply the Belfast Volunteer Company, thus generating confusion for historians. It adopted a
blue uniform faced with blue, and blue hats adorned with gold lace.[6]
The 'Blue Company' it was to remain through all the vicissitudes of
the following decades. There were other Belfast companies, but the
Green and the Blue always took pride of place, and from the outset
there was a rivalry between them, underpinned by social and other
distinctions.

The Volunteers of Belfast had thus been in existence for several
months when Banks, on the sudden rumour of invasion, made his
appeal to Dublin Castle. The reply he received was neither as despair-
ing nor as unconcerned as legend depicted. What the Chief Secretary
actually wrote was that *for the moment* the Lord Lieutenant could
send no further military aid *than a troop or two of horse or part of a
company of invalids* to augment the two troops actually stationed at
Belfast. It was a formal communication, not a cry of helplessness, and
the Lord Lieutenant was at pains to add that he very much approved
the spirit of the inhabitants of Belfast in forming themselves into
companies for the defence of the town.[7]

In this he was being disingenuous. In reality there were few things of which John Hobart, Earl of Buckinghamshire, approved less, but he dared not say so in public. The initial effect of the war with the American colonists had been drastically to reduce the number of troops in Ireland, a matter of some importance for the stability of Irish society. The soldier was also the policeman of the eighteenth century, or could be if occasion demanded, and when service overseas relieved him of this duty, the landed gentry reacted nervously. Menaced by the activities of Whiteboys, Oakboys, Steelboys and other shadowy agrarian organizations, the gentry put pressure on the government to raise a new militia. A Militia Bill was duly introduced in the Irish House of Commons, but no practical steps were taken to implement it.[8] In the third year of the American war, Ireland was without adequate forces either to maintain internal order or to repel foreign invasion. Of the 12,000 soldiers considered necessary to garrison the island, only a third remained, and these were concentrated in two or three large barracks in the South. Worse still, the Irish executive was bankrupt, obliged to suspend all salaries and pensions and to borrow £20,000 from La Touche, the Dublin banker.[9]

In these circumstances, some members of the House of Commons declared that, if authorized, they would raise independent companies of Volunteers among their own tenants. The Lord Lieutenant advised London that this offer should be accepted, and that the government should supply them with arms, accoutrements and pay. He soon discovered that even such limited support was beyond the financial means of his executive. The government then determined, in Charlemont's words, to steer with a current it could not stem, 'to make use of the volunteers as a sure protection against invasion, and to take every possible method of gaining their confidence'. Sixteen thousand muskets were issued from the arsenal and divided among the County Lieutenants for distribution to corps throughout Ireland.[10]

The precise time and place of the birth of the Volunteer movement which was to have so significant an impact on Irish politics are difficult to determine, since almost every part of the country subsequently claimed precedence. Some historians would say that it really began when the inhabitants of Carbery, Bantry and Bere in Co. Cork formed a Volunteer company in 1774, or when the Protestants of Birr and Roscrea formed companies in 1776 to suppress the Whiteboys. In King's County (now Offaly) a corps of light infantry was raised by a Mr Tottenham, who had once served in the army and had 'an old attachment to red clothes'.[11] Most of the companies in the list which Thomas MacNevin compiled in the nineteenth century have 1778 or 1779 as the date of their incorporation, but a few are older.[12] There can be little doubt, however, that it was in 1778, and in the North, that individual companies began to form an articulate Volunteer association, and it was the Belfast companies in particular that created and maintained a radical initiative in politics over the next twenty years.

Within a year there were thirty-four companies in Co. Down and twenty-one in Co. Antrim, with an approximate total of 3,500 men. They received no pay from government and took no oath. They elected their own officers. Every man provided his own uniform and weapons and some of the corps acquired artillery. At the zenith of their fame the Volunteers boasted a nominal roll of 100,000 men from the whole of Ireland, and of these 34,152 belonged to the Province of Ulster. In July 1781 the Northern regiments mounted a three-day mock battle to defend Belfast from an invading force. Visiting observers were immensely impressed, and one of them reported his satisfaction that in three days and four nights he had not heard of one individual being drunk or disorderly 'except a lord and two blackguard sailors'.[13]

One company in Co. Armagh adopted for its colours the device of a cock crowing, and the motto: 'Arise! the day approaching'. Another chose the Irish harp and the motto: 'I am new-strung and *will* be heard'.[14]

Volunteering might seem to enter Irish history as a national event in 1778, but in truth there had always been a reason of one sort or another for raising Volunteers in Ireland, and especially in the North. There Volunteers had been hastily assembled in the first shock of the rebellion of 1641 which all but swept away the Ulster Plantation; in the protracted civil war which had followed; and again in the turbulent days of Derry and the Boyne at the end of the century. They had been levied during the Jacobite scares of 1711 and 1715; and in 1745, on a rumour that Prince Charles Edward and his Highlanders were preparing boats for an invasion of Antrim, Belfast raised two Volunteer companies and sent them to strengthen the defences of the great Norman castle of Carrickfergus, 10 miles to the north-east, on the shore of the lough.

A letter in the Joy manuscripts captures the *frisson* of that year. It was written by Henry Joy to his brother Robert in Belfast.

Carrickfergus Castle, October 30, 1745

Dear Bro^r.

We are sent here to keep Garrison, how long we are to remain I can't tell. There are upwards of 80 volunteers and 90 Independents of us here and in the highest spirits, and I don't believe this place was better garrisoned these many years. The reasons of our coming here you'll find in our Paper enclosed. There is no getting furloes and I don't know how we'll get our business managed and my Father begs you may come down – there are 4 out of our house, viz^t. Father, I, Mich^l and Billy Dunn . . . You must excuse my seldom writing, we are prodigiously hurried and in continual alarms.

Yo^rs in great haste,
Henry Joy[15]

The Joys were an enterprising family of Huguenot stock who contributed much to eighteenth-century Belfast, not least in compiling materials for its history. Francis Joy, the father of Henry and Robert, had migrated to Belfast early in the century from the tiny Co. Antrim village of Killead, married the daughter of the town sovereign, and set up as an attorney. In 1737, when he acquired a small printing-press in settlement of a debt, he used it to produce the town's first newspaper at the sign of 'The Peacock' in Bridge Street. *The Belfast Newsletter* still appears as a morning paper, and claims the longest history of continuous printing in the British Isles. In the year of the Jacobite alarm Joy bought a paper mill in Ballymena, and with it produced enough paper not only for his own press but for the needs of the whole Province of Ulster and far beyond.[16]

The Volunteer companies were re-embodied in the autumn of 1756 when there were serious riots in Belfast provoked by shortages of grain and provisions. Some of the rioters were imprisoned, and when a mob gathered to try to release them,

the alarm drum was beat, and in less than half an hour, 200 of the principal inhabitants appeared in arms, and an order being signed by the sovereign and another Justice of the Peace they marched under the command of Stewart Banks, Esq, Captain of the Guard, through the principal streets and suburbs of the town and searched the houses of several ringleaders of the late riots, against whom examinations had been lodged.[17]

In the following year Banks was sworn in as sovereign of the borough, and, immediately after, his company of Volunteers received him under arms and presented him with a fine sword and a scarlet silk belt on which was wrought in gold twist 'The compliment of the Young Volunteer Company of Belfast to Stewart Banks, Esq., their Captain, Sept. 29, 1757'. The company thanked him for his care in having them trained to meet any emergency. They could scarcely have foreseen how soon that emergency was to arise.[18]

# 2

## In the Hour of Danger

On the morning of 21 February 1760 the inhabitants of Island Magee, a small peninsula just to the north of Belfast, awoke to the astonishing sight of three French warships standing inshore towards the Bay of Carrickfergus.[1] They were the forty-eight-gun *Maréchal de Belle-Isle* and the smaller *Blonde* and *Terpsichore*, and towards 10 o'clock they came to anchor scarcely 3 miles from the town. The garrison of Carrickfergus consisted of four companies of the 62nd Regiment of Foot, commanded by Lieutenant-Colonel Jennings, and at that moment they were exercising in a field half a mile south of the town on the Belfast road. Some French prisoners of war were being held in the castle (the Seven Years War was still in progress) and at 11.15, following an established routine, a guard was made up and marched to relieve the soldiers on duty there, while the rest of the men resumed their drill. Soon afterwards news was brought to them that the ships in the bay, at first taken to be East Indiamen, were putting off cutters crowded with sailors and soldiers.

Colonel Jennings had no way of knowing whether these soldiers were friends or foes, but he acted with admirable dispatch, sending word to the Castle that both guards were to continue under arms, and marching his men briskly back to the market-place. He then sent his adjutant, Lieutenant Benjamin Hall, and a small party out to reconnoitre. From the high ground overlooking the sea, where they cautiously stationed themselves, Hall could see soldiers in French uniform disembarking in great numbers and forming up in companies on the shore. He hurried back to Carrickfergus with this alarming intelligence, and the mayor, Willoughby Chaplin, at once called on Jennings to defend the town.[2]

Jennings was unable to see how he could do this. He pointed out that all attempts at resistance would be futile. His force was too small; he had only 200 men, the rest of the regiment, under Major-General Strode, being stationed at Belfast. The Castle was in a ruinous state, with a 50-foot breach in the sea wall and not a single cannon mounted. The mayor angrily insisted, and at last Jennings gave way. The men of the 62nd prepared to make a brave token stand.

The story of Thurot's landing at Carrickfergus has usually been told from an Irish perspective and indeed largely as an isolated and interesting episode of local history. We now know a great deal more about its complex background. The war which began in 1756 has been seen as 'a decisive stage in the struggle between England and France for world colonial pre-eminence',[3] and the key factor in England's ultimate victory was naval strength. The incident at Carrick-fergus was a small part of a much larger strategy, and in itself an example of the French failure to win and retain command of the seas.

Legend holds that François Thurot was really an Irishman called Farrell and that this is why he knew the Irish waters so well. There does not seem to be any evidence for this. It has been established that he was born on 21 July 1727 in Nuits St-Georges, a town now synonymous with good burgundy, and that his father was, among other things, a wine merchant. Apprenticed to a surgeon in Dijon, Thurot left home after some obscure scandal and in 1744 joined the privateer *Le Cerf Volant*. In August of that year the vessel was captured and he became a prisoner of war in England, but he escaped in 1745 and crossed the Channel in a small boat. This so impressed the Duc de Belle-Isle, who had himself been an English prisoner, that he undertook to give the young man a proper naval education. From being the great man's protégé, Thurot in time became his friend and confidant, and in 1748 he was given his first command.

When war with England broke out again in 1756 Thurot was appointed *lieutenant des frégates du roi*. He then became a highly successful privateer, capturing no fewer than sixty prizes in the same year. Bankers and merchants began to invest in his expeditions. In 1757 he was given command of a squadron of privateer frigates, one of which was the *Maréchal de Belle-Isle*, named after his patron. With this squadron he began to raid English shipping in the Baltic, the North Sea and round the shores of Ireland, perfecting the technique of never staying in one area long enough for the Admiralty to send a fleet after him. In the late summer of 1758 he anchored for several days in Lough Swilly and took on supplies.

This record persuaded Belle-Isle that Thurot had a key part to play in a projected French invasion of the British Isles. He was told that 'it has been decided to employ you on an important mission for the king, which could contribute decisively to the addition of your own fortune,'[4] and he was summoned to Versailles. He was received by Louis XV and promoted to *capitaine de vaisseau*. While at Versailles he also became a kind of popular idol, as John Paul Jones was to be twenty years later.

Thurot's 'important mission' was to lead what would now be called a commando raid on the British coast, involving six vessels and 1,500 men. This force would land, cause as much destruction as possible and re-embark before the enemy could marshal an effective retaliation. It was intended to divert attention from the much more formidable French invasion being planned elsewhere. At the same time Thurot was allowed to form a private company to capitalize on the profits of the expedition. The state provided the soldiers, arms, ammunition and two warships, the *Blonde* and the *Terpsichore*. Paris bankers, individual merchants and smaller investors furnished the *Maréchal de Belle-Isle* and two more frigates and a cutter, along with substantial working capital.

Thurot's chief problem was to recruit enough sailors for the expedition, especially as the French Atlantic fleet was being assembled by Admiral Conflans at Brest and another invasion force was being prepared in Brittany, but by July 1759 he had his required complement, which incidentally included some Irish sailors. The 1,500 troops were recruited from six crack regiments of guards.[5] They were assembled and reviewed by their commander, Brigadier Flobert, a seasoned soldier in his fifties, who had served in the Spanish and French armies and had given up command of the Genoese army in 1758 to serve his country in time of war.

From the outset it was clear that Thurot and Flobert disliked each other intensely and had different opinions on how the expedition should be conducted. Flobert resented being under the command of a sailor, and one whose humble origins he despised. The King's orders made it clear that while at sea all personnel would obey the orders of the naval commander who would decide the time and place of landing. Only when the troops were fully disembarked would the military officers take command.

Tedious and complicated financial arrangements, and the settling of Thurot's debts, delayed their departure until September. Flobert complained bitterly about Thurot's inactivity, while Thurot alleged that Flobert was going soft in the head; 'he worries about everything, wastes his time and finishes nothing that he has begun'.[6] By now the enemy had got wind of the enterprise and an English squadron was gathering outside Dunkirk harbour. There was genuine concern in Britain that Thurot's ships were part of an invasion fleet bound for Ireland. Thurot *did* have Ireland in mind, but secret instructions identified his targets as Newcastle and Bristol, with alternatives should he be able to take advantage of English naval deployments. Dunkirk was full of English spies, and Thurot's own agent in England was able to tell him that all his instructions had been sold to the English, who expected him to land between Newcastle and the Scottish border, destroy the port and blow up the coal-mines. Meanwhile provisions were being consumed, soldiers were falling sick and debts were accumulating.

It was not until 5 October that Thurot, taking advantage of bad weather, was able to slip out of Dunkirk and reach Ostend, where he shook off the English frigates left to shadow him, and his little squadron vanished into the mists of the North Sea. While the English searched for him there, he slipped into the Kattegat, reaching Gothenburg on 26 October. Thereafter the autumn storms dispersed the fleet. A rendezvous had been arranged at Bergen in Norway, but there Thurot had to wait in vain for weeks, since some of the damaged vessels had limped home to Dunkirk. He next sailed for the Faroes where he encountered further storms. A council of the officers on New Year's Day 1760 was overwhelmingly in favour of turning back, but Thurot was determined to carry out an offensive operation of some kind and he received support from Cavagnac, Flobert's second-in-command. He wanted to raid Londonderry, but contrary winds forced him to abandon the plan. On 12 February, after a riot on the *Maréchal de Belle-Isle*, he gave the order for a course to be set to take them back past the north of Scotland.

On the following day the winds went around. Secretly harbouring the idea of another attempt on Derry, Thurot declared that they would return to France through the Irish Sea after all. The captains of the *Blonde* and *Terpsichore* protested that their ships were in no condition to face the English fleet in St George's Channel. The soldiers on the *Terpsichore* then took control and ordered the captain to sail away from the others. Furious, Thurot pursued her in the *Maréchal de Belle-*

*Isle*, trained his guns on the frigate and forced her to surrender. He promised to land as soon as possible and collect provisions.

Next Flobert, discovering that they were in reality on course for Londonderry and not the North Channel, tried to arrest Thurot and take command of the ship. Thurot retired to his cabin and emerged with a pair of loaded pistols. Flobert ordered his grenadiers to arrest him, but rescinded the order when they hesitated. Thurot suggested nailing the King's orders to the mast, but compromised by having them read out instead. On the surface the quarrel was patched up. But once more the elements intervened and the ships were blown back towards Scotland.

On 16 February, flying English colours, the vessels anchored off Islay. Though he had been deceived into putting out in a boat to greet the ships, a local gentleman, Archibald Macdonald, hospitably entertained Thurot and his officers to dinner. When he told them about the French defeat at Quiberon in November, the Frenchmen dropped their knives and forks on the table and bowed their heads in silence.

Louis XV's orders had expressly forbidden any attack on Scotland, a potential ally, and Thurot insisted on leaving bills of credit for the provisions collected on the island. The three vessels entered the North Channel on 20 February and that evening Thurot told a dumbfounded Flobert that they would enter Carrickfergus Bay during the night and land at dawn at Whitehouse. He was undoubtedly thinking that to put a ransom on the prosperous town of Belfast was his last chance to avert personal financial ruin. Flobert agreed to attack Belfast, but only if Thurot acquiesced in *his* plan, which was to land instead at Kilroot and take Carrickfergus first.

The landing force, now reduced to 600 effective troops, was given the last of the French brandy before being put ashore. Not surprisingly, Flobert was eager to take command at last and see some military action. He immediately led 200 of his French guards through Kilroot, entered Carrickfergus by the Water Gate on the east, and tried to rush the Castle. The guards, attempting to smash the gates with axes, suffered casualties from the 62nd's first volley, and Flobert, wounded in the leg by a bullet, had to be carried into the shelter of a neighbouring house. Command of the French was then taken by a young nobleman, the Marquis d'Estrées. It is said that as he came up the High Street, sword in his right hand, a child ran out of a house in the path of the advancing French troops. D'Estrées scooped the child up with his left arm and carried it to the door of the nearest house. A few minutes later he was killed at the Castle gates.

Meanwhile Cavagnac had assembled the main force in proper formation and advanced slowly on the town. Before they arrived, however, Commandant du Soulier had taken command of the assault and called upon the garrison to surrender. He proposed to destroy the town if they refused, but at that moment an officer emerged from the Castle under a flag of truce. Articles of capitulation were drawn up and signed by du Soulier and Jennings. The garrison would be deemed prisoners of war, but would be allowed to stay in Ireland on parole. They were not to carry arms until repatriation. The French undertook not to plunder or burn the town or misuse its inhabitants. Jennings agreed that all possible care would be taken of any wounded officers or soldiers left behind when the French re-embarked. They were not to be treated as prisoners of war, but would be returned to France as soon as possible. These conditions turned out to be important and were scrupulously observed.[7]

Cavagnac had little to do but to occupy and secure the town, and that night Thurot anchored his three frigates close under the Castle walls. He came ashore in the morning and repeated his view that they must attack Belfast without delay. The French had lost nineteen men and had thirty wounded, against the loss of four by the defenders, with twelve wounded. It would be an expensive victory if Belfast was not taken. Once again, Flobert flatly contradicted Thurot, arguing that by now the militia would have been called out and that his soldiers were too weak to walk to Belfast. He was in no condition to proceed there himself.

Instead he proposed making a demand for provisions, which Carrickfergus could not supply. If Belfast responded favourably, the French would re-embark and not wreak havoc in Co. Antrim. Accordingly, the Rev. David Fullerton, a Presbyterian minister, left for Belfast accompanied by a French officer with a flag of truce and a letter to the sovereign demanding '30 hogsheads of Wine, 40 of Brandy, 60 barrels of Beer, 6,000 lbs of Bread and 60 bullocks'.[8] If these provisions were not forthcoming, the French proposed to burn Carrickfergus, then proceed to Belfast and burn it as well.

In Belfast the news of the French landing had caused alarm and confusion. Men sent their wives and children to the country and buried their valuables. Major-General Strode, doubting his ability to hold the town with his remaining battalions of the 62nd, called out the militia, then still in existence under the old militia laws, and sent an urgent dispatch to the Lord Lieutenant, the Duke of Bedford. The inhabitants of Belfast thought it prudent to comply at once with the French demands and loaded the provisions on to a lighter, but 'the weather being tempestuous the lighter could not sail down the lough that day'.[9]

This was on Friday, and on Saturday morning a message was sent to the commander of the French forces explaining the delay. Two lighters would sail with the evening tide if possible. It was very difficult to get anyone to man them, but one lighter managed to leave that afternoon. However, she was at once stopped and forced to heave-to by an Admiralty tender in the lough; the authorities were beginning to get a grip on the situation. The French reply was swift. If the provisions were not on board their ships by 8 o'clock on Sunday morning, they would hang Mr Fullerton, put the inhabitants of Carrickfergus to the sword and reduce the town to ashes. Then they would march on Belfast. The provisions were hastily loaded on to carts which set off along the Carrickfergus road.[10]

While these exchanges were going forward, something very remarkable was happening throughout the countryside. Bedford's first move had been to order four regiments of Foot and three regiments of Dragoons to assemble at Newry, but most of the Irish garrison was still quartered in the South, where the main French invasion was expected to take place. At the same time he wrote to the Prime Minister, the Duke of Newcastle, saying that he feared Belfast might fall and that the Carrickfergus landing, small in itself, might be the prelude to a full-scale invasion.[11]

In the event the first of these regular troop reinforcements did not reach Belfast until after the French had re-embarked. In the meantime, companies of Volunteers sprang up everywhere in Antrim and Down, and in Co. Armagh as well. Late on Friday evening the Antrim Volunteers marched into Belfast (Lieutenant James Finiston, commandant; four sergeants, four corporals and two drums). Lisburn Volunteers came to Belfast the same evening with some French prisoners under guard. Shane's Castle Volunteers arrived on Saturday night, well armed with nine rounds of cartridges, and were followed next day by seven pieces of small cannon, which were planted on the breastwork at Three Mile Water. Ballymena sent two companies, and from Broughshane came Captain John White's company, 'nine of them with scythes fixed on poles'.

An even greater number of companies was raised in Co. Down. Volunteers poured into Belfast from Purdy's Burn, Castlereagh, Hillsborough, Moira, Dromore, Waringstown and Magheralin, from Comber, Ballybeen, Killyleagh, Donaghadee, Downpatrick and Newry. Co. Armagh, farthest from the scene of the action, contributed five companies, including the Lurgan Volunteer troop of Dragoons and Volunteers from Armagh City who arrived all armed and on horseback at 10 o'clock on Sunday morning.

In Belfast itself Banks's Volunteers were reactivated and divided into three companies, the other two under the command of James Ross and John Brown. On Saturday morning they marched to the Three Mile Water, 'as did all the companies that were then arrived'. An entrenchment was dug near the Three Mile Water Bridge to defend the town from attack to the North and 'planted with some small ship cannon'.[12]

Meanwhile, with the Lord Lieutenant's permission, Lord Charlemont travelled to the invaded county to take charge of operations. He found Belfast crowded with defenders.

The appearance of the peasantry, who had thronged to its defence, many of whom were my own tenantry, was singular and formidable. They were drawn up in regular bodies, each with its chosen officers and formed in martial array; some few with old firelocks, but the greater number armed with what is called in Scotland the Lochaber axe, a scythe fixed longitudinally to the end of a long pole, a desperate weapon, which they seem determined to make desperate use of.[13]

Charlemont was extremely critical of Strode's handling of the military situation.

Unused to command, his orders were confused and contradictory. Upon the first arrival of the country auxiliaries, he had ordered a body of the best armed among them to march towards Carrickfergus with the avowed intention of attacking the French. They instantly and cheerfully obeyed, but by the time they had gotten half way, his mind had changed and he sent orders to them to halt. In this also he was obeyed and the corps lay upon their arms the whole night, unsheltered and exposed to the inclemency of the season. In the morning he was asked by a brother officer what he had done with this body of men; he replied he had forgotten them and desired that they might be recalled.[14]

In the event the Volunteers were not needed. Thurot declared that since Flobert did not propose to move against Belfast it would be pointless to stay any longer in the area. He had no intention of waiting for the English frigates. On the afternoon of 25 February the French troops began to re-embark. The cannon in the Castle were spiked and the powder and shot from the keep were thrown into the sea. The embarkation was not complete until the following day, and contrary winds kept the ships from putting to sea until 8 o'clock on the evening of 27 February. Flobert, Cavagnac and a dozen other wounded were left ashore under the terms of the capitulation. The mayor, Mr Chaplin, and three other local notables were taken away on board the *Maréchal de Belle-Isle*.

It was midnight before they cleared Carrickfergus Roads, and towards 4 in the morning they were intercepted by Captain John Elliot RN, commanding the *Aeolus, Pallas* and *Brilliant*. As the frigates closed in, Thurot put on sail and tried to run for it, but the English ships easily caught up with the heavy French vessels, foul from months at sea. Thurot signalled the *Blonde* and *Terpsichore* to rally, but they continued their course and the *Maréchal de Belle-Isle* turned to fight the three English ships alone. Thurot's only hope was to grapple the *Aeolus* and use his soldiers to board her, but the attempt to use the grappling-irons failed. The *Maréchal de Belle-Isle*'s mizzen mast was shot away and the ships collided. As they drifted apart, the English gunners continued to pour shot into Thurot's vessel below the water-line. She now had 6 feet of water in the hold, but Thurot refused his officers' plea to strike the colours. Instead he ordered his gunners to fire one more broadside. Moments later he was shot through the chest and died instantly. All the French vessels now surrendered and were rounded up.

Thurot, in accordance with his wishes, was buried at sea. As the sailors from the *Aeolus* scrambled aboard, his body, wrapped in the carpet from his cabin, was lowered into the water, and some days later it was washed ashore on the Mull of Galloway. Thurot was identified by his uniform and a silver snuff-box with his name engraved on the lid. Sir William Maxwell of Monteith had the body buried in Kirkmaiden churchyard with full military honours.

In 1791 the revolutionary Assemblée Nationale declared Thurot a Hero of the People and gave his daughter a state pension. His grave at Kirkmaiden cannot now be identified, but in 1960 members of COLDIN, a secret society to which Thurot belonged, placed a memorial plaque on the church, and in 1966 a party of French naval cadets laid a wreath there in his honour.[15]

Elliot took his prizes into Ramsay Bay in the Isle of Man. The French casualties were very heavy, between 250 and 300 men, and more than 1,100 French soldiers and sailors were brought ashore as prisoners. Men from the regiment of Artois were taken to Whitehaven and the sailors to Kinsale, but the majority of the soldiers were sent to Belfast, where they were 'received with every politeness'. Those officers who had taken the precaution of travelling with letters of credit found that these were readily accepted by the merchants of Belfast. This was not the end of the story, however. In some respects the prison authorities did not fulfil all the obligations of the articles of surrender, and committees were formed in Belfast to provide comforts for the French prisoners until such time as they were exchanged.

Charlemont arrived in Carrickfergus not long after the French had left and found that the whole episode was not without humour. 'A few ancient matrons' told him 'in terms at least as positive as querulous that the violation of their property was not the only species of violation which they had to lament'. He condoled with them; but to remedy their complaints was, of course, beyond his power. Flobert, delighted to find someone who could speak French, was eager to pour into Charlemont's ear the story of his tribulations. Was he not right to secure Carrickfergus first? Would Charlemont (*vous, milord, qui êtes du métier . . .*') have left such a strong place in his rear? Charlemont was wryly amused, both at the attribution to him of military experience and the over-estimate of the strength of Carrickfergus and its Castle.[16]

Soon Carrickfergus was to have a more remarkable visitor. John Wesley arrived there on 5 May 1760 on one of his interminable preaching circuits of the British Isles, and his *Journal* and correspondence are unexpected sources of eye-witness accounts of the French landing. After preaching in Belfast he travelled to Carrickfergus, 'where I willingly accepted of an invitation from a merchant in the town, Mr Cobham, to lodge at his house; the rather when I heard that M. Cavagnac, the French lieutenant-general, was still there'. He asked

Cavagnac if the French had really intended to burn the town. 'Jesu Maria! We never had such a thought,' was the reply. 'To burn, to destroy, cannot enter into the heart of a good man.'[17]

Meanwhile Flobert had gone to Dublin to stay with Francis Rawdon, the Earl of Moira, and later, with Charlemont's help, he obtained the Lord Lieutenant's permission to return to France on parole. Charlemont happened to be going to London, so they went together. At Chester he entrusted his whole stock of money to Charlemont, 'entreating that I would carry it for him to London, as he heard there were robbers on the road, who would not, he imagined, attack me'.[18]

The Volunteer army which sprang into existence overnight in the eastern parts of Ulster faded from the history books, but it was not forgotten by people who were alive at the time, and this helps to explain why, when the threat of French invasion recurred eighteen years later, the Volunteer companies were raised and coordinated so quickly. The matrix of local military action was already in place. There were, however, subtle complications in the process. In theory, at least, the companies levied in 1760 were embodied by the government under the old Militia Act of 1715, which defined their function as 'suppressing . . . all such insurrections and rebellions, and repelling of invasions' as might threaten the kingdom at any particular time.[19] In practice the initiative was largely spontaneous. Major-General Strode lamented to the Lord Lieutenant that he was unable to supply them with arms, and Charlemont was frankly surprised at their good order, given that they were totally undisciplined,

for though the old militia laws were at that time still in force, we all know the futility of the old militia laws. But the conduct of the people upon this occasion was a foretaste of what has since happened, and from such men the renown of Irish Volunteers might even then have been foreseen.[20]

However, on 17 March 1778 the members of the Belfast First Volunteer Company went out of their way to make explicit in a written engagement that they were quite independent of government.

The declared principle of their association was the defence of the town and country; the expense of array to be borne by themselves; and no manner of pay accepted from government nor any military oath whatever taken . . . the preclusion of an oath of military duty prevented the officers from having the offer, or having it in their power to accept, either of commissions or pay under the Crown.[21]

Moreover this example was followed by new Volunteer companies in other parts of the North. The First Newry Volunteers declared: 'We engage to bear our own expenses, accepting neither pay nor commission from government.' The Armagh Volunteers resolved not 'to receive any reward or wages from the government as a Volunteer company'.[22]

In the South and West of Ireland the 'armed societies' were formed on more conventional lines, and did not, indeed, at first call themselves 'Volunteers'. It is probable that if the government had chosen to implement the new Militia Act of 1778 the gentlemen commanding these armed associations would have accepted militia commissions without demur. As one authority writes, 'it is only from 1779, when this older tradition of armed service joined *faute de mieux* with the new radical version pioneered by Belfast, that we can speak of the Volunteer "movement" '.[23]

The Belfast insistence on independence was therefore an explicit political gesture, for reasons presently to be examined, and it is hardly surprising that these Northern Volunteers were regarded with some suspicion by government. The rapid progress of the First Company was an index of its support among Belfast's weightier citizens. On 16 April 1778 sixteen survivors of the Volunteers who had manned the walls of Carrickfergus Castle in 1745 dined together in the Donegall Arms 'to give their countenance and approbation to the spirit springing up in the place for self-defence'.[24] Robert Joy acted as recruiting officer for the men, attending their drills and exhorting them to persevere, until they mustered ninety men and held their first church parade in full uniform at the end of June. Their captain was Stewart Banks and the first lieutenant Waddell Cunningham, another prosperous Belfast merchant.

# 3
# The Story of the Injured Lady

Every man, observed Dr Johnson, thinks meanly of himself for not having been a soldier. The Volunteer movement allowed thousands of men of the middle classes to indulge that fantasy. The companies formed at levels of society clearly defined by economic limits. To be a Volunteer, a man needed to be in a position to provide his own uniform and accoutrements, and to have sufficient leisure to attend drills, musket practice, parades and manoeuvres. In the counties the bulk of the Volunteers were farmers and tenants in fairly comfortable circumstances; the companies tended to be centred on the society of small towns and villages rather than on the estates of the great landowners. If the landlords came in, it was generally to continue to influence their tenants; since all the officers were elected, the Volunteers chose their aristocrats, so to speak, rather than the other way round. This, in itself, was novel.

In the towns the lead was taken by the professional and mercantile classes, with a strong element of merchants and small traders. All were Protestant, since Catholics, of whatever social rank, were prohibited by the penal legislation from possessing arms. Nevertheless, many Catholics expressed a willingness to join the movement and offered to raise subscriptions for its support. After 1784, when there was a change in Volunteer policy, they joined the ranks in considerable numbers.

For the rising mercantile class, largely excluded from the exercise of political power, whether they were Church of Ireland or Dissenters, and bored by a century of unwonted peace in Ireland, the movement offered many excitements – the satisfaction of playing soldiers, of displaying wealth and dressing up in military fashion at a time when uniforms were becoming very splendid; of taking healthy exercise in the open air; of hobnobbing with their social superiors and (above all) of discussing politics with them. The custom flourished of dining together convivially after the reviews and manoeuvres, drinking toasts and entering into resolutions. The companies rapidly became debating societies.[1]

A whole class, politically excluded, found in the organization of the Volunteers an instant 'chain of national communication', a conduit for the expression of grievance to an oligarchic and unrepresentative Irish Parliament. Within a short time the Volunteer movement appeared almost as an alternative to Parliament. The Volunteers spoke with the voice of 'the People', meaning the Protestant middle class, and of 'the Nation', meaning the Protestant nation. Both these voices alarmed the government. As Lord Charlemont expressed it,

A great army, wholly independent of the Crown, self-raised in time of griev-ance and of universal complaint, in a country deemed and affectedly termed subordinate, when England was weak beyond all former example, beset on every side by enemies whom her own arbitrary follies had brought into action, would certainly have been an object of terror even to the wisest and strongest administration, and the present one was neither wise nor strong.[2]

The speed with which the various Volunteer companies throughout Ireland coalesced into larger associations and eventually into one national movement is matched only by the speed with which that movement became political. Within the next six years it was to change the face of Irish politics, and, as a result, the course of Irish history. In that short period it set itself four enormous political aims – to win the right for Ireland to trade freely with the colonies, to establish the independence of the Irish Parliament, to reform that Parliament, and to restore the franchise to Roman Catholics – and achieved two of them. Little of this programme could have been discerned in 1778 or 1779, but the movement's first demands established an uneasy relationship with Parliament which was to pass through all the stages from honeymoon to divorce.

For almost a century Ireland had enjoyed a spell of unusual peace and stability. The long tug-of-war between the two religions, which had been going on since Tudor times, ended in a decisive victory for the Protestants in the Jacobite war, a victory which had the appearance of being complete and permanent. Twice at least during the seven-teenth century the Catholic cause had been revitalized and had taken the field in arms, only to go down in renewed defeat and humiliation. The war had subsumed purely Irish discontents in a wider European conflict, but there was no mistaking the local significance of its outcome. The Battle of the Boyne in 1690, and the Treaty of Limerick in the following year, ushered in the era of the 'Protestant Ascendancy', though the term itself was not coined until the very end of the eighteenth century. Within a short time the stipulations of the Treaty were broken in the letter and in the spirit, and the passage of harsh anti-Catholic legislation in both the Irish and English Parliaments excluded Catholics from political influence and gave Protestants of the Church of Ireland (the only ones to be called 'Protestants') a virtual monopoly on power.[3]

The focus of that power was the Irish Parliament, in which neither Catholic nor Protestant Dissenters were represented. Although in almost every respect it was modelled on the Parliament at Westminster, the Irish Parliament had not experienced the same continuity of tradition. From its medieval origins onward, in fact, its history had been patchy. In Ireland parliaments were called only when royal policy in Ireland urgently required them, and intervals between them were lengthy. Only six parliaments were summoned during the entire seventeenth century. All this changed with the Hanoverian succession, and the Irish Parliament began to meet regularly for six months of every two-year cycle. It rapidly made up for lost time, assuming traditions and customs from its English counterpart. Its authority derived less from its own historical evolution than from imitation of the Mother Parliament, and the gradual assumption of that Parliament's privileges. This process accelerated rapidly during the eighteenth century. The Irish Parliament developed its own *esprit de corps* and a greater consciousness of its own rights and responsibilities.

In theory it was the independent Parliament of a sister-kingdom. In reality it had no independence. The early Tudor monarchs had been obliged to govern Ireland through the most powerful of their former Irish enemies, the Yorkist Earls of Kildare. In 1494, during one of the brief spells when the king attempted to break the Kildare stranglehold by appointing an Englishman as Lord Deputy, Sir Edward Poynings compelled the Irish Parliament to pass an Act which was to perpetuate his name for centuries to come. By Poynings' Law all legislation proposed by the Irish Parliament had to be vetted by both the Irish and English Privy Councils before it received royal licence to pass through the various stages of parliamentary procedure in the normal way. The original purpose was to curb the authority of over-mighty subjects in Ireland, but it served other uses as conditions changed. At

times in the seventeenth century the Irish Parliament even regarded
Poynings' Law as a safeguard of its rights. One way or the other,
however, it remained a permanent shackle on the institution, and by
the early eighteenth century the cumbersome procedure it enforced
was seen as a major Irish grievance.[4]

To make matters worse, the English Parliament claimed an immem-
orial right to legislate for Ireland, if and when such action was appropriate. The Revolution Settlement had created a new situation which
greatly complicated this relationship. The turmoil of the seventeenth
century had advanced the English Parliament to the central position
in the constitution. The House of Commons was now the real seat of
government, although in theory Ireland was still ruled in the old way
by the King in Parliament. In Ireland the King's place was taken by
the Lord Lieutenant, but the realities of politics meant that he was a
servant of the State, accountable to the Cabinet in London and not to
the Irish Parliament.

Ireland had therefore neither representative nor responsible government. Nor was there in the Irish Parliament a two-party system in the
modern sense. It was true that during Anne's reign something like it
had emerged from the ferocious quarrels between Whigs and Tories,
which took an even sharper form in the religious climate of Ireland
than they did in England. With the Hanoverian succession a new
situation was created, since both Whigs and Tories were obliged to
assert in fulsome terms their adherence to the Crown and the Revolution Settlement. The temper of the country gentlemen who sat in the
Irish House of Commons was generally Whiggish in tone, and they
could on occasion be critical of government and form an ill-defined
'Country' interest against 'Court' influence. At the same time they
were jealous guardians of the privileged status of the Established
Church, and vigilant for any machinations against it by Catholics or by
Protestant Dissenters. They were also very susceptible to government
manipulation.

The loyalty of MPs was given not to parties but to 'interests' headed
by the most powerful and influential of the Irish borough-owners. For
most of the time the Lord Lieutenant was able to manage Parliament
and facilitate the passage of government business by the time-honoured methods of bribing members with patronage and pensions, but
there was a continuous process of re-alignment as the Members were
attracted to, or repelled by, this or that 'interest', like iron filings

moving in a field of magnets. As time went on, and more systematically after the 'Wood's Halfpence' affair in the early 1720s, when an attempt was made to provide a new copper coinage for Ireland without consultation with either the Irish Commissioners of the Revenue or the Irish Parliament, the government came to rely on managing Parliament through the powerful groups in the House.

The native parliamentary managers, who were known as 'undertakers', smoothed the path of government legislation in return for control of a substantial slice of government patronage. The arrangement was to the advantage of both parties. It made for less friction between the administration and Parliament, while on many sensitive issues the undertakers were able to forward 'Irish' policies. In the end, the undertakers threatened to become more powerful than the Lord Lieutenant, appointing their own agents in London to intrigue against him, and holding him to ransom to demonstrate their indispensability or to settle their internecine feuds. Such a situation was bound to become intolerable, and in the 1760s, after several abortive attempts, the government succeeded in 'bringing administration back to the Castle'.

Only twice in the period before 1775 did the government lose control of the Irish House of Commons, during the agitation over 'Wood's Halfpence' and the disputes over Money Bills between 1751 and 1755. On each occasion the MPs gave way to the strength of nationalist feeling outside Parliament, and it became impossible for the Lord Lieutenant and his advisers to build up a majority in the House.

The fact that reality did not accord with theory in the early eighteenth century provided the mainspring of Protestant politics. Throughout the century, the claims of the Irish kingdom were put forward by an apostolic succession of Protestant patriots. The first was William Molyneux, who as early as 1698 published *The Case of Ireland's being bound by Acts of Parliament in England, stated*. The contents of the book lived up to its catchy title. Molyneux, a friend of John Locke, and one of the most versatile savants of his day, was married to the daughter of Sir William Domville, who had been Attorney-General for Ireland. From his father-in-law's papers Molyneux drew up a long list of dry legal precedents for asserting the independence of the Irish Parliament. The House of Commons at the time gave its verdict that the book was 'of dangerous consequence to the Crown and people of

England'. A legend grew up in the eighteenth century that the book had been ordered to be burned by the common hangman, but this is not true. Molyneux's *Case*, however, became as popular as if it *had* been.[5]

Molyneux especially resented the claim that Ireland was only an English colony and should be governed by laws made at Westminster. He protested that Ireland was 'a complete kingdom itself. Do not the kings of England bear the style of Ireland amongst the rest of their kingdoms? Is this agreeable to the nature of a colony? Do they use the title of kings of Virginia, New England or Maryland?'[6]

When the union between England and Scotland was carried through in 1707, Irish Protestants wondered if this might be the solution to their problem. But when it became clear that a union with Ireland would not take place, Jonathan Swift vented his feelings about Ireland's neglect by writing *The story of the injured lady, being a true picture of Scotch perfidy, Irish poverty, and English partiality*. He did not dare to publish it, though, and it did not appear in print until after his death forty years later. It told how the lady was jilted and ill-used by her rich and powerful suitor, who then married his neighbour to the North.

Ireland's sense of injury was sharply accentuated in 1720 when the Declaratory Act was passed by the British Parliament. This short Act 'for the better securing the dependency of the kingdom of Ireland on the crown of Great Britain' stated in uncompromising terms that the British Parliament had the right to make laws for Ireland, and that the British House of Lords was the supreme court of appeal for all Irish cases.[7]

The British ministry had no wish to stir up resentment in Ireland at this time, but it was forced to act because the British House of Lords had overturned the verdict of the Irish House of Lords in a case of disputed inheritance (*Sherlock* v. *Annesley*) in 1719. The Declaratory Act, popularly known as 'the sixth of George I', was bitterly resented in Ireland and became a rallying cry for the Protestant patriots.

All the resentment at the Declaratory Act surfaced in the national agitation over 'Wood's Halfpence' in 1724. Swift came forward as a powerful, if unlikely, champion of the rights of Ireland, and by writing the anonymous *Drapier's Letters* earned himself the title of the 'Hibernian Patriot'.

In the mid-century Swift's mantle descended upon Charles Lucas, an obstreperous apothecary who fought his way as a Dublin ward politician to membership of the House of Commons. He promptly made Parliament too hot to hold him and fled briefly to France. But the cause was actively advanced by more sedate MPs, the group of so-called 'Patriots' led after 1768 by Henry Flood, a brilliant parliamentary orator who was the son of a wealthy judge. In the Lords they were represented by a solitary Liberal peer, the Earl of Charlemont.

The grievances of the Protestant nation, keenly felt as they were, had all been hatched within the shell of a much larger grievance which had not yet been made articulate. It was simply that the Protestant Ascendancy had unselfconsciously assumed the identity of the Irish nation. Even patriot writers began the history of Ireland no earlier than the twelfth century, while siding in spirit with the native Irish against the Anglo-Normans.[8] The vast bulk of the population, which was Catholic, was excluded from the political process by the formidable barrier of the penal laws which the Ascendancy in Parliament had erected around itself.

Penal laws were not peculiar to Ireland in the eighteenth-century. France, Spain, Italy and England itself had such laws, and the persecution of Protestants in the Catholic States of Europe was indeed used as the justification for measures against Catholics in Ireland. Moreover, the legislation has to be seen against the background of the European war. Thousands of the 'wild geese', the Jacobite soldiers who left Ireland under the terms of the Treaty of Limerick, were in the service of the armies of France and Spain, and the Irish Parliament feared that they might be used to invade Ireland and raise the Catholic population in the cause of the Stuarts. Ireland was unique, however, in that the penal laws were applied not to a religious minority but to four-fifths of the population.

The real motive of the penal code was political rather than religious, though recent historical research has tended to suggest that the hope of proselytism, and of weakening, or even extirpating, the Roman Catholic Church, was stronger than earlier historians have sometimes allowed. If such was the case, the result was precisely the opposite. Those of the penal laws which were directly concerned with the practice of religion were not vigorously enforced, and were soon allowed to fall into disuse. The collusion of well-disposed Protestant landlords was a factor in mitigating some of the worst consequences. But even this aspect of the penal years had a lasting effect on the Church as such, influencing its architecture, its self-image, and its attitudes to the State and to Protestantism.

The most important of the laws related to real property, that is, to land. No Catholic could legally purchase an interest in land except for a lease of not more than thirty-one years. He could not acquire land from a Protestant by inheritance or marriage, nor could he dispose of his own land by will and testament. On his death it was automatically divided among all his sons. If his eldest son became a convert to the Church of Ireland, however, the whole estate would go to him, and if he conformed during his father's lifetime, the law considered the father to be merely a life tenant.

These provisions were enforced more effectively than restrictions on worship, and they almost achieved their objective of eliminating what was left of the Catholic gentry. A few Catholic families conformed rather than see their lands eroded in this way; others managed to retain theirs by collusion with Protestants, or by finding ways round the law. Fake 'discoveries' were sometimes arranged by lawyers, to put trustworthy Protestants, hired for the purpose, into nominal possession without disturbing the real ownership. Happy were the families who had only one son, or good Protestant friends.

One of the most comprehensive of the penal laws was the Act of 1704 'to prevent the further growth of popery.' It reinforced laws passed since 1690 and added new ones. Catholics were not permitted to send their children abroad to be educated, nor could they act as guardians to children under age. In William's reign, it had been decreed that no Catholic could bear arms 'except gentlemen comprised in the Treaty of Limerick'. No Catholic could be apprenticed to an arms-maker, nor could he own a horse worth more than £5. A clause added to the 1704 Act imposed a sacramental test on all office-holders, and this meant that no Catholic and no Protestant Dissenter could henceforward hold any office under the Crown.[9]

The penal laws had consequences very different from those intended. In time they were to prove a source of enormous strength to the Roman Catholic Church. Any Church will thrive under persecution, and the totality of the ban imposed upon Catholics taking part in public life made them aware that their common interest could lie only with their own Church and people. To some extent this was countered by the rigid social distinctions of the time, but by the same token the laws helped to erode those distinctions faster in Ireland than elsewhere. The Church became in fact an alternative State which commanded the loyalty of Catholics, and to which they turned for guidance in all things. Clergy and laity were brought closer together, more so perhaps than in any other Catholic country. If the eighteenth century is the century in which the Protestant nation ruled, it was also that in which the Catholic nation was created.

The second consequence of the penal laws was to undermine respect for the law amongst the majority of the population, as Prohibition tended to do in the United States in the twentieth century. This had a deeper significance for the future than the mere resentment of injustice. The law in Ireland became permanently associated in Catholic eyes with British rule in Ireland, and more accurately with the Ascendancy and Protestantism. The fissure already created by religious allegiance in previous centuries was widened and made permanent, and its baneful legacy is still to be seen today.

The penal code bore most heavily on the Catholic upper classes, on those levels of society which, in eighteenth-century terms, ought to have been influential in politics. Rather than risk the confiscation of their estates, the natural leaders of Catholic society preferred to stay out of political life, and this is the chief reason why there appears to have been no Catholic political organization of any kind until 1760. The tenantry were less directly affected by the laws, since they took virtually no interest in national affairs, but their resentment was sharpened by the imposition of tithes. Catholics and Protestant Dissenters alike were obliged to pay tithes for the upkeep of the Established Church. A Catholic had thus to pay tithes to the Church of Ireland by law, and to his own Church by tradition and loyalty. It gave a sharper edge to rural poverty, and helped to pave the way for agrarian unrest, which became almost endemic in the second half of the eighteenth century.

The overall effect of the penal age was to distort Irish society. The only sphere of activity left open to Catholics was that of trade and industry, and they made certain areas, notably the provision trade, distinctively their own. By the end of the century a strong trading middle class had grown up in the towns, and it was to become a potential ally to the aggrieved Protestant middle class.

# 4
# *Dungannon*

In 1779 the Patriot members of Parliament suddenly realized the immense potential of the Volunteer movement, and lost no time in harnessing it to their political programme. Flood, Grattan and many other MPs hastened to appear in uniform. The first effective demonstration of Volunteer power came that autumn, with the customary parades to mark the anniversary of King William III's birthday on 4 November. The Volunteers turned the event into a vast demonstration in favour of 'Free Trade', a scene vividly preserved for posterity in Francis Wheatley's splendid painting, now in the National Gallery of Ireland.

The Volunteers placed their cannon round the King's statue, with placards reading 'Free Trade or This'. The implication was that the guns could just as easily be trained on the Parliament building nearby. Dublin was *en fête*, and the red, blue and gold of the uniforms, the glittering standards, and the smoke and thunder of repeated *feux de joie* could not but create a sense of excitement and drama. The voice of the people had been heard, and it spoke directly to Parliament. What it demanded was not free trade in its more familiar and modern sense, but the right of Ireland to trade directly with British colonies rather than through England.

Faced by a combination of popular tumult and skilful opposition, Lord North's government gave way and granted some concessions including the right to trade directly with the colonies. The Patriots, exhilarated by their success, began to think of pushing through all their demands to an English government weakened and made compliant by the war with America. Yet there was still a great deal of uncertainty and unease among the Volunteers at the dangerous and revolutionary path they seemed to be treading. Even some of their leaders had been opposed to the orchestration of the Free Trade agitation. Besides, the first flush of Volunteer enthusiasm was subsiding. In the winter of

1779–80 many companies were depleted, parades and reviews were fewer, and the Volunteers almost ceased to publish resolutions.[1]

In retrospect the Volunteer movement appears as a force gradually strengthening until it was able to achieve the culminating triumph of 1782, but it has been shown that the graph of its rise is more erratic. The reality is that the Volunteers became very quiet and subdued in the winter of 1780, to the dismay of the Patriots. For them the session of Parliament had been anything but successful. Expecting further triumphs, they found themselves instead attacked on all sides, and defeated in every measure they sought to introduce. A kind of political deadlock set in, and by 1781 it was clear that some bold initiative was called for, if the momentum was not to be lost. At this point Lord Charlemont and his friends took a calculated political gamble which, had it failed, might have destroyed their entire cause.

The man who was now propelled to the forefront of Irish politics was an intriguing mixture of timidity and political resolution. James Caulfeild, the 1st Earl of Charlemont, was born in Dublin in 1728 and came into his inheritance at the age of six. The first Caulfeild in Ireland had been an Oxfordshire gentleman who served as a captain in the war against Hugh O'Neill and was rewarded by James I with a title and extensive lands in Co. Armagh. The 4th Viscount and 1st Earl was a delicate child, educated by a succession of able tutors, the last of whom, the Rev. Richard Murphy, accompanied him abroad when, at eighteen, he embarked on what was to prove a protracted Grand Tour of Europe and the Middle East. He lived for some years in Holland, Italy and France, with excursions to Spain, Sicily, Greece, Egypt and Turkey, becoming in the process an accomplished scholar, a connoisseur and a bibiliophile.

He was the patron of important artists, including Hogarth and Piranesi. After Hogarth's death, he continued to correspond with, and buy prints from, his widow. Piranesi, a man of touchy disposition and violent temper, quarrelled with him, and removed his name from the plates of his celebrated *Veduti di Roma*.[2] Throughout his life Charlemont was happiest when he could be left alone with his pictures and prints, and first folios of Shakespeare. His travels brought the acquaintance of a variety of interesting and important figures, including David Hume, Montesquieu, and Pope Benedict XIV who,

Charlemont's biographer tells us, regarded him 'with a kindness and benevolence that was almost parental'.[3]

The youthful Charlemont was much impressed by Montesquieu at their first meeting. He had been looking forward to it with some trepidation, but the author of *L'esprit des lois*, then in his mid-sixties, put him instantly at ease by leaping over a three-foot high gate to show him round the property. It may be said in passing that Charles de Secondat, Baron Montesquieu, had some interesting Irish connections. His secretary was Irish, as Charlemont was disconcerted to learn, just before he took his leave (they had been talking all the time in French).[4] The wine-exporting aspect of Montesquieu's estate brought him in business contact with a number of English and Irish importers. Among them was John Black of Belfast who had a house at Bordeaux close to Montesquieu's residence. It was there that his son, the famous chemist, Joseph Black, was born. A few of Montesquieu's letters are preserved in Joseph Black's papers in Edinburgh University; in them, Black describes the philosopher as an intimate friend of his father, who had shown the family great kindness. Years later, John Black was to provide ships for the repatriation of the French prisoners captured in 1760.[5]

One of Charlemont's earliest experiences might have been taken directly from the pages of Bram Stoker. Travelling southward through Germany, he was seized with a desire to see the source of the Danube, and made a detour from his planned route.

My way lay through that immense tract known by the terrific name of the 'Black Forest', at the extremity of which the capital of the landgrave is situate, and as I approached his residence, I was surprised and shocked to observe that most of the trees bordering the highway were hung with human limbs, so as to have the appearance of a shambles in a country of cannibals. Hands, feet, arms, legs and even hands were everywhere to be seen, and my first idea was that some numerous gang of robbers had been taken and executed. I stopped the chaise, and, enquiring of the postilion into the nature and circumstances of these supposed banditti, was thus answered: 'No, sir, there have been no robbers: those limbs belonged to certain desperadoes who were audacious and wicked enough to kill the prince's game . . .'

'I shall only say', adds Charlemont, 'that such atrocities invite rebellion, and that the true means to prevent revolution is to govern so as to make the people happy.'[6]

Charlemont came home, after eleven years abroad, to find that his own country was just then undergoing a sharp bout of political cannibalism. The Money Bill dispute, as it became known, was the only serious crisis apart from 'Wood's Halfpence' to disturb the Augustan calm of Irish politics before 1775. In essence it was a trial of strength between two sets of parliamentary 'Undertakers'. Henry Boyle, the Speaker, who had reigned virtually unchallenged as chief Undertaker since the 1730s, felt his party to be menaced by a combination of the ambitious Ponsonby family and George Stone, the English Archbishop of Armagh.

In 1753 there was a surplus in the Irish treasury. By custom it belonged to the Crown. The House of Commons wished to appropriate it for Irish purposes, and Boyle's party made the issue one of the rights of the Irish Parliament. This was a very popular cause, and Boyle became a Patriot hero overnight. The House did not get its way, nor indeed did it expect to, at the first trial. A surplus arose again in 1755. The administration sought a compromise. The surplus could be appropriated, but a clause must be added to the Bill saying that this was done with the King's consent. Anthony Malone, the Speaker's deputy, refused to put in the clause, and public opinion was inflamed to a fever.

It was at this point that Charlemont reached Ireland. The borough of Charlemont, for which his brother sat, was one of those included in the Boyle interest, but Charlemont was also a friend of the Lord Lieutenant, Hartington, and on good terms with the Ponsonbys, so that he was the obvious person to act as mediator. Boyle was, in the end, happy to abandon his patriotic opposition to an earldom and a pension of £3,000 per annum for thirty-one years. The infuriated Dublin mob, who had made him a Patriot saint, now burned his effigy in the streets.

Charlemont thus discovered that his mediation 'was strongly seconded by motives of personal emolument', the terms of which were unknown to him. He became aware for the first time that 'the mask of patriotism is often assumed to disguise self-interest and ambition, and that the paths of violent opposition, are too frequently trod as the nearest and surest road to office and emolument'. He reflected that in one respect 'the pseudo-patriot resembles the Christian whose hopes are fixed upon an hereafter, and the death of patriotism is not unusually succeeded by a glorious resurrection into the paradise of court favour'.[7]

Aside from these sardonic reflections, Charlemont was convinced that the commotions had done some good. 'By them people were taught a secret of which they had been hitherto ignorant, that government might be opposed with success.' A spirit was raised in the nation, and men's minds were turned to constitutional subjects. What Ireland needed was a permanent and respectable opposition, and Charlemont formed his plan of keeping 'one individual at least of rank and property wholly independent, as a standard to which, upon any emergency, men might resort'.[8] He determined never to receive any favour from government, nor to solicit one for anyone else.

This was not an easy course, given the nature of eighteenth-century patronage, but Charlemont stuck to it, and became a most valuable acquisition to the Patriots in Parliament. Unfortunately, his effectiveness was marred by a crippling nervousness which inhibited him from speaking in the House of Lords. 'No man was ever, I suppose, born with a greater degree of nervous diffidence,' he confessed. It was all part and parcel of his hypochondria. He suffered much from eyestrain, and for the last thirty years of his life felt himself unable to read or write except in natural light. His rheumatism was an even greater affliction. Once, with the help of lawyers, he prepared a Bill for the better regulation of juries, but when he was ready to speak on it, a violent attack (brought on doubtless by his fear of public speaking) laid him low for two years, 'during which time I was an absolute cripple, and went through an excruciating course of pains and physicians, until I was at length restored to health by the tender care and effectual abilities of the excellent Dr Lucas'.[9] Lucas's contribution to the Patriot cause was not confined to his political activities.

Nevertheless, from 1757 until 1760, rheumatism kept Charlemont from taking an active part in public affairs. On Thurot's seizure of Carrickfergus, he came North, as we have seen, to take command of the raw levies raised in Ulster, and this exciting activity seems to have been very beneficial. The menace of the French was soon succeeded by an internal one, posed by the shadowy agrarian organizations which seemed to spring up after 1760. It began with the Whiteboy movement in the South, but in 1763 disturbances of a rather different kind, initiated by the Oakboys, or Hearts of Oak, broke out in various parts of the North. They were associated with protests against the county cess, or tax, for the repair of roads, and their focus was in Co. Armagh, of which Charlemont was Lieutenant. Mobs of men, wearing sprigs of oak in their hats, waylaid travellers (including Charlemont himself on one occasion) and attacked some isolated houses at night. Charlemont played a very active part in organizing the local gentry to suppress these disorders, and the incidents eventually ceased.

As a reward he was raised to the dignity of an earldom, but his determined opposition to the Address returning thanks for the Treaty of Paris prevented further Court favours. In 1764 he went to London, where he was to keep a town house until 1773 and devote himself to his literary and artistic tastes, in the congenial company of Burke, Sir Joshua Reynolds, Goldsmith and Johnson. He appears fitfully in the pages of Boswell's *Life*, on one occasion being put up to ask Johnson if there was any truth in the newspaper story that he was taking dancing lessons. This was risking a good deal, thought Boswell, and 'required the boldness of a General in the Irish Volunteers to make the attempt'. Johnson's reaction was everything his tormentors could have wished for, but then, entering into the joke, he asked, 'Why should not Dr Johnson add to his other powers a little corporeal agility? Socrates learned to dance at an advanced age.'[10]

In 1768 Charlemont married a Miss Hickman, the daughter of an impoverished gentleman of Co. Clare, a quiet and modest girl (in contrast to some of his earlier conquests), and in about 1770 he embarked on building a magnificent town house in Rutland Square in Dublin, and restoring his existing residence at Marino. He had come to the conclusion that, much as he enjoyed English society, it was his political duty to live in Ireland.

Meanwhile Charlemont had not neglected his role in the Irish House of Lords, and with Flood he shared the honour of the Patriot victory when the Octennial Bill was passed in 1768, limiting the duration of Parliament to eight years, instead of the lifetime of the monarch. The end of the 1760s saw also the final overthrow of the power of the Undertakers, when Lord Townshend skilfully and decisively 'brought administration back to the Castle'. Like most of these changes, it was brought about more by contingent circumstances than the character of any one individual, but it undoubtedly made the way clear for the rise of a Patriot party in the House.

The immediate result, however, was an increase in defections from the opposition. The most shocking of these did not take Charlemont entirely by surprise, though it caused him great chagrin. Only months before the outbreak of war with the American colonies in 1775, Flood, with disastrous mistiming, accepted a post in the government as Vice-

Treasurer. He had been won over, not without immense difficulty, by the assiduous wooing of the Lord Lieutenant, Lord Harcourt, and his Chief Secretary, John Blacquiere. 'Flood the champion of his country', lamented Charlemont,

the bulwark of her liberties, her strong tower of defence against all assailants – Flood, my friend Flood, – the dear partner of my heart and all its councils – anchor of my hope, and pillar of my trust – Flood gave way and deserted the glorious cause in which he had been for fourteen years triumphantly engaged.[11]

Providence was to compensate this loss in an ambiguous and grievous way. Charlemont's brother Francis Caulfeild, along with his wife and two daughters, was drowned on his passage from England in November 1775. The borough of Charlemont lay vacant, and Charlemont nominated for it the young lawyer Henry Grattan. Despite some differences which later grew up between them, Grattan's admiration for Charlemont never dimmed.

The stupendous success of the Volunteer movement in the Free Trade agitation had carried Charlemont to a position of national renown that he was by no means eager to occupy, but he could not now draw back when his parliamentary colleagues proposed to keep up the momentum of Volunteer reform. The first move to break the deadlock was made by his officers in the Southern battalion of the Ulster Regiment. Meeting at Armagh in the last days of 1781, they registered consternation that so little attention was being paid by their representatives in Parliament to the constitutional rights of Ireland, and called upon all Volunteer associations in Ulster to send delegates to a Convention in Dungannon (which they held to be the central location in the province) on 15 February 1782.[12] The resolutions for the Convention were carefully drafted in Charlemont's town house in Dublin where Flood, Grattan, and Francis Dobbs were present, along with James Stewart of Killymoon, one of the MPs for Tyrone, who was a friend to the Dissenters.

The resolutions were a summary of the principal Patriot demands, and it was agreed that Dobbs should move them. A further resolution was added, strongly urged by Grattan, though it aroused little enthusiasm from the others, who doubted its wisdom on tactical grounds. It called for the relaxation of the penal laws against the Catholics. This resolution had come up from the Volunteer associations, with the backing of the Dissenting ministers, and it was to find a permanent place in the history books even if, as so often happens, its survival was a close thing.[13]

Flood had already expressed to Charlemont his unease over the potential of the Catholic question to cause division in the Volunteer ranks.

I am frightened about the popery business [he wrote]. It ought to be touched only by a master hand. It is a chord of such wondrous potency that I dread the sound of it, and believe with you that the harmony would be better if, like that of the spheres, it were, at least for a time, inaudible.[14]

At 10 o'clock on the morning of Friday, 15 February, 250 delegates from 143 Ulster Volunteer companies marched into the parish church at Dungannon 'two and two, dressed in their uniforms and fully armed'. With Colonel William Irvine in the chair they deliberated on the resolutions until nightfall, voting overwhelmingly for their adoption. The first resolution asserted that 'a citizen, by learning the use of arms, does not abandon any of his civil rights'. They went on to agree that a claim by any body of men, other than the King, Lords and Commons of Ireland, to make laws to bind that kingdom, was unconstitutional, illegal and a grievance; that the powers exercised by the Privy Council of both kingdoms under Poynings' Law were unconstitutional and a grievance; that the ports of Ireland were open to all foreign countries not at war with the King; that a Mutiny Bill of unlimited duration was unconstitutional; and that the independence of judges was as essential to the administration of justice in Ireland as it was in England. The Volunteers declared their unalterable determination to seek redress of these grievances, and to support only those candidates for Parliament who would endorse them. Finally, 'as men and as Irishmen, as Christians and Protestants', they rejoiced in the relaxation of the penal laws against their Roman Catholic fellow-subjects, 'a measure fraught with the happiest consequences to the union and prosperity of the inhabitants of Ireland'.[15]

The following day these resolutions went out in Charlemont's name to Volunteer companies in every part of Ireland. For tactical reasons he had, along with Flood and Grattan, stayed away from the Convention, but he gave his unqualified approval to the resolutions, including the one which called for Catholic emancipation. In the House of Commons Grattan now moved for the second time the abolition of

Poynings' Law and the Declaratory Act. The motion was lost by 137 votes to 68. For the moment, at least, it did not seem that Dungannon had achieved much for the Patriot cause.

But the real drama still lurked in the wings. The Irish Parliament adjourned for the Easter recess on 14 March. Ten days later in England Lord North's government suddenly resigned, and the King reluctantly asked the Whig Lord Rockingham to form a cabinet. A new Whig Lord Lieutenant, the Duke of Portland, was sent to Ireland. The Patriots took heart again. During the recess a vast mobilization of opinion began. More than 450 Volunteer companies individually or in groups gave public support to the resolutions. In twenty-one counties support was expressed by the grand juries, and in eight by county meetings of freeholders. A few counties remained silent, and, ominously, one of them was Armagh. But the machinery set up at Dungannon had achieved its object. A great current of excitement was running through the entire island, and even before the end of March it was taken for granted that the new government would give in to all the Volunteers' demands. The playwright, Richard Brinsley Sheridan, was told by his brother, an Irish MP, that

a declaration of the independency of our Parliament upon yours will certainly pass our House of Commons immediately after the recess. Government here dare not, can not, oppose it. You will see the volunteers have pledged their lives and fortunes in support of the measure.[16]

At this critical moment Grattan fell ill and had to undergo surgery. The fate of the nation now seemed to rest on the shoulders of his patron, Charlemont. Fortunately the Marquis of Rockingham and Charles James Fox were old friends of his. Both wrote to him to beg that he would help procure a further adjournment of the Irish House of Commons 'in order that the British ministry might obtain necessary information as to Ireland'. The new administration desperately needed to play for time, to avoid at all costs a direct collision of English and Irish interests. Charlemont sent for Flood to advise him, but Flood sulked in his tent, and would not come up from the country. Then Charlemont went to see Grattan. The sick man propped himself up in bed and croaked out, 'No time, no time.' The English ministry must not be allowed a way out – the iron was to be struck while it was hot.[17]

Courteous as ever, but with a dignified firmness, Charlemont replied to Rockingham that 'they could not delay, they were pledged to the people'.[18] Writing to Fox, he expressed his lifelong admiration for the Whigs:

I know and respect their principles, and should be truly unhappy if anything should prevent my perfect co-operation with them; for, my dear Sir, with every degree of affection for our kingdom – with every regard for the empire at large – *I am an Irishman*.

He hoped that the government would not insist on an adjournment since the eyes of all the nation were eagerly fixed on the meeting of Parliament on 16 April.[19]

For two days before that date every approach to Grattan's house in Dame Street was jammed with carriages and excited crowds, as deputation after deputation waited on him with expressions of esteem and good wishes for his speedy recovery of health. When the day came, the galleries were packed with spectators, 'every heart panting with expectation'. Hundreds of Leinster Volunteers had come up to the capital for a provincial review the following day, and they ceremonially lined the streets for the Lord Lieutenant's progress from the Castle to College Green.

Still deathly pale, Grattan rose to address the House, his voice faint but growing stronger as he warmed to his theme. This time it was not a recital of old grievances and demands, but a hymn of triumph for a victory already won.

I am now to address a free people! Ages have passed away, and this is the first moment in which you could be distinguished by that appellation . . . I found Ireland on her knees; I watched over her with an eternal solicitude; I have traced her progress from injuries to arms, and from arms to liberty. Spirit of Swift! spirit of Molyneux! your genius has prevailed. Ireland is now a nation. In that new character I hail her, and bowing in her august presence, I say, *Esto perpetua*.[20]

For the third time Grattan then moved for the Declaration of Rights. This time it was carried unanimously in both Houses, and on 27 May the Lord Lieutenant announced that 'the British legislative have concurred in a resolution to remove the causes of your discontents and jealousies'. Soon afterwards the Declaratory Act was repealed by the Westminster Parliament, and Bills to repeal Poynings' Law and the Perpetual Mutiny Act, and to secure the independence of judges, were introduced in the Irish Parliament and rapidly passed. Overnight

Grattan became a national hero, and Parliament voted £50,000 to purchase an estate for him at Tinnehinch.[21]

This wholesale sweeping away of ancient grievances came to be known as the 'Constitution of 1782'. It was not, however, like the British Constitution, the result of an evolutionary process over a great period of time. Nor was it, like the American Constitution, a written instrument arrived at by careful thought. Like so much in Irish history, it was the product of a particular set of chance circumstances, a chemical fusion which was not entirely foreseen, and not completely understood. It was only with time that its weaknesses became apparent. It gave the Irish Parliament more power in theory than in practice. The two Parliaments might now be independent of each other in abstract terms, but the Lord Lieutenant and the machinery of government remained in Dublin Castle. Unlike the Prime Minister in England, the Lord Lieutenant was not accountable to the House of Commons, nor did he have to depend on a majority in that House to carry on the King's government. By the same token, neither Grattan nor anyone else could form an administration or implement a national policy in opposition to the Lord Lieutenant.

The settlement of 1782 failed to address the two basic problems of Irish politics: first, the precise nature of the relationship between the two kingdoms; and second, the relationship between the government and Ascendancy on the one hand and the bulk of the Irish population on the other. After 1782 Ireland still had neither responsible nor representative government. There were, besides, any number of technical problems unresolved, concerning defence, for instance, or diplomatic relations with other countries. Above all, the Irish Parliament still had no control over the revenue, and this in itself was enough to make independence illusory.

Grattan was a genuine Whig. He derived his political principles from the Revolution of 1688, and believed that the strengths of the British Constitution stemmed from that necessary but unique revolution. The Volunteers had played their part in bringing the Irish Constitution back to its pristine purity; their proper role was now quietly to disband and resume their normal vocations. They had given a Parliament to the people, he told them, and they must now leave the people to Parliament. The country needed to rest after the turmoil of the previous four years, to allow Irishmen to set about the business of internal administrative reform. But in the shadows, just outside the circle of limelight, was the brooding and saturnine figure of Flood. A bitter jealousy had awakened in his breast against the man who had entered Parliament as his acolyte. All those thrusts about bribery were now paid back with compound interest. He smarted still over his disastrous desertion of the Patriots just before they scented victory, and his undignified scramble back in order to enjoy the *réclame*. His intentions were manifest to all, but he had to wait his opportunity.

It came to him fortuitously when two rather pedantic lawyers, Bradstreet and Walshe, pointed out in the Commons that Britain's repeal of the Declaratory Act meant just that and nothing more, not the renunciation of the *right* to legislate for Ireland.[22] To secure the country's rights, simple repeal was not enough. Flood took up the cause of 'Renunciation' with all the considerable skill at his command. He had the backing of the Lawyers' Corps and the majority of the Volunteer associations, but it was only when he turned to Ulster that the campaign began to make headway.

A second Dungannon Convention convened on 21 June, this time in the Presbyterian church, and gave overwhelming support to Flood on the Renunciation question. It also called for the reform of Parliament and a more equal representation of the people. This was an even more sensitive issue, since Charlemont and some of the other senior officers owned closed boroughs, controlling safe seats in the Commons. Charlemont was now elected general of all the Volunteers of Ulster, and was presented with an illuminated copy of the resolutions which he had framed and hung in his library.[23]

On 27 June the members of the Belfast First Volunteer Company sent an address to Grattan on the subject of simple repeal. They said that doubts had arisen as to whether the repeal of the 6th of George I was a sufficient renunciation of the power formerly exercised over Ireland. They thought it advisable that a law should be enacted similar to the Address which had been moved to His Majesty and which embodied a declaration of the rights of Ireland. Grattan's answer was short, and brusque to the point of rudeness. He said that he had given the fullest consideration to their suggestions; he was very sorry he differed from them, but he conceived their doubts to be ill-founded.[24]

On the same day the Company wrote to Flood, in very much more complimentary terms:

Sir – Your unequalled abilities, your unrivalled eloquence, your knowledge, which seems bounded only by the limits which the author of our nature has prescribed to the greatest of our kind, and the sacrifices you have made to serve your country, oblige us to look up to you as one of the first of men. We have seen your remarks on the repeal of the 6th of George I which perfectly co-incide with our sentiments; and we thank you for the clear and extensive view you have given us of that subject.[25]

Flood replied that he was happy to have the honour of agreeing with them about the inadequacy of simple repeal. 'We sought for the certainty of express law, and we have not attained it.' He feared that his humble talents were unequal to the exaltation and energy of their style, but such as they were, they were wholly at their service. Enchanted by this reply, the First Company resolved unanimously 'That the Rt Hon Henry Food be, and he hereby is, admitted *a member of this corps*'.[26]

Grattan had tried to steer the Volunteers into the path of moderation. Carefully selected delegates met as a National Committee and declared themselves satisfied with simple repeal, provincial assemblies obediently repeating the formula. But the two Belfast companies protested vigorously at this stage-management, and pointed out that the three Ulster delegates on the committee, Mervyn Archdall, Joseph Pollock and Francis Dobbs, had been given no mandate to take decisions which would be binding on the Province. Dobbs took this as a personal affront, and engaged in a series of angry clashes with the Belfast companies, in which he managed to strike exactly the wrong note. Though well-informed, he told them, they were not capable on their own of making such 'nice decisions' as those involved in supporting simple repeal.[27]

On 18 July the First Company published an address to the various Volunteer corps that were preparing to take part in the annual review. It declared that

the rights of this kingdom are not yet secured, not even acknowledged by Britain, partly owing to the delusions of many sincere friends, to the perfidy of pretended ones, and to an error committed through precipitancy by our representatives in the Senate. Unless a spark of that sacred flame which but a few days ago glowed in every breast in Ulster be again excited, the glorious attempt of this country to procure its emancipation, instead of producing any permanent good, will probably be the means of depriving us of our rights forever.[28]

What these rhetorical phrases meant was that the First Company had become the spearhead of the Renunciation campaign.

On the last day of the month Charlemont reviewed 4,000 Volunteers at Belfast. Three days later Dobbs, as the exercising officer, moved the address of thanks to Charlemont, in which there was a clause expressing full satisfaction with the concessions granted by Great Britain. Incensed, the Belfast men moved an amendment that the clause should be expunged, and after a marathon debate of eleven hours the amendment was carried by two votes.[29]

It was now obvious that the Renunciation dispute had divided the Volunteer army, and it was hardly a coincidence that towards the end of 1782 the government introduced a measure which was clearly designed to take advantage of the division and to draw the political sting of the Volunteers. The idea was to embody new 'Fencible' regiments of soldiers, raised locally for home service only, commanded by local landowners and armed and paid for by the government. Such Fencible regiments were raised successfully in England, Scotland and Wales, and they were later to play an important military role during the Napoleonic Wars. By a strange irony the only theatre in which they were to see active service was Ireland. But in Ireland the proposal enraged the Volunteers and greatly complicated the bitterness over simple repeal. Volunteer officers who accepted Fencible commissions were execrated, and in some cases expelled from their Volunteer companies. The plan was eventually abandoned at the end of 1783.

The Renunciation dispute ended early in that year when the British Parliament finally passed a Renunciation Act, explicitly giving up the right to legislate for Ireland. But the mischief had been done. Renunciation was the first split in the political unity of the Volunteers, as men sided with Grattan or Flood. It also had the effect of ending the cooperation between the Volunteers and Parliament. In a sense it had been a Volunteer victory, won at the cost of Parliament's goodwill. The Volunteers were not prepared to be moved away from the centre of the stage which they had occupied for so long. And the more radical companies, especially in the North, had begun 'to question the integrity of a parliament which had been prepared to accept imperfect securities for Ireland's independence'.[30]

# 5
# The Edicts of Another Assembly

While the Renunciation dispute was still at its height, the Volunteers began to take up the cause of parliamentary reform. The initial impulse came from resolutions of the Munster companies, but these were taken up at once by the Northerners, who again put themselves in the vanguard of the campaign and made Belfast its headquarters. They determined to call a general meeting of the Ulster corps at Dungannon on 8 September 1783, and a meeting of delegates of forty-five corps at Lisburn in July set up a special Committee of Correspondence to collect the opinions of the great and the good in the world of representative reform. Irish notabilities were canvassed, but the views of a wide selection of campaigners abroad were also sought.

The chairman of the committee was William Sharman of Moira, Lieutenant-Colonel of the Union Regiment of Volunteers and MP for the Borough of Lisburn. The secretary was Henry Joy, junior, the proprietor of the *Belfast Newsletter*, who threw himself into the task with considerable enthusiasm. Not all the recipients of his circular letter took the trouble to reply, but among those who did were William Pitt, Benjamin Franklin, the Duke of Richmond, Lord Effingham, the Abbé Raynal, and the English radicals Dr Price, Major Cartwright and the Rev. Christopher Wyvell.[1] Pitt, writing from Brighthelmstone (Brighton) was politely non-committal, but Wyvell's reply was in Mrs McTier's opinion 'elegant, and expressive of much warmth and affection to their cause'.[2]

Joy also wrote to Charlemont, whose response was guarded. He said that while he fully approved of some attempt being made to ameliorate popular representation, he feared the Volunteers were apt to move too rashly in undertaking responsibility for the attempt. It was not only that they were unequal to the task, a very delicate one, but such an action on their part would be seen as a usurpation of the powers of the legislature. Grattan reacted in the same cautious way, and privately communicated his fears to Charlemont.

There is another difficulty which I feel, and don't wish to express except to you and a few more very select friends, and it is a difficulty which I am sure you feel as I do. The repetitions of the Dungannon meetings will alarm Parliament, as if the delegates were coming in the place of the legislature.[3]

By the time the third Dungannon Convention met on 8 September 1783, the main issues had become parliamentary reform and the political rights of Catholics, the latter introducing yet another cause of contention into the Volunteer ranks. This time there was an assembly of 500 representatives from 276 Ulster corps, and colour was added to the proceedings by the flamboyant arrival, in a garb half-military and half-ecclesiastical, of Frederick Augustus Hervey, the Earl of Bristol and Bishop of Derry, an ardent and unswerving advocate of Catholic rights. He made an able speech in which he described the assembly as 'a faithful, honest and spirited representation of the people', but he was then stricken by gout and had to depart early. Flood was to have attended as a delegate of the Belfast First Company, but the same malady claimed him on the road, and he turned back. An even more ignominious fate awaited the unfortunate Francis Dobbs. He was refused admission because he had accepted a commission in the Fencibles.[4]

The chief decision taken was that the specific details of a plan for the reform of Parliament should be subject to further consideration by a National Convention, which it was proposed to summon to meet at the Royal Exchange in Dublin on 10 November. The plan of parliamentary reform which the Ulster Committee of Correspondence to the Provincial Assembly proposed for the National Convention included the 'extension of suffrage to such a description of Roman Catholics as the National Convention . . . may deem proper objects for that great trust'[5] and this evasive line was followed in the debates, a stronger resolution in favour of the Catholics being negatived.[6]

The National Convention was for Charlemont the turning-point in his relations with the Volunteers. It was with considerable trepidation that he agreed to take the chair. That he should do so was vital, for Hervey had now emerged as a potential leader of the Volunteers, with the backing of the more radical elements, including many of the Northerners. He was a vain, eccentric and rather ridiculous figure, so generally unepiscopal in character that his contemporaries, and many writers since, have been tempted to dismiss the sincerity of his views on parliamentary reform, and more particularly on Catholic emancipation. He was, in most ways, his own worst enemy.

Charlemont's contempt for Hervey was absolute, and his description of him is a deliberate character assassination, though not entirely inaccurate.

His genius is like a shallow stream, rapid, noisy, diverting, but useless. Such is his head, and . . . I fear that it is much superior to his heart. He is proud and to the last degree vindictive; vain to excess; inconstant in his friendships, if such they may be called, which are never formed but to serve some private purpose; fond of intrigue in gallantry as well as in politics, and sticking at nothing to gain his ends in either. . . . Possessed of no firm principle, public or private, he is continually assuming, and as continually forfeiting, the character of a patriot and a virtuous man. A bad father, both from caprice and avarice; a worse husband to the best and most amiable of wives; a determined deist, though a bishop, and at times so indecently impious in his conversation as to shock the more reprobate.

Charlemont's denunciation of Hervey takes up two whole pages of his memoirs. He accuses him of seeking popularity by throwing out the best-adapted lure to every class of people. The Presbyterians were won over by his affectation of patriotism, his unbounded professions of liberty in Church and State, his violent abuse of his fellow-bishops and, above all, his 'coinciding with them, and even going beyond them, in their favourite plan of reform'. The Protestants he allured by his affability and condescension, 'a never-failing bait for the vulgar'. 'And with regard to the Papists – to whom from his long residence in Popish countries, *and from the levelling influence of that new philosophy of which he wished to be deemed an apostle*, he was, I believe sincerely addicted' [my italics].[7]

In all this Charlemont is less than fair to Hervey's very complex character, and the fact that the Earl–Bishop seems to have been intermittently prey to some kind of insanity does not in itself invalidate two of the very rational springs of his political actions. One is indicated by the passage in italics quoted above, and to that it will be necessary to return. The other is that his travels abroad, unlike Charlemont's, had given him special information about Irish Catholic intrigues on the Continent, and some prophetic insight into the probable course of Irish history in years to come. This led him to condemn the maintenance of the penal code, and to lay stress on the serious danger to the connection between England and Ireland involved in the refusal to sanction the free exercise of the Roman Catholic religion, 'a Gordian knot which only the sword of civil war can cut'.[8]

As early as 1778, Hervey had seen the threatened war with France as the second act of the American tragedy, and appreciated the key relevance of the penal laws should it occur. From Rome in May 1778 he wrote to Edmund Pery, the Speaker of the Irish House of Commons: 'Ireland, if the war with France takes place, must inevitably be thrown into the greatest confusion.'[9] Two months earlier, he had written to Sir John Strange that

the Ministers have not the least idea of their danger, yet *I have the most authentick* intelligence that the first impression will be made upon Ireland ... I know likewise that there is resumed the original idea of attempting a coalition between the Papists and Protestants of Ireland in order to declare an Independence under the protection of France and Spain.[10]

Whatever credit might be given to the Earl-Bishop for his astuteness, however, was always likely to be undermined by the extravagance of his behaviour. On the opening of the National Convention he entered Dublin in state, like a monarch heading a victorious army of occupation. Dressed entirely in purple, with diamond knee and shoe buckles, and with long gold tassles hanging from his white gloves, he sat in an open landau, drawn by six horses caparisoned with purple ribbons. His own mounted servants, in gorgeous liveries, attended on either side of his carriage. In front rode a squadron of dragoons, commanded by his nephew, George Robert Fitzgerald, an old Etonian who was to be hanged for aggravated murder three years later.

A second squadron brought up the rear in equal splendour and thus, with slow and regal pace, the procession passed on, the volunteers falling in with bands playing and colours flying, the crowd shouting 'Long live the Bishop!', the Bishop bowing to the crowd.

At the doors of the Parliament House the cavalcade halted, and the Earl-Bishop had his trumpeters sound a loud fanfare, which startled the Members inside, so that some of them tumbled out like sleepy dormice emerging into the sunlight. The Earl-Bishop saluted them with royal dignity. The Volunteers presented arms, the band played the 'Volunteer March', and then, with a defiant blast on the trumpets, the procession went on its way. The Earl-Bishop's message to Parliament was as resolute as it was unsubtle.[11]

When the Convention assembled, it at once adjourned to the

Rotunda, where there was more space. Charlemont was duly elected chairman, no cause of comfort to him, though a setback for the Earl-Bishop. This was largely because most of the delegates were country gentlemen of character and position, and included 'several experienced and constitutional politicians, who had been induced by Charlemont to offer themselves as delegates for the express purpose of moderating its proceedings'.[12]

None the less, there were some demagogues and incendiaries present, and Charlemont noted 'some signs of violence' at the outset.

A certain Mr Bruce, a dissenting clergyman, proposed as one of the regulations that in all questions when sentiments were divided, the names of those who voted on either side should be taken down by the secretary, and published with the daily minutes of the convention.

The motion was carried without a division, 'any opposition to it having been deemed imprudent'.[13]

A committee was appointed from among the delegates, which began to debate various plans for the reform of Parliament. Charlemont listened with growing incredulity as delegate after delegate took the floor.

Hundreds of plans were sent in of the wildest and most ridiculous nature. Every schemer laid before them the crude production of his shallow understanding, and the farrago of matter was such as absolutely to confound the members; until at length, and after the toilsome confusion of many days, the Bishop of Derry moved that Mr Flood, who had not been put upon the Committee, should, with the leave of the convention, be called in as an assessor and assistant.[14]

Flood was still trusted by even the most radical delegates, and he rapidly and skilfully drew the strands of the debate together, and imposed on the committee what was effectively his own plan of reform. Charlemont made a public gesture of giving up control of his borough 'which I had ever held in trust for the people, and which I now most cheerfully re-delivered to them as the original proprietors'.[15] The Earl-Bishop tried hard to bring forward the question of the Catholic franchise, but, while he found considerable support from the delegates, he was defeated by the combined tactics of Flood and Charlemont. At the end of three tedious weeks the blueprint for parliamentary reform was ready, and on 29 November Flood proposed that he and other Members of Parliament present should at once proceed from the

Rotunda to Stephen's Green and move for leave to bring in a Bill corresponding to the plan, and that the Convention should not adjourn until its fate was known.

It was a foolishly precipitate step, as Charlemont sensed. His opinion was that all direct confrontation between the Convention and Parliament should be sedulously avoided, and that the plan should be carried down by the delegates to their respective counties for further discussion and, if approved, should come back to the House of Commons from the great body of constituents. But private interest fatally interfered. Flood had to sail in a few days for England, and he could not brook delay.

Charlemont has left a curiously moving account of the hours which followed. It was about 4 o'clock in the afternoon when Flood proposed his course of action and promptly set off for the House of Commons.

Three long hours elapsed, and no news arrived; when, at length, guessing from the delay . . . at what had passed, and dreading the effect which such a report as I now expected might produce upon minds inflamed with zeal, enraged at disappointment, heated with animosity, and rendered still more intractable by the impatience with which they had long waited, I, with much difficulty, prevailed on the assembly to adjourn, hoping that the intervention of a day, the morrow being Sunday, might in some degree calm the perturbation of men's minds, or, at the least, give time for prudent counsels.[16]

Flood, with William Brownlow and others, had gone down to the Commons in Volunteer uniform. The Members had only to look at them to see in graphic terms the nature of the challenge that was being presented. Was Ireland to have a civil or a military government? The placemen and the borough-mongers snuffed the air and knew that the game was theirs. Once again, as in 1775, the impetuous Flood had made a colossal error of judgement. Two assemblies representative of the people had sat within a mile of each other to debate the affairs of the nation, and the illegal one was now proposing legislation to the legal. The truth was that the alliance between Parliament and the Volunteers had broken down. They had united to achieve the patriotic goals of free trade and legislative independence. They were certain to disagree on parliamentary reform and the repeal of the penal laws.

For six years Parliament had been in thrall to the Volunteer movement, eager to exploit its command of popular opinion, but half-afraid of the military threat which it posed. Now, however, the American war had ended; and 'Gentleman Johnny' Burgoyne, who had surrendered to the Americans at Saratoga in 1777, was back in town with 20,000 troops under his command.[17] Parliament had nothing to fear from the Volunteers. It was time, even for the Patriots, to put the genie back in the bottle.

'We sit not here', said Barry Yelverton, now exalted as Attorney-General, 'to register the edicts of another assembly, or to receive propositions at the point of a bayonet.' And John Fitzgibbon, who was to be the architect of the Union, declared that he did not think life worth holding at the will of an armed demagogue. Towards 3 o'clock on Sunday morning the vote was taken. By 157 votes against 77 the House refused to receive the Bill. The Attorney-General moved a resolution that it had become necessary to declare 'that this House will maintain its just rights and privileges against all encroachments whatever', and even Grattan voted for it, though in silence.[18]

# 6

## True Old Whig Principles

For the Protestant Dissenters, enrolment as Volunteers was, in the words of their historian James Seaton Reid, 'the grand secret of their political influence' after 1778.[1] In the North most Volunteers were Presbyterian, and they frequently elected the more well-to-do members of their community as officers in preference to the episcopalian gentry. The *Belfast Newsletter* boasted that nine-tenths of the delegates at the Dungannon Convention of 1782 had been Dissenters.[2] Presbyterians supplied the rank and file of the whole organization in the North, and their ministers conducted drum-head services in full regimentals. A great many ministers and ruling elders of congregations were Volunteers, though they were, of course, acting as private citizens and not as representatives of their Church. By custom only the General Synod, the supreme court of the Church, was supposed to make political pronouncements, and political allusions did not normally appear in session or presbytery minutes. At times of intense political excitement, however, congregations and even presbyteries sometimes inserted declarations in the public prints, which made known, in forthright terms, their opinions on current affairs.

At the end of the eighteenth century the number of Presbyterians in Ireland was estimated at about half a million. The first ecclesiastical census, taken in 1834, revealed that approximately 8 per cent of the total population of the island was Presbyterian. The great majority of them were settled in the nine counties of the Province of Ulster, and almost three-fifths in the Counties of Antrim and Down alone. In Antrim they made up more, and in Down slightly less, than one half of the county population. There is no reason to believe that any significant change in these proportions took place during the preceding half-century.[3]

There were at that time five main bodies of Presbyterians in Ireland. Four of them were in Ulster, and the fifth consisted of the Synod of Munster and the Presbytery of Dublin, for historical reasons rather anomalous, and only loosely connected to the rest. The largest, and by far the most important, of these bodies was the Synod of Ulster, the original Irish Presbyterian Church, and an offshoot of the Church of Scotland. Closely associated with it, but less orthodox in theology, was the Presbytery of Antrim.

The other two bodies, the Reformed Presbytery and the Secession Church, were not really of indigenous growth, since they owed their origins to the schisms which afflicted the Mother Church of Scotland. The Seceders, carrying this tendency to schism to absurd lengths, divided amoeba-like into two associated synods, calling themselves Burgher and Antiburgher (the subject of contention was the Burgess Oath in Scotland). They were to reunite in 1818 as the 'Presbyterian Synod of Ireland distinguished by the name of Seceders'. The Reformed Presbytery, generally called Covenanters in Ireland, had nine congregations at the end of the eighteenth century, and the Seceders had forty-six.

At the beginning of the nineteenth century the Presbyterians were to be described as a people who had 'partaken so deeply first of the popular and since of the democratic politics of the country as to be an object much more of jealousy than of support to the government'.[4] There is ample evidence to prove that this description was justified. The first part of it refers to their intervention in the Volunteer movement between 1778 and 1785, and the second to their radicalism after 1790.

The process which brought the Presbyterians to the centre of Irish national politics really began in 1768 with the passing of the Octennial Act. Henceforth, elections were held every eight years, and not only on the demise of the Crown, making Parliament in theory more responsive to popular opinion. In 1776, during the first excitement of the war in America, the Presbyterians succeeded in electing James Wilson, a half-pay naval officer, to represent their special interests as one of the members for Co. Antrim. He undertook to submit all his actions in Parliament to the scrutiny of the local congregations, and in his campaign he had the full support of the General Synod. The Dissenters took the novel step of imposing on him an elaborate test. He had to agree not to accept any place or pension under the Crown, to obey his constituents' instructions, and to work for the reform of Parliament and the repeal of Poynings' Law, restoring to Ireland her rights as a free country. The adoption of this form of test was very significant both because of its content, and because it became the model for those which the Volunteers were later to impose upon their representatives during the campaign for legislative independence and parliamentary reform. Ultimately, the United Irish oath of association was to be called a 'Test'.[5]

Wilson resigned his commission in a memorial to the King which was highly critical of the government's actions against the American colonists, and he begged to be released from the awful choice of having either to disobey His Majesty's commands or 'rushing into the blood of his kindred fellow-subjects and countrymen'.[6] When Wilson was elected, the reaction of local Presbyterians was ecstatic. At a civic reception for him in Ballymena

ten thousand men with blue cockades, and hearts elated by the restoration of Liberty to the county, went foremost in array: next to these 400 freemasons, attired in their jewels, armed with carabines for the purpose of saluting, and preceded by a large band of music, and colours made for the occasion, descriptive of their different lodges, and embroidered with various emblematical figures; to these succeeded 500 young women, habited in white, ornamented with blue ribbons, and carrying green boughs in their hands; the leader of those patriot virgins bore a large garland richly decorated; and the animated daughters of liberty closed their fair train with a female band of music, who with infinite spirit and address, played 'Britons strike home' and several other tunes suited to the joy of the happy multitude.[7]

Despite the hyperbole in this account, particularly with regard to numbers, it does indicate fairly clearly some of the main elements in the campaign – good old true-blue Whig principles, a Masonic involvement, solidarity with the Americans, who were often literally cousins, and simple patriotism. Two years later, the threat of invasion and the popularity of the Volunteer movement caused a wave of patriotic and nationalist feeling to sweep through the country. In this the Northern Presbyterians enthusiastically participated. From the government's point of view, their nationalism was the most dangerous kind, for it was pro-American and tinged with republicanism. 'Presbyterians in the north', reported Lord Harcourt, 'in their hearts are Americans.'[8]

There is no lack of evidence for this, and it is clear that the links with kindred on the other side of the Atlantic remained close. Differing views on the American conflict could, and often did, divide Presbyterians from fellow-Protestants at village level. John Caldwell, who died in the United States in 1850, had childhood memories of the little club

which met to discuss politics in the house of his father or grandfather
in Coleraine.

On hearing news from America favourable to their cause, indeed the entire
village seemed but as one family, united in praying for the success of their
efforts. This continued until the famous declaration of 4 July 1776 arrived,
when Mr Lecky withdrew from the club, and his brethren of the village who
were members of the Established Church thought it incumbent on them to
join in the hue and cry against the rebels.[9]

The ministers were among the most ardent supporters of the American cause. In Tyrone the Rev. Thomas Birch drafted the address which
the Yankee Club of Stewartstown sent to Washington, expressing joy
that America had thrown off the yoke of slavery. Washington returned
his thanks.[10] In Co. Down the Rev. William Steel Dickson condemned
the war as 'unnatural, impolitic and unprincipled'. It is hardly surprising that many Presbyterian ministers were Volunteer officers and
among the most effective speakers at Volunteer conventions. These
were the years when, in Dickson's oft-quoted words, 'the rusty black
was exchanged for a glowing scarlet, and the title of Reverend for that
of Captain'.[11]

On 28 March 1779 Dickson preached a sermon to the Echlinville
Volunteers on *The Propriety and Advantages of acquiring the knowledge and use of arms in time of public danger*. Birch, when he moved
to Co. Down, became chaplain to the Saintfield Light Infantry, and
styled his manse 'Liberty Hall'. Dr Crombie, the minister of First
Belfast, published a sermon *On the experience and ability of volunteer
associations for national defence and security in the present critical
situation of public affairs*. On one famous occasion the minister of
Third Belfast, the Rev. Sinclair Kelburn, preached in Volunteer uniform with his musket leaning against the pulpit door. The Rev. William
Bruce joined the Lisburn True Blues as a private, and we have a
description of him preaching to his congregation 'in short blue
swallowtail coat, with brass buttons lettered LTB, red cuffs, collar
and facings, white breeches and black leggings'. At the Dungannon
Convention of 1782 the resolution in favour of Catholic emancipation
was seconded by the Rev. Robert Black, the minister of Dromore. The
Rev. Samuel Barber was captain of the Rathfriland Volunteers and
later colonel of the First Newry Regiment.[12]

Aside from the great national issues of 1779 and 1782, the Volunteers achieved much for the Presbyterians as a community. In June 1778 a vigorous attempt was made in the House of Commons to remove the most bitterly resented of the Dissenters' grievances. A Bill had been prepared to relieve Catholics of some of the penal disabilities. It was proposed to add to it a clause repealing the Sacramental Test, which had been added in the same way to the most notorious of the penal laws in 1704, 'the Act to prevent the further growth of popery'. This clause, by its insistence on communion being taken according to the usage of the Church of Ireland, had excluded Presbyterians from a wide range of civil and military offices. When the Bill was returned from England, the addition had been obliterated. The Bill passed and Parliament was prorogued.

During the long recess of Parliament, however, from August 1778 until October 1779, the Volunteers had increased rapidly. On the first day of the new session, Sir Edward Newenham moved for leave to bring in a Bill for the relief of the Dissenters, and the Speaker, accompanied by the entire Commons, carried it to the Castle. But on Christmas Eve 1779 the government disclosed that the Bill had not yet been transmitted to England, and it was not until 11 March 1780 that the Bill was finally, and rather ungraciously, conceded. Far from mollifying the Volunteers, this delay simply whetted their appetite for reform. To quote Reid, the Dissenters felt they were indebted for this piece of tardy justice, not so much to the enlightened wisdom of their rulers, as to the brilliant array of their own armed advocates.[13]

Among the Acts passed in 1782 was one which affirmed the validity of marriages among Dissenters celebrated by their own ministers. Another Bill, introduced by the Hon. John O'Neill and the Hon. Isaac Corry, was of great importance to the Seceders, who had always refused to kiss the Bible when swearing an oath. They were now permitted to swear with the right hand upraised. More was promised. The Whig Lord Lieutenant, the Duke of Portland, was drawing up plans to augment the *regium donum*, the royal bounty paid to the ministers, when the Marquis of Rockingham died on 1 July 1782. The scheme was not taken up again.

The first opportunity for the Presbyterians to demonstrate their renewed political confidence came little more than a year after Grattan's triumph. In the summer of 1783 Ireland was thrown into a state of excitement by a general election. In several of the Northern constituencies Presbyterian Volunteer influence turned the scales. Two candidates supported by the Independent interest, Hercules Rowley and John O'Neill, were returned for Co. Antrim. The Earl of Hertford, one of the great landed proprietors, had both his candidates defeated in the borough of Lisburn, where his influence had been considered absolute. The successful candidates were two very active and popular Volunteer officers, William Todd Jones (later to be a prolific writer of pamphlets) and William Sharman, a former revenue official.

In Co. Down, however, the contest was bitter and protracted. The Earl of Hillsborough had put forward his son, Lord Kilwarlin, as a candidate. Edward Ward of Castleward and Robert Stewart of Newtownards entered the fray in the popular interest. Stewart was then still a Presbyterian, as all his ancestors had been, and he felt sufficiently confident of the Dissenters' support to defy the combined strength of the landed families who still regarded him as a *parvenu*. Because of an undertaking he had once given to Hillsborough, however, he declined to enter into an electoral pact with Ward. To complicate the affair, the Seceders, who were very strong in this part of Down, were under a debt of gratitude to Hillsborough, who had acted as their patron in the oath-swearing business, and they turned out in strength for Kilwarlin.

The Dissenters of Belfast and Down threw themselves into Stewart's campaign with all the energy and enthusiasm of which they were capable. On one occasion the Rev. William Steel Dickson brought forty freeholders to the door of the candidate's lodgings in Downpatrick, after parading them on horseback through the town. In a rather contrived anecdote Dickson has the future Lord Castlereagh, then a lad of fourteen, rushing into the street, crying, 'See! See! Father! See what Mr Dickson has brought! I would rather be at the head of such a yeomanry than be the first lord ever a king created!' (Stewart had reputedly said that a peerage was an honour much inferior to that of representing the electors of Down.) The day would come when Dickson would be arrested and imprisoned on Castlereagh's order, and would describe him as 'the unblushing betrayer of his country to a foreign sanhedrin'.[14]

Birch, too, was campaigning. A burlesque history of the election attacked him as 'Blubbering Birch', a nickname which his enemies were not to forget. But his service to the Stewart family was not forgotten either, and one day he would owe his life to it. After a protracted contest of twenty-three days, Stewart finished at the bottom of the poll. The Presbyterians of the General Synod were irate, and they were inclined to think that he had lost the election by his over-scrupulous neutrality in refusing any pact with Ward, and perhaps also by his cold and distant manner towards his friends and supporters.[15]

A by-election later in the year gave the Independent interest another opportunity. Barry Yelverton resigned as the MP for Carrickfergus, a borough virtually controlled by Lord Donegall. One Amyas Griffith, a revenue officer from Cork who had recently settled in Belfast and single-handedly created a revival of Freemasonry there, stood as a candidate. Almost at once he withdrew in favour of Waddell Cunningham, then the captain of the Belfast First Company. The election lasted a week, and Cunningham was returned by 474 votes to 289 cast for Lord Donegall's nominee, Joseph Hewitt.

The Independents' satisfaction was all too short-lived. In March 1784, a petition lodged in the House of Commons alleged 'an undue election and return for the borough of Carrickfergus, effected through violence and other means'. Complaints were also made against the Constitutional Club of Lisburn, to which Griffith belonged, and its members were summoned to appear before a committee of the House in April. The hearing was twice postponed, and did not finally take place until February 1785. Griffith was the first witness to be called, and, with misplaced pride, he confessed that he had used every exertion in his power in favour of Cunningham 'not only as a private gentleman, but as a revenue officer'.

This damned him completely. The committee found that Cunningham had been elected illegally, and a new election was called. Cunningham stood again, only to be defeated by Ezechiel Davys Wilson, another nominee of Lord Donegall. The unfortunate Griffith was duped by John Pollock, Donegall's attorney, into taking the opposite side, in the hope of saving his post with the Revenue. Unknown to him, the Commissioners of the Revenue had already decided on his dismissal, it having been proved that he had used his position to induce a poor seaman, who sold an occasional unlicensed barrel of beer from his roadside cottage, into voting for Cunningham.[16]

During this eventful year, the Synod had been applying in Dublin for an increase in *regium donum*, through the advocacy of one of its most able ministers, the Rev. William Campbell of Armagh, who was chaplain of Charlemont's regiment of Volunteers. The new Lord Lieutenant, Lord Northington, received Campbell with great civility, but it soon became apparent that powerful interests at Court were opposed to the Dissenters' cause. Lord Hillsborough had seen the opportunity to revenge himself on the Synod. As a former Secretary of State for the colonies (in which office his inflexible views had helped to bring about the American war), he still enjoyed considerable favour at Court, and had plenty of incentive to oppose the Presbyterians on political and ideological grounds. Northington told Campbell that London considered the North of Ireland to be 'in a disturbed state, and ready to break the peace of the kingdom' and that 'very unfavourable representations had been made of the Synod of Ulster'.[17]

Campbell's reaction was to set about producing a polished vindication of his brethren, and to such good effect that Northington was won over. 'The principles you advocate', he told Campbell, 'are the old whig principles I revere, and I wish you to support the character of your forefathers.' After some delay he sent for Campbell again to tell him that 'the king's letter was come over, with a grant of one thousand pounds a year'. This was the largest increase ever made in the *regium donum*. Still the Presbyterians were not satisfied. Portland's abandoned scheme had promised them at least £5,000 and probably £10,000. And the knife was turned in the wound when it became known that Hillsborough had persuaded the King to grant £500 to his old friends the Seceders.[18]

The American war, the repeal of the Sacramental Test, the winning of independence for the Irish Parliament, the Renunciation dispute, and the subsequent campaigns for parliamentary reform and Catholic emancipation, were all subjects of burning interest to the Presbyterians of the North of Ireland, and nowhere more than in Belfast. We can see with great clarity how they impinged on the Dissenters in the fortunately preserved correspondence of a man who in these years was drawn ever closer to the eye of the storm.

# 7

# *The Blue Company*

On St Patrick's night in 1778, when the First Belfast Volunteer Company was born, a young Irish medical student in Edinburgh and a few of his friends dined together to honour their patron saint. William Drennan was twenty-four years of age and preparing for his final examinations. He was the son of the Rev. Thomas Drennan, sometime minister of Belfast's Old Congregation, who had died in 1768. The minister's wife had born him eleven children in all, but of these only three survived infancy – William and his sisters Martha and Anne. Martha (Matty) was the eldest of the three, born in 1742. She married a widower in her father's congregation, Samuel McTier, who had a grown-up daughter, Margaret. The second sister, Anne (Nancy), remained unmarried. Withdrawn in personality and eccentric in behaviour (at least in her family's opinion), she concerned herself with domestic affairs and, in contrast to her brother and sister, took little interest in public or political matters.

Drennan had at first intended to become a minister like his father. He attended a small school for local children conducted by the Rev. Matthew Garnet, a Church of Ireland clergyman. At fifteen he matriculated at the University of Glasgow and at some stage, perhaps on the advice of Dr Alexander Haliday, a family friend, he decided to become a physician. He enrolled as a medical student at Edinburgh in 1773 and graduated MD in September 1778. His family began to preserve his letters from 1775 onwards. On his arrival at Edinburgh, he soon discovered that for students from the North of Ireland, the city was not quite as congenial as Glasgow. He was very conscious of his Irishness, fiercely independent, inclined to be critical of the townsfolk, and rather homesick. 'Never, never, had a man a more burning affection for relations, for friends, for country than I have,' he wrote, 'and the pleasure I used to feel on the first day of my return to Ireland is a sufficient reward for the pains of Purgatory which I suffer here . . . I am the continual joke of the lads here for making Belfast the eternal subject of my conversation. I dream of Belfast.'[1]

By 1777, however, Drennan was comfortably installed in rooms at the end of Nicolson Street ('half-a-crown a week and a shilling for coals') and able to give his family a detailed account of the routine of his life as a medical student.[2] One reason why he missed Belfast was that its inhabitants were just then beginning to display such independence in politics. These citizens were not slaves, and scorned to be courtiers. His brother-in-law, Samuel McTier, seemed to him to be the very epitome of this independent outlook. Drennan had the hypersensitivity of the young and insecure. After some fancied slight from one of the professors, himself of Belfast extraction, he burst out,

What would I give to see Sam for one week among them. I declare to God I am ashamed and I blush this moment at the thought of having crouched so to them. I have the pleasure once a week of venting some of my rancour in the Speculative Society, which I could not do in private company, and as most of them take me for an American, I can do it with the greater safety.[3]

Like so many of his co-religionists in Ulster he was warmly sympathetic to the cause of the American colonists. It annoyed him to hear the Scottish divines praying for the success of British arms. 'Pray on ye men of blood, but if ever I forget thee O Jerusalem may my tongue cleave to the roof of my mouth, may this right hand forget its cunning. . . . Gentle spirit of my father, woulds't thou have prayed so?'[4]

However, it was prudent for a final year student to keep such thoughts to himself, or at least confine them to his letters home. Drennan suspected that some who knew more medicine than he did might have failed on account of their politics, 'one in particular last year having dedicated his thesis to his uncle, Mr Zubly, a member of the Continental Congress, the Principal threw his roll at him, and the poor fellow's laurels were blasted the same instant that he gathered them'.[5]

In the same letter Drennan rejoices at General Burgoyne's defeat at Saratoga. It was quite probable, he thought, that future historians would date the fall of the British Empire from 16 October 1777.

No object can be thought more melancholy than a great empire that has thus outlived itself, and is now degenerating into a state of political dotage,

prophetical of its final dissolution. Was it for this shameful day that Sidney
suffered and Hampden bled?[6]

Scotland had been gripped by war fever. Nothing was going on but
the raising of regiments for America. Every order of men from the
highest to the lowest were emptying their pockets. Nevertheless there
was some evidence of dissent. Although the Speculative Society had
raised 100 guineas, Dr Robertson, the Principal of the University, had
contributed only ten, and Drennan's friend Dugald Stewart but two.
Every Church of Scotland minister in the city had given what he could
to edge the sword of war except Dr Dick, who on the appointed Fast
Day had preached on the text 'How shall I curse whom the Lord hath
not cursed; how shall I judge whom the Lord hath not condemned?'[7]

In April 1778 Drennan got wind of the Volunteering in Belfast.

I see there is to be a militia established on a better footing. When and how is
it to take place? Were it in any degree compatible with necessary avocations,
I would greatly long to obtain some rank in it. You'll be so good as to ask
Sam.

Meanwhile, with six other Irish students he was receiving military
instruction from a sergeant in Edinburgh Castle.[8] By July his sister
Matty was able to tell him that the two Belfast companies were making
a good figure. The First was the most numerous, and Captain Banks
was fond of showing his men off marching to church, a parade which
others declined. Sam had been chosen as an officer in the Blue Company, 'a very inconvenient, because an expensive, honour'.[9]

In August Drennan took his degree, presenting his thesis on vene-
section in the treatment of continued fevers 'though not in elegant, at
least in good medical Latin, as well at least as some of my examiners'.[10]
When he returned home to Belfast he was swept into the Volunteer
movement with all the enthusiasm of a young and public-spirited
Irishman, joining the Blue Company, and taking a keen interest in
Volunteer politics. The correspondence with his family necessarily
ceased, frustratingly, at the beginning of the most critical phase of
Volunteer history, but he continued to write to his friend William
Bruce in Dublin, and from this correspondence we get a few tantalizing
references to company politics. A letter written in the summer of 1782
relates how Francis Dobbs had defended his support for simple repeal
to the Belfast Volunteers and been censured. Drennan was shocked by
the vehemence of the attack on Dobbs, whom he describes as 'a weak

vain honest man', singled out for vengeance. While the debate was going on there was a mob in the street, and he thought that the less vocal minority did not wish to make the Belfast Volunteers 'the first in the nation who have given a precedent to anarchy'. 'Flood is invited down here', he told Bruce,

and the first company intend to elect him their delegate. Every man in that company thinks himself fit to decide on the affairs of the nation, and on his Atlantean shoulders bear the weight of this mighty question. . . . It is a perilous adventure this Town is engaged in, to alter the voice of four provinces and two Parliaments and to reverse their decrees.[11]

The Renunciation dispute had unfortunately coincided with a crisis in Sam McTier's affairs. He owned a tan-yard in North Street in Belfast, but a disastrous fire had put him out of business and reduced him to penury. He and Matty were obliged to move in with Mrs Drennen while he looked around for some new employment. Both mother and daughter had strong wills, and Nancy and Margaret McTier were also under the family roof. Matty was rapidly brought to a nervous breakdown, and all of this put enormous pressure on her husband.

To a man in such a position, with a high standing in the Volunteers, the offer of a Fencible commission seemed like a godsend. He announced his intention of accepting, only to fall foul of the general indignation. The Volunteers' outright rejection of the government's proposals to raise Fencible regiments had begun with the Galway Independents, and their resolutions were considered by the Blue Company on 9 September 1782. The sixth resolution declared 'that we shall consider any volunteer who shall accept of a commission in any regiment of Fencibles to be raised in Ireland justly entitled to our severest censure'. It was endorsed, but with two dissentients, one of whom was presumably McTier.[12]

Similar resolutions were entered into by the six corps of the Belfast Battalion, with Colonel Banks in the chair, but they were not accepted with unanimity by all the inhabitants of the town, and a protest against them was published, signed by over forty leading citizens including George Black, Dr Haliday and McTier.[13] The tide of opinion was against them, however, and Sam was deeply hurt by the bitter attacks of his old friends. The scheme to raise the Fencibles was dropped, but in the meanwhile McTier resigned his command in the company.

Drennan was angry and embarrassed, the more so because he was privately in agreement with the critics.

Fortunately he had taken his sister Matty to Edinburgh in September, both to give her a change of scene and to seek medical advice from his old teacher, Professor Cullen. Cullen was a friend of Dr Haliday and of Doctor Mattear (Sam's cousin, though he spelled his surname differently) and at first he refused to accept any fee. He at once diagnosed Matty's complaint as nervous in origin, and assured her that a change of air would soon work wonders.[14] In fact her health had begun to improve dramatically as soon as she left Belfast, confirming the accuracy of Cullen's diagnosis. Drennan thus had an excuse to stay out of the way until the Fencible storm was over, but he confided his true feelings in a letter to Bruce.

You have no doubt heard of Sam's particular situation and must along with me have pitied the misfortunes that obliged a man of such principles to seek a livelihood in that line. . . . I know not whether it will give you pleasure or pain to hear that the fascinating voice of self-interest, backed by one or two puny arguments, had completely changed his views with regard to this branch of politics and made his understanding perfectly callous to impositions of which it was formerly peculiarly sensible. He has resigned his command of the Company, which perhaps he should have done the moment he formed a resolution of becoming a Fencible and all the other officers resigned.[15]

This was the disagreeable situation in which Drennan found himself on his return home. He decided to continue in the company for the time being, first because he agreed with the principles of the majority, second because he did not feel obliged to take part in squabbles which had occurred in his absence, and third because joining another corps might prove expensive. 'I shall endeavour to conduct myself as free in politics as a man of principle and an Irishman can do in times like these.'[16]

The visit to Edinburgh had been very successful. Everywhere they went they were asked about the Volunteers, and Drennan waxed ardent in the Volunteer cause. Mr Berkeley, the son of Bishop Berkeley the philosopher, was so interested that he left a large company to get sight of Drennan's blue uniform, 'which he returned with in his hand, saying, that was the dress of the common men in the Irish army'.

While they were away Mrs McTier gave her husband the benefit of her opinions on Volunteer politics, and in not very comforting terms. Brother and sister were of the same mind on the Fencible affair.

I am hurt that you are no longer an Irish volunteer: much hurt that you have lost next to Lord Charlemont's the most honourable post in it – and for what? I am at the same time perfectly assured that in such case you'd consider and act right, but be cautious of throwing blame on the Company. Though you are right, it does not prove them wrong. If they are in an error, it is an excusable one and what I am more inclined to admire than condemn. Perhaps their country may yet thank them for it. I cannot blame them in regard to the Fencibles, though I should never blush for you being one. Yet with an independence I would have gloried in refusing it. It sure will be peculiarly hard neither to be one or the other.[17]

All this helps to explain why Drennan eventually resigned from the Blue Company and moved to Newry to set up in practice there, though neither he nor Sam was finished with Volunteer politics by a long chalk. Obstetrics was the branch of medicine in which Drennan chose to specialize, and he began to practise as an *accoucheur*. His sister Nancy undertook to transform his blue Volunteer uniform into a coat suitable for a doctor on his rounds. The gold epaulettes were removed, and the coat was sent to the tailor for a new lining and lapels. 'This was but half-accomplished when the Taylor's fear of the Patriot stopped his hand. He came here and represented your displeasure at this sacrilege, *his* certainty that you would be here at the next Review, and your disappointment at finding you could not join the Company.' In the end a new coat was bought and sent to Drennan at Newry.[18]

He was not altogether displeased. For him it *was* a kind of sacrilege that Nancy should strip the gold epaulettes from his uniform. He might, after all, attend the review. The most exhilarating moment of his life had already passed, though he would come to realize this only gradually in the years ahead. It was the moment when he had stood on the *mons sacer* of Dungannon, and seen the word INDEPEN-DENCE flash on his imagination in letters of gold.[19] To him, as to so many of the Volunteers, it had seemed to be the dawn of a glorious day for Ireland.

# II
# A DEEPER SILENCE

# 8
# *An Honest Ghost*

All through his life Drennan walked with a ghost. The beckoning
shade, which constantly exhorted him to a high level of virtue, public
and private, was that of his father, the minister of the First Belfast
Congregation. Drennan was barely fourteen when his father died, and
his memories of him were the intense but incomplete memories of
childhood. He recalled walks in the country when he had been gently
chided for striking down nettles with a stick or treading on an insect.
Everything, his father told him, had an equal right to life. He remembered sitting silently under the table with the family cat for company,
listening to his father comfortably discoursing with Jack Ross, one of
his elders, over their tobacco and pewter tankards of ale. Above all,
he remembered his lessons in the classics, and his father bending over
him with benign approval at his school work, and planting on his
forehead a kiss that was the reward for diligence. Like many another
man, he later felt a vague remorse for a debt which could never be
repaid. At times of temptation or indecision the image of his father's
benign countenance came vividly to his mind, and he would dissolve
into tears.[1]

At a critical moment in 1792 Drennan's old friend John Pollock
came to his lodgings to try to persuade him to give up radicalism and
put his pen at the service of the government. Drennan was tempted,
but stood firm.

I said that I had early formed my principles in politics and that my father to
his last hour had desired me never to forsake them, and here, on recollecting
that best of men, and thinking that I saw his meek and venerable form and
face bending over me with a placid and approving smile, I burst into tears
and remained for some time much affected.[2]

Drennan once asked another of his friends, Dr William Bruce, to
provide a suitable Latin inscription for a tablet to his father's memory
which he proposed to place in the church. At length he took on the

task himself. There are several versions, and he seems to have worked on it at various times throughout his life, though the tablet was never inscribed.

'*Placida in morte quievit [Feb. 14, 1768]*', it begins, in fairly conventional terms, '*Thomas Drennan vir, integer vitae, scelerisque purus, amabilis, venerandus . . .*' It goes on, however:

You will not desert me, Best of Fathers . . . I hold you, and shall hold you, in memory. . . . I embrace the image of your morals, your virtue, your piety, the sophistication of your mind, your simple and open manners, the sweetness of your conversation, your popular eloquence and graceful erudition.[3]

A particular debt which Drennan felt he owed his father was the early introduction to Homer. While still a small boy he had been told the story of Ulysses, and lines to 'My Father', which Drennan published in 1815, ask:

> Who, with Ulysses, saw me roam,
> High on the raft, amidst the foam,
> His head uprais'd to look for home?

> What made a barren rock so dear?
> 'My boy, he had a country there!'
> And who, then dropt a *prescient* tear?

'Prescient', one assumes, because this boy would be remembered as a founder of the Society of United Irishmen, and as the poet who first called his country 'The Emerald Isle'. The lines continue:

> Who now, in pale and placid light
> Of mem'ry gleams upon my sight,
> Bursting the sepulchre of night?[4]

'Bursting the sepulchre of night' has an evocative ring. In 1785 Drennan suddenly begins to quote Shakespeare's *Hamlet*, and especially the scenes of Hamlet's encounter with the ghost of his father. In August he wrote to his friend Bruce that he had come up from Dublin to Belfast to see 'the buried majesty of the people arise and cross the stage for the last time. The ghost of volunteering was dressed in its habit as it lived, and shook in vain its visionary sword.'[5]

Criticizing Lord Charlemont's desertion from the ranks of reform, he says, 'The ghost of volunteering might now be made by the witchery of a master poet to rise and upbraid him.' Again, he writes, 'I vex not the ghost of volunteering with such cruel forgetfulness', and in the same year we find him talking about 'preparing an antidote to the poison which is daily coming in drop by drop, and all tending to this incestuous, accursed union'.[6]

From all this we might infer that Drennan had read the play, or seen it performed in that year, when the Volunteer movement was foundering, and that he had been particularly moved by it. Both he and his sister Matty continued to express enthusiasm about *Hamlet*, comparing different versions they had seen, and as late as 1801 she asks him, 'Why was Hamlet at thirty only just come from the university? Why does he swear by St Patrick?' And she adds, 'Oh that Shakespear, the world's wonder, had been born in Ireland. It could never have been that ill-fated, despised, degraded, swindled country.'[7]

In what sense did Drennan feel himself to be Hamlet to his father's ghost? What was the ghost's message? And to what did it enjoin obedience? The answers are in the play. Horatio, on first encountering the ghost, says:

> Speak to me
> If thou are privy to thy country's fate,
> Which haply, foreknowing may avoid.[8]

When Hamlet thinks that in his agitation he has offended Horatio, the latter says:

> There's no offence, my Lord.

and Hamlet replies:

> Yes, by St Patrick, but there is, Horatio
> And much offence too. Touching this vision here,
> It is an honest ghost, that let me tell you.[9]

At first sight, the helmeted spectre groaning from the wings is the defunct Volunteer movement. In his correspondence Drennan makes no secret of his view that the movement left its major work undone, and that there was a responsibility devolving on him, and those who thought like him, to redeem the Volunteer honour. He knew also the mixture of boldness and irresolution in his own character, his deep uncertainty about the course he should take, both in his career and in politics. He felt an irrational guilt and remorse about his father. There were so many things that he would like to discuss with him, now that he was a grown man.

Remember thee!
Ay, thou poor ghost, while memory holds a seat
In this distracted globe. Remember thee!
Yea, from the table of my memory
I'll wipe away all trivial fond records,
All saws of books, all forms, all pressures past
That youth and observation copied there.[10]

On the surface there might seem little to connect the mild Dissenting minister of Rosemary Street with the majesty of buried Denmark. But these tantalizing allusions awaken a curiosity about the Rev. Thomas Drennan and his political principles. The trail at first seems unlikely to prove rewarding. The biographical evidence is slender. There are a few side references, uninformative, scattered here and there – the tender memorial in Latin to his lost children, a single page of writing in an exquisite regular hand, an entry in church *Fasti*[11]. One feels like Sir Walter Scott's 'Old Mortality', scraping the moss from a weathered tombstone on a winter's evening in a dreary kirkyard.

Even Thomas Drennan's children seemed hazy about the details of his early life. In 1805 Mrs McTier told her brother that Dr Bruce had been asking her for some reliable facts and dates.

I assured him that I did not know the date of my own birth or any other. 'Oh,' said Bruce, 'you know that he lived at the corner of Dorset Street [in Dublin]?' 'No indeed.' 'That he was educated by, and the friend of Hutcheson? And I beg you to try and get me the information.'[12]

Bruce was trying to put together a history of Nonsubscription in Irish Presbyterianism, which was ultimately published in parts in *The Christian Moderator*. In this he describes Thomas Drennan as an elegant scholar, a man of fine taste, overflowing benevolence, and delicate sensibility.

His voice was solemn and pathetic, and, as he advanced in years, acquired a tremulous tone, particularly in reading the metrical psalms and in prayer, when in the fervour and tenderness of his devotion, the tears would sometimes trickle down his cheeks.[13]

In 1794 William Drennan was put on trial for seditious libel on the grounds that his 'Address to the Volunteers' was an incitement to armed rising by that body. He prepared his own defence, which his lawyers dissuaded him from using, as lawyers customarily do. No doubt their advice was good, for the eloquence of John Philpot Curran eventually secured his acquittal. But Drennan preserved the document among his papers, and even published it many years later. In it he declares:

I am the son of an honest man, a minister of that gospel which breathes peace and goodwill among men, a Protestant dissenting minister in the town of Belfast, to whose spirit I am accustomed to look up in every trying situation as my mediator and intercessor with Heaven. He was the friend and associate of good, I may say great, men; of Abernethy, of Bruce, of Duchal and of Hutcheson . . .

This sentence was the slender clue. It is the key to a door which leads us from the drear churchyard into a well-lit room in the early eighteenth century.[14]

For Francis Hutcheson was indeed a great man, remembered today as a philosopher who played a leading role in the development of the Scottish Enlightenment. He was born at Drumalig, halfway between Belfast and Saintfield in Co. Down in 1694, the son and grandson of Presbyterian ministers.[15] His grandfather, Alexander Hutcheson, who came originally from Ayrshire, was appointed by the Commonwealth government as the Puritan pastor of Saintfield in 1657 at an annual salary of £60. Evicted from the parish church at the Restoration, he eventually became the Presbyterian minister of Saintfield, and apart from a year at Capel Street in Dublin, he spent the rest of his life there.

He purchased the townland of Drumalig from the 3rd Viscount Clandeboye, and it was in the manse there that Francis Hutcheson was born. His earlier years were spent very much under his grandfather's tutelage. His father, the Rev. John Hutcheson, 'a man of good sense and excellent moral character, but of a modest and retiring nature',[16] was minister of Downpatrick from 1690 until 1697, when he was called to Armagh. In the 1720s, towards the end of his life, he was to emerge as a champion of the orthodox party in the Synod of Ulster, in contrast to the views of his son. John Hutcheson married twice, first a Miss Trail who bore him three sons, of whom Francis was the second, and then a Miss Wilson of Co. Longford. There was another family from this marriage.

When he was eight, Francis and his older brother Hans went to live with their grandfather at Drumalig, and Alexander Hutcheson seems to have taken a special interest in his grandsons' education. Their first school was a disused meeting-house at Saintfield, and then at fourteen

Francis was sent to an academy at Killyleagh conducted by the Rev. James McAlpine, who was held by the Presbyterians to be a teacher learned in philosophy. This was one of the earliest of the academies which the Presbyterians hoped to build up into a recognized seminary for the training of their ministers at home – an ambition which persisted throughout the eighteenth century – and it had a considerable local reputation, though it eventually disappeared. Here Hutcheson would first have encountered his cousin William Bruce, the son of the minister of Killyleagh. Bruce was later to be his Irish publisher.[17]

Alexander Hutcheson died in 1711, leaving his considerable property divided between his son and his grandson, Hans. John Hutcheson's portion was entailed to Francis, and was charged with annuities to the other dependents. In the same year Francis matriculated at Glasgow University (where he was entered as *Scoto-Hibernus*), probably along with friends, for more than half of the names entered with the Regent, John Loudon, are so described. After taking his MA in 1713, he began his theological studies and came much under the influence of the Professor of Divinity, John Simson, who was soon to be in the midst of his trials upon charges of holding heretical opinions.

There is an old, and no doubt much embellished, story which purports to illustrate the extent to which Hutcheson may have imbibed Simson's views while still an undergraduate. The Rev. John Hutcheson suffered from rheumatism, and one wet Sunday morning when Francis was at home during the vacation he yielded to the temptation of sending his son to preach in his place. An hour or so later the rain eased, and, grasping his walking-stick, the minister set out for his church, only to meet his entire flock on the road coming the other way.

'We a' feel muckle wae for your mishap, Reverend Sir,' said one of the elders, who was a Scot,

'But it canna be concealed. Your silly loon, Frank, has fashed a' the congregation wi' his idle cackle; for he has been babblin' this 'oor aboot a gude and benevolent God, and the sauls o' the heathens themselves will gang tae Heaven if they follow the licht o' their ain consciences. Not a word does the daft boy ken, speer nor say aboot the gude auld comfortable doctrines o' election, reprobation, original sin and faith. Hoot, man, awa' wi' sic a fellow.'[18]

Despite such distressing Simsonite tendencies, Hutcheson was licensed as probationer by the General Synod of Ulster in 1719, and shortly afterwards received a call to the congregation of Magherally. He probably stayed on in Glasgow after completing his studies, but evidence of his activities at this juncture is sparse. He was briefly tutor to the Earl of Kilmarnock's son, a connection of some significance as will later become clear, but he may have spent some time at home as well. It is possible that the growing crisis in the Synod of Ulster over subscription to the Westminster Confession of Faith delayed his entrance to the ministry, for he took the opposite side to his father.

He was not, however, destined to be the minister of Magherally. The passing of the Toleration Act at the end of 1719 allowed the Presbyterians to contemplate opening a private academy in Dublin, and some of the ministers there invited Hutcheson to take charge of it. He accepted the challenge at once. In 1720 he rented the house on the corner of Dorset Street and Dominick Street. (Dorset Street was then still called Drumcondra Lane and Dominick Street was in the process of being built.) At first he appears to have done all the teaching himself, but at some point after 1720 there were enough pupils for him to require an assistant. The assistant chosen was Thomas Drennan.[19]

Drennan was two years younger than Hutcheson, but went up to Glasgow while Hutcheson was still there. In the University records the name Thomas Drennan, *Scoto-Hibernus*, appears on the laureation (graduation) list under the date April 1716. Dr William Bruce in his notes on Nonsubscription says that his family came originally from Larne in Co. Antrim. Drennan's father carried on trade in Belfast, and was 'induced by the early promise of his abilities to spend on his education more than came to his share'. He was amply repaid, however, by his son's brilliant academic progress. In later years Drennan's widowed mother, 'when bereft of all her other children', took refuge with him and lived to the age of ninety.[20]

Drennan was not licensed by the General Synod of Ulster until 1726, and he seems to have carried on the work of the academy after Hutcheson left Ireland in 1730. In 1731 he was called to the congregation of Holywood in Co. Down, whence he moved to Belfast in 1736 to become assistant to the Rev. Samuel Haliday in the First Congregation.[21]

# 9

# *The Belfast Society*

Any account of the influences which moulded the young Drennan must begin not with Hutcheson, however, but with Abernethy. Born in 1680 in Co. Tyrone, John Abernethy belonged to that generation whose lives were indelibly marked by the events of the Williamite war in Ireland, and in particular by the Siege of Londonderry. In 1689, when the Revolution came, his father was the minister in Moneymore, in the neighbouring county of Derry. The elder Abernethy, with the Rev. Patrick Adair, had been chosen by the Synod to present an address of congratulation to the Prince of Orange, and he was in London when Tyrconnell's army swept down on Ulster. John, the eldest child, had been sent to stay with a relative in Ballymena. After the skirmish known as 'the Break of Dromore', when the Protestants were routed and Hamilton's troops overran Co. Antrim, the relative went to Scotland with the boy, giving him into the care of his maternal grandfather, Walkinshaw of that Ilk. Meanwhile Mrs Abernethy fled from Moneymore with the rest of her children to seek refuge behind the walls of Derry. During the siege all the children perished.[1]

John Abernethy entered Glasgow University, where his gifts were soon recognized, and after taking his MA there he moved to Edinburgh to study theology. Declining offers made to him in Scotland, he returned to Ireland where in a short time he received a 'call' from the congregation at Antrim. Meanwhile he had preached at Wood Street in Dublin, and that congregation were also determined to have him as assistant to their minister, the Rev. Joseph Boyse. By now Abernethy's father was old and ailing, and he decided to stay in the North. The Synod was called upon to arbitrate between his father's charge at Coleraine and Antrim, and sent him to Antrim.[2] He stayed there for twenty-seven years.

In 1705, with two other Co. Antrim ministers, Abernethy formed what came in time to be known as the Belfast Society. It consisted of local ministers, some divinity students and candidates for the ministry 'whose places of residence rendered their attendance practicable'. The Society devoted itself to consideration of the scriptural terms of the unity of the Christian Church, the nature and mischief of Schism, the rights of conscience and private judgement, the sole dominion of Christ in His Kingdom, and other subjects of that kind. At each meeting two members were appointed to study chapters of the Old and New Testament, and to present their interpretations at the following meeting, with any doubts that should have occurred to them.

Another function of the Society was the pooling of the members' reading and study. Each member undertook to tell the others the substance of anything remarkable which he had found in his reading since the last meeting. In this way they acquired knowledge of 'a great variety of curious books, which no single man among them had the leisure to read, or perhaps the money to purchase'. Care was taken that the same book should not be bought by two members.[3]

At first the Society attracted little attention, but some ten years after its foundation it began to become more widely known, not to say notorious. The accession of new members, and a change in the situation of the old ones, made it convenient for them to choose Belfast as their central meeting-place, and the Society acquired its familiar name. Orthodox Presbyterian historians have had little good to say about it. While reluctantly recognizing the intellectual abilities of its members, they have deplored their ecclesiastical indiscipline, and accused them of opening a door to Schism and heresy. Undoubtedly it created the nucleus of the ministers who would come to be called 'New Light', and through them it precipitated the great storm over doctrine which was soon to break over the Synod.

The two leading members of the Belfast Society were Abernethy and the Rev. James Kirkpatrick, the minister of Second Belfast. Both had been fellow-students with Simson in Glasgow and corresponded regularly with him.[4] Many of the younger members of the Society had studied theology under Simson, and reflected his opinions, sharing his desire to find a rational basis for the teachings of the Church.

In 1719 Abernethy preached a sermon before the Society on the text from Romans 14:5, 'Let every man be fully persuaded in his own mind'. The sermon owed a great deal to an even more famous discourse on 'The Nature of the Kingdom of the Church of Christ', which the Whig Bishop Benjamin Hoadley preached before George I two years earlier, and which sought to prove that the Gospels afforded no warrant for any visible Church authority. To save Hoadley from the wrath of the orthodox clergy, the King prorogued the Convocations of Canterbury and York, which did not convene again, except as a formality, until 1852. This was the the so-called 'Bangorian Controversy'.[5]

Abernethy's sermon was published, with consequences which were not dissimilar. For the next seven years the Synod was convulsed by a controversy that grew increasingly bitter and personal despite all attempts at mediation. In 1705 the Synod had enacted that thenceforth all persons licensed or ordained should be required to subscribe to the Westminster Confession as the confession of their faith.[6] That formula had been the historic one adopted by the Long Parliament in 1643 for the Puritan reform of the English Church, and agreed to by the Scottish Commissioners. Though its acceptance in England was partial and only temporary, it at once established itself as the definitive statement of Presbyterian doctrine.

Until 1705 the General Synod of Ulster had not insisted that ministers should sign the Confession, and its being made obligatory was the main reason for the Belfast Society's formation. As time went on, the outright rejection of the rule by Abernethy and his friends awakened suspicions that they had secretly espoused the Arian heresy, and no longer believed in the Divinity of Christ. The Nonsubscribers argued vehemently that there was no foundation for these suspicions, and that their objection was solely to man-made definitions of faith, but the occasional detection of heresy, as in the case of the unfortunate Thomas Emlyn, provided plenty of ammunition for their critics.[7] The Rev. John Malcolme, an elderly minister who published a pamphlet in reply to Abernethy's sermon, referred sarcastically to the Belfast Society providing a 'New Light'. The term was not original (it had been coined during the fierce theological debates of the mid-seventeenth century) but henceforward it was used constantly of the Nonsubscribers.[8]

One of the ministers suspected of Arianism was the Rev. Samuel Haliday, whose unusual early career had taken him well outside the bounds of provincial Presbyterianism. The son of the minister of Ardstraw in Co. Tyrone, he was born in 1685 and went to Glasgow University in the normal way when he was about fifteen. After taking his MA, he went to study theology at the University of Leyden in the Netherlands, and defended his thesis against Witsius, the celebrated critic of Spinoza. He was licensed at Rotterdam in 1706, and two years later chose to be ordained at Geneva 'because the terms of communion there were not narrowed by any human impositions'. He next became chaplain to Colonel Anstruther's regiment of Cameronians, and served with them throughout Marlborough's campaigns in Flanders. The Synod of Ulster accepted him as 'an ordained minister without charge' in 1712, but for some years he settled in London, where he seems to have moved in influential circles. Reid says that he was 'well known to the leaders of the Whig party, both in and out of government'.

In 1718 Haliday played some part in bringing about a substantial increase in the *regium donum*, the royal bounty paid to the Presbyterian ministers, and in 1719 he was present at the Salters Hall debates, which, in Caroline Robbins's words, 'marked the cleavage in the sects between the old fanatic and the modern rational dissenter'.[10] An attempt was now made to settle Haliday with the congregation of Plunket Street, Dublin. This failed, but in 1719, on the death of the Rev. John McBride, he received a call to First Belfast.[9]

It so happened that the Rev. Samuel Dunlop, a minister of one of the Southern congregations, and a man of orthodox views, had been in London at the time of the Salters Hall debates, and had formed the opinion that Haliday was not only an adherent to the Arian heresy, but an enemy to all Church government. He wrote this to a colleague in Belfast, and the rumour spread rapidly. However, the Synod which met in June 1720 found that Haliday had 'sufficiently cleared his innocency', and the accuser was rebuked. Justice having been done to Haliday, the Synod moved to quiet the fears of those Presbyterians who were becoming suspicious that some of the ministers proposed to throw over altogether the Westminster Confession of Faith.[11] They agreed on the so-called Pacific Act, expressing their determination to adhere to the Confession, but permitting any person required to subscribe, and who scrupled at any phrase therein, to express himself in his own words, and leaving it to the discretion of the Presbytery to accept the explanations or not.[12]

It was generally understood that this resolution was taken to meet the case of Haliday, whose installation at First Belfast was imminent. When the date arrived, Haliday dramatically refused to sign the Confession in *any* form, declaring that the Scriptures were the only rule of revealed religion. The Presbytery of Belfast went ahead with the installation, but the orthodox portion of the congregation withdrew, and set up a third church in Belfast. Haliday's disingenuous and tactless handling of the subsequent ferment was largely responsible for provoking the theological war which followed.[13]

Haliday's principal ally, apart from Abernethy, was the Rev. James Kirkpatrick, minister of the Second Congregation, which in its time had been the 'overflow' of First Belfast. He wrote an able defence of Nonsubscription, which appeared under the auspices of one of his elders, Dr Victor Ferguson. It came to be designated *Ferguson's Vindi-cation*, though Kirkpatrick was the real author. Dr Ferguson was an active member of the Belfast Society and a prominent Nonsubscriber. In his younger days he had travelled on the Continent, and claimed to have seen something of the Reformed Churches there, particularly the Protestant Church of France. Kirkpatrick and Ferguson have another curious claim to celebrity, though one that lay far in the future. The Empress Eugénie of France, the bride of Louis Napoleon, was descended from the family of Kirkpatrick, and Ferguson is the direct ancestor of Sarah Ferguson, the Duchess of York.[14]

One consequence of Haliday's installation at Belfast was that part of his congregation withdrew in the time-honoured way and announced their intention of creating a new congregation. The Synod gave its approval in 1722, and dismissed appeals against it by Haliday and Kirkpatrick. There was some unseemly wrangling over church property – 'cloaks, palls, flagons and cups' – and the orthodox party indicated that they were anxious to have the new meeting-house built, and a minister installed, before the next winter.[15]

That seemed an over-ambitious objective, but one Samuel Smith, a merchant with extensive business contacts in Scotland, set about fund-raising with a will. In the autumn he led a delegation to Glasgow, and on 22 September they laid their plans before the city's magistrates and council, stressing heavily that they were not only people who came from the Church and nation of Scotland, but firm adherents to the doctrine and government of the Scottish Church as defined in the Confession.

They received a sympathetic hearing, and on the following day, a Sunday, a collection was announced in the Glasgow churches. On Monday James Arbuckle, a graduate of Glasgow University, distri-buted to the council a printed hand-bill vindicating Haliday and Kirk-patrick from certain 'artful insinuations' against them which he pre-sumed were to be found in the petition. An irate Samuel Smith then printed his petition, which contained no such references, and added a few observations on the ungraciousness of Arbuckle's accusations. Arbuckle, who was studying divinity under Simson and was a strong supporter of the Nonsubscribers, published his rejoinder, with which the exchange ended.[16]

The Synods of Glasgow and Ayr, meeting in Irvine, organized another collection, and Smith and his friends were soon able to begin building their church. In gratitude for Scottish generosity, they designated three pews in the gallery for the perpetual use of visitors from Scotland, one reserved for merchants and master mariners, the other two for ordinary seamen. Flushed with success, Smith now asked the Synod's permission to extend his campaign to the east of Scotland, which knew little about Belfast and its affairs. This application was hotly resisted by the Nonsubscribers, and Haliday reported that he had had a letter from Professor Simson, who said that Smith in Glasgow had alleged that the Nonsubscribers held principles which might be dangerous to the Church, though he did not suspect them of Arianism. Smith demanded that the letter be produced. Haliday declined to produce it, and so appeared to be unable to substantiate his charge.

At this point Colonel Upton of Templepatrick, a prominent elder and one of the MPs for Co. Antrim, entered the fray with devastating consequences. What matter if Smith had used these words? Were they not the plain truth? In his opinion the Nonsubscribers *did* maintain principles which 'opened a door for error and heresy to enter the Church'. His intervention initiated another prolonged and bitter process of discussion. Upton was eventually defeated, but he automatically appealed to be heard again at the next Synod. Meanwhile Smith, undeterred, set out for Scotland, and spent the next three months raising funds in Edinburgh, St Andrews, Perth and Dundee.

In Edinburgh the Nonsubscribers had influential friends. A pamphlet was printed and distributed claiming that the Irish delegation then in the city was not worthy of public support. A letter of more moderate tone, signed by Haliday and Kirkpatrick, was also published, accusing the new congregation of promoting Schism. Smith returned to Belfast in April, well satisfied with the results of his mission. The church of Third Belfast was already roofed and glazed, and the Rev. Charles Masterton had been called to the charge of its congregation.[17]

Part of Haliday's original popularity had arisen from his role in having the *regum donum* augmented in 1718. Through the agency of Haliday and two of the Dublin New Light ministers, the Rev. Joseph Boyse and the Rev. Richard Choppin, the King had been persuaded in that year to add a further £800 from the English Civil List, one half of which was allocated to the ministers of the Synod of Ulster, and the other to the six ministers in Dublin. This augmentation had really been achieved largely through the influence of the English Dissenters. In 1723 the Synod received a letter from Boyse stating that the *regium donum* would no longer be paid directly to the Synod's agent, but instead made over in trust to the Rev. Dr Calamy and other Dissenting ministers in London. Boyse hinted that some in the Synod who were 'like to carry matters too high in Church affairs might find themselves obliged to walk more soberly'.

The Synod reacted with fury to this blackmail, and the Nonsubscribers were driven into the arms of the English Dissenters to an extent they did not desire. In 1725 there was a head-on clash with Calamy, who threatened to suspend the payment of the bounty, and the Dublin ministers, headed by Boyse, even approached the Lord Lieutenant, Lord Carteret, achieving the pained response that the divisions among the Northern Presbyterians were displeasing to His Majesty and ought to be healed.[18]

# 'O Domus Antiqua'

James Arbuckle, the student who distributed the handbills to Glasgow Town Council in support of the Nonsubscribers, was a close friend of Thomas Drennan. Their friendship, he says in one of his letters, went back 'almost to infancy'.[1] Arbuckle was a cripple who abandoned preparation for the ministry in favour of poetry and philosophy in 1724. He was not a great poet, but he does not deserve the obscurity which has enveloped his memory, and he has suffered from being confused with one or other of the James Arbuckles who seem positively to infest the scenery of contemporary Dublin and Belfast. He was probably the son of the James Arbuckle who was an elder in the Second Congregation, and who may be the Belfast merchant whose death, in the Isle of Man, was recorded in 1739.[2]

In 1719, while he was still at Glasgow University, Arbuckle published *Snuff*, a mock heroic poem with much interesting lore about snuff-boxes and snuff-taking. In downgrading smoking, it provides propaganda which would prove handy for any anti-smoking campaigner of today.

> No more th' unwary Youth whom Beauty fires,
> Through naseous Tube polluted air respires,
> Whose putrid Smack his humid lips retain
> And makes each Maid his loathsome Kiss refrain.[3]

In the same year Arbuckle wrote *An Epistle to Thomas Earl of Haddington on the death of Joseph Addison, Esq*, and in 1721 there appeared his best and longest work, *Glotta*, a description in verse of the city and University of Glasgow. His verses are for the most part innocuous imitations of Pope, whom he obviously admired.

The doggerel letters Arbuckle sent to his friends did not attempt that level, but they are generally amusing. In the year of his *Epistle* to Haddington, he wrote to Drennan, complaining of his slackness as a correspondent, a complaint that was to be echoed many times by his friends in the years to come:

> Dear Tom, tho' 'tis indeed provoking
> And past excuses, shams or jocking,
> That I cou'd never get my eye on
> One Line of yours these six months bygone.

Drennan is recalled to his obligations with a wealth of joky reference to classical anecdotes until the writer, in his relentless pursuit of rhyme, loses the thread of his discourse and reverts to news of the University, where smallpox and fever have made dreadful inroads on the 'collegians'.

The letter was brought to Drennan by John Smith, another friend, whom Arbuckle recommends to him in his place, as he is unavoidably detained in Glasgow

> Far from Lagana's* lovely Flood,
> Whom, when her grovy Honours stood,
> Oft in the dear, the sacred Shade
> Serenely cheerful have I stray'd.[4]

Within a short time after this, both Arbuckle and Smith were deeply involved in serious disputes with the University.

Students at Glasgow in the early eighteenth century got into the kind of scrapes which students have been involved in since universities began. They showed a propensity for staying out too late at night, drinking in low taverns, insulting the townspeople and taking part in riots. They wrote skits and poems to caricature their professors, drawing cruel attention to their mannerisms and physical appearance. They affected to believe that these mentors knew little or nothing about the subjects they were professing, and that they made a comfortable living at their students' expense – literally so, since the fees were then paid directly to the professors.

More surprisingly, perhaps, they were every bit as agitated as their modern counterparts about student rights, and anxious to establish democratic control of the Faculty and the College. There were frequent complaints that the Principal or the Faculty was acting in a despotic manner and encroaching upon the ancient rights and privileges of undergraduates. In the second decade of the century these complaints

---

* The River Lagan on which Belfast stands.

became more serious, and students were not infrequently 'extruded', that is, sent down, for breaches of discipline or intemperate behaviour.

In 1713 one William Carmichael was extruded for absenting himself from public worship, uttering Jacobite sentiments, attacking Presbyterianism and calling the ministers 'bloody-minded villains' and the Principal 'a greeting [weeping] hypocrite'. In the following year John Satcher was imprisoned in the steeple for writing an insolent letter to the Principal. He was rescued by the other students but recaptured, and then dramatically 'threw off his gown', signifying his withdrawal from the University. Even he was pardoned eventually. Indeed the authorities seemed to have tempered justice with mercy, or at least with indulgence for the predictable follies of youth.[5]

In 1716 a body of students burst open the door of the room in which the masters were sitting on a case of discipline, and bitterly accused the Faculty of injustice. More serious grievances lay behind this incident, however, arising from the fact that the Principal, John Stirling, a domineering and high-handed man, had antagonized the students over the method of electing the Rector. In November 1716 the University had once again declared Sir John Maxwell, Lord Pollock, to be the Rector, without involving the students. The dispute which followed was complicated, but in general terms the students were demanding a return to the former method of election, as laid down in the statutes, in which the undergraduates voted in their 'nations', along with their professors, whereas Stirling had been operating through a party in the Faculty, and latterly through an inner circle of his confidants. A Royal Committee of Visitation in 1717 effectively ruled in favour of oligarchy.

The students now alleged that Maxwell was exercising his office unjustly, and they authorized nine of their number to take action in the courts to have the election declared null and void. One of the nine was Francis Hutcheson. At this stage the students had the support of some of their masters, in particular the Regent, Gershom Carmichael, who in 1717 had delivered 'a noble Harangue to them in one of the publick Halls in Praise of Liberty' and continued to support their cause for some years until he was bought over to the Principal's side by some favours shown to his family.[6]

This was part of Stirling's triumph. With the help of influential aristocratic allies he managed to rout the opposition and exclude the students from the rectorial elections of 1721 and 1722. In the latter year an anonymous pamphlet was printed in Dublin with the title *A Short Account of the Late Treatment of the Students of the University of G . . . w*. It was distributed in Glasgow, and most of the copies were seized by the magistrates there and destroyed. Only a few copies survived. The pamphlet chronicles in some detail the cases of Arbuckle and Smith, and a reference at the beginning to 'the Authors hereof' would suggest that it was written by them jointly. Smith probably organized its printing and distribution.[7]

Headed by a classical epigraph, *O Domus antiqua, heu, quam dispari Dominare Domino*, and purporting to be a plain narrative of matters of fact, the *Short Account* gives a simple explanation of the corruption of the students' rights 'founded on the Old Gothick Rule of governing All by All'. These rights had not been questioned for centuries.

But soon after the late happy Revolution, the College being then in an unsettled condition, the Managers at that Time thought it might occasion strife and debates among the students to call them to a general meeting once a Year with the Figure and solemnity of a Corporation, and therefore took it into their heads that it would be most convenient to agree upon a rector among themselves, and afterwards intimate it to the students for their concurrence.

At the time, the students were too weak to oppose the Principal's measures, which was a great pity when one considers how the State itself had so recently been saved from tyranny.

an unhappy affair truly, that so soon after our Fathers had gloriously rescued themselves, and their children, from slavery, the Rights of their children at the University should be wheedled away, their tender minds depressed under the worst sort of tyranny, that of schoolmasters.[8]

*A Short Account* tells how the students had been browbeaten and abused for putting on performances of plays, Addison's *Cato* and Rowe's *Tamerlane*. They had been called wicked and ungodly for endeavouring to raise in their minds the sentiments of liberty and virtue. The ostensible objection of the Principal and Carmichael was that it was indecent for men to dress up as women to act the part of the ladies in the play.[9] The real reason was, of course, that these were both very political plays, Whig and Williamite in sympathy, in which civic virtue was contrasted with tyranny and corruption.

Nicholas Rowe's *Tamerlane*, written in 1701, was an implicit panegyric on William III, and one of the most popular plays in the early eighteenth century. Addison's *Cato*, first performed in 1714, seems to us a creaking drama (C. S. Lewis observed tartly that if Addison is not the most hated of English writers, it is only because he is so little read), but such was not the opinion of people at the time. *Cato* was an enormous box-office success, was reprinted scores of times, and acted continuously throughout the century. Pope was proud to write a prologue for it, and Queen Anne begged that it should be dedicated to her (but begged in vain).[10]

The Whigs seized upon it as their own, and the Tories quickly tried to wrest it from them. Party strife, at its most acute in 1714, ensured the play's popularity. But the antique virtues of the Roman Republic were the stock-in-trade of the Real Whigs and Commonwealthmen who kept alive the levelling principles of the Civil War. Both these plays had a special significance for Ireland and were always popular in Dublin. It must be remembered also that Addison had been Chief Secretary in Ireland between 1708 and 1710 when Lord Wharton was Lord Lieutenant. Wharton was brought up as a Dissenter, and is given the credit of writing the words of the Orange song 'Lillibullero'. Macaulay wrote that his first years were passed amid Geneva bands, heads of lank hair, upturned eyes, nasal psalmody and sermons three hours long. Once he emerged from this control, he went to the other extreme, and became the most notorious libertine in England, 'an emancipated precisian'.

Rightly or wrongly, he was believed to be sympathetic to the Irish Dissenters' efforts to have the Test Acts repealed, and this drew down upon him the hostility of the Established Church.

> Republicans, your tuneful voices raise,
> And teach the people whom to thank and praise,
> Lord Wharton first, for being High Church's terror
> And confuting that antique vulgar error
> That poysonous creatures could not in Ireland live,
> 'Til he came thither ...[11]

For the Glasgow presentation of *Cato* in 1720 a prologue was written by Arbuckle and an epilogue by a Welsh student, Thomas Griffith. 'It happened very unluckily that there were some passages in both which the Principal and his friends would needs understand to be meant for themselves.' Griffith had attacked 'those gloomy mortals who look upon theatrical representation to be the devices of Satan, and remanents of popery. This was reckoned to be a plain satyr upon the Principal and a wounding of religion through his sides.' Arbuckle for his part had mentioned that the tragedy of *Tamerlane* had been opposed by a tyrannizing faction on a neighbouring stage. The neighbouring stage could signify nothing but the Church, and the tyrannizing faction the Faculty, though it was really a reference to the Dublin stage. During the late reign 'a set of honest gentlemen' had been prosecuted for encouraging the production of *Tamerlane* in the Royal Theatre in Ireland.[12]

The Principal severely reprimanded Griffith, who was disgusted with the management anyway, and went to pursue his studies elsewhere. Stirling was also determined, with Carmichael's help, to break up the student societies, and one in particular, the Trinamphorian, of which Arbuckle and Smith were prominent members. Though it included some Glasgow merchants and ministers, the original members were all English and Irish, and it was looked upon as 'a set of Latitudinarians, Free-thinkers, Nonsubscribers and Bangorians, and in a Word, Enemies to the Jurisdictions, Powers and Divine Authority of the clergy'.[13] The Principal and his friends failed to suppress the society, but they found ways and means of gratifying their spleen against its members on all occasions, 'of which Mr Arbuckle and Mr Smith could, if they pleased, give the World very authentick Proofs'.[14]

Since the case of Arbuckle was 'more privately managed' by the University authorities, the *Short Account* could report only 'what in the instant of Mr Arbuckle's Resentment escaped him in conversation with his friends'. Smith's case was to become much more public. He had 'very early interested himself in the Liberties of the College, while yet only a Student of Philosophy', and by 1721, when he entered the Divinity School, he was a veteran of several clashes with authority. He had formed a poor opinion of his Professor of Divinity, the controversial Simson, who appeared to be

a Man of such trifling Genius as has exposed him to the Fury of the Bigots on the one Hand, and the just Ridicule of Men of Sense on the other. His empty metaphysical Speculations in Divinity are Proof of the first, as his annual Experiment, which he exhibits to his Scholars with a great deal of Solemnity, of kindling a Turf Clod at *Christmas* through a piece of cold Ice, to the great Terror of his Majesties peaceable Subjects, is an Evidence of his being studiously serious in Vagaries.[15]

Underlying all this unrest was the continuing saga of the rectorial election, and in 1722 the students began to seek the aid of more powerful allies:

All other Means having proved ineffectual, it was found necessary at last to apply to the House of Commons, and interest the Representatives of the Nation in a Matter of such great Consequence to the Publick. A Petition for that End was prepared, and several Honourable Patriots in Parliament were so sensible both of the Justice and Importance of the Cause of the Students of *Glasgow*, that they very warmly espoused it, and promised them such Assistance as it became Men of Honour, and Lovers of publick Liberty to give.[16]

The initiative was very successful. Several opposition members at once demonstrated support, though this fell away when more urgent matters claimed their attention. The students found their most steadfast friend in Robert, 1st Viscount Molesworth, who had a seat in the English Commons and in the Irish Lords. Molesworth's father fought on the Parliament side in the Civil War, and was rewarded with 2,500 acres of Irish land in Co. Meath. Subsequently he became a rich Dublin merchant and rose high in Cromwell's favour during the Commonwealth. Robert Molesworth was born in Fishamble Street in Dublin, and educated at Trinity College. Attainted like so many other Protestant landowners by James II's 'Patriot Parliament' in 1689, he went to Denmark on a secret mission to persuade the Danish king to send troops to aid the cause of William III. The result was the Danish force which fought at the Boyne.[17]

William made him Privy Councillor and in 1692 sent him to Denmark as his envoy extraordinary, but two years later Molesworth had a blazing row with the Danish Court and withdrew abruptly to Flanders, where he expressed his resentment by writing *An Account of Denmark as it was in the year 1692*.[18] His object was to show that a monarchy subservient to a Protestant clerical establishment could be more tyrannical than any Catholic autocracy. This ruffled some Whig feathers, but the book became very popular with radical thinkers, and brought Molesworth to the favourable notice of Locke and the 3rd Earl of Shaftesbury. It was soon identified as a kind of textbook of Real Whig principles, though these were even more clearly set out in the preface which Molesworth wrote in 1713 for a translation of Francis Hotoman's *Franco-Gallia*.

After a few stormy years in Anne's reign, he was restored to favour by George I, and created Viscount Molesworth of Swords. He won the admiration of Swift, in spite of his pronounced anti-clericalism, and it was as a tribute to him as an Irish patriot that Swift dedicated the fifth of the *Drapier's Letters*. Molesworth was ageing and unwell by 1722, but he took up the cause of the Glasgow students with enthusiasm. Only the calling of a general election that spring prevented him from presenting their petition in the Commons, and in the resulting contest he unexpectedly lost his seat and retired to his home at Breckenstown on the outskirts of Dublin – not, however, before a false report of his success reached Glasgow.

The Irish students were elated and, with some sympathetic townsfolk, they lit a large celebration bonfire in the High Street opposite the main gates of the University. There was no objection to a bonfire as such, but this particular one was regarded by the Principal as a piece of insolent sedition on the part of the wild Irish. Carmichael rushed out and ordered them to extinguish the fire at once. Smith told him that he had no authority outside the University, and Carmichael, losing his temper, began to drag out the burning timbers himself. Smith caught his arm and pulled him to the ground. Although he had been at Glasgow for six years without any complaint being made against him, Smith was summarily expelled for the very serious crime of assaulting a regent, though five of the Faculty entered protests in his support.[19]

Smith took his case all the way to the Court of Session, which, within a month, granted him a Bill of Suspension against the University. Incredibly, the University paid no attention to it, and did not even bother to lodge answers to his complaint. The Professor of Divinity genially told him, 'he might light his Pipe with his Suspension, because it was not worth a F––t'.[20] Smith immediately went back to the court, and this time the University condescended to answer the complaint. It argued that it was the business of students to study, not to concern themselves with government and public affairs. The Lord Advocate added this gloss: 'Mr *Smith* is an *Irishman*, and if he, and his *Irish* Brethren take the Liberty to put on Bonfires when they think fit, others may do it upon very unlawful Occasions.'

Smith's reaction was to interpret this as a racist remark, all the more unmannerly 'when we consider against whom it is levelled, viz. the numerous body of Britons transplanted, who have done and suffered more for the British and Protestant Interest than any Twenty imperious Ministers of State had ever either the will or capacity of doing'.[21]

The legal wrangle dragged on, and was not finally resolved until 1727. Smith went to Dublin when the Court of Session rose for the summer recess on 1 July 1722, and never returned to the University. It is no surprise to learn that he handed over a letter of thanks to Lord Molesworth from the Glasgow students.[22] The efforts of the discontented students and their friends to enlist Molesworth's support can be traced in the published extracts of his surviving correspondence. On 5 March 1722 one William Stuart assured him that his 'approbation of our proceedings will be a powerful incentive to us to imitate that love of liberty and our country, for which Your Lordship is so justly celebrated'.[23]

In August Molesworth received a letter from Dr George Turnbull, lately made Professor of Philosophy in 'the new College of Aberdeen'. Turnbull was a loquacious supporter of the students and his letter is one of fulsome compliment: 'Good and honest surely must he be who is the friend and trustee of the truly good and upright Shaftesbury . . .' Turnbull says that he has made a close study of Shaftesbury's works, and laments that none of the philosopher's friends has given the world an account of his life. He assures Molesworth that 'even in this narrow bigoted country' there are several of his acquaintance who are sincere lovers of truth and liberty.

There is an intriguing postscript. When Turnbull was just about to seal the letter, a friend called on him, one to whom he owed his introduction to Shaftesbury's works.

He was educated by his Presbyterian friends for the sacred function, and e'en commenced preacher, before he came to his present free state of mind and just notion of religion and virtue, but is now a very sincere promoter of liberty and true virtue, by his sermons and otherwise, and indeed he is very well fitted to do service here in the honest cause, being wise as well.[24]

Another of the students' supporters, the Rev. William Wishart, wrote to Molesworth in similar terms in October, rejoicing with him in the revival of ancient virtue and the love of true liberty, and mentioning particularly the proofs of that noble spirit which the learned youth of the University of Glasgow had lately given.[25]

After his return to Ireland in the summer of 1722 John Smith, having tasted the joys of publication, set up in business as a publisher and bookseller 'at the Philosopher's Head' on the Blind Quay in Dublin, taking into partnership one William Smith, to whom he may have been related. This William Smith was the son of the merchant Samuel Smith, whose prodigious fund-raising for the Belfast Third Congregation has already been described. In 1724 he married into the Dutch publishing family of Wetstein and settled in Amsterdam, where he spent the rest of his life. To replace him John Smith took, as his new partner, Hutcheson's cousin, William Bruce. By 1725 they were ready to bring out their first title, under the imprint 'Smiths and Bruce'. It was *An Inquiry into the Original of our Ideas of Beauty and Virtue* by Francis Hutcheson.

# 11

# 'A Contempt for Tyranny'

Hutcheson's *Inquiry* was a direct and youthful response to the works of Shaftesbury, and a defence of them against the criticism of Bernard Mandeville, a hard-headed, anglicized Dutchman, who had published his thoughts in 1714 as *The Fable of the Bees*. Mandeville, who was as much as anything a self-taught satirist of humanity, argued that the origin of virtue was to be found in 'selfish and savage instincts', and pointed out that public prosperity depended on private vices, a theory which is now fashionable, but which was condemned as pernicious in the early eighteenth century. Most of the moralists execrated it, however, Dr Johnson was later to write that the *Fable* did not puzzle him, but 'opened his views into real life very much'.[1]

Shaftesbury had taken the view, all the evidence notwithstanding, that benevolence was a natural human instinct. Hutcheson took this premise and developed it as the basis for a whole ethical system. The purpose of the *Inquiry* was clearly enough set out in the book's extended title: *An Inquiry into the Original of our Ideas of Beauty and Virtue; in two treatises, in which the principles of the late Earl of Shaftesbury are explained and defended, against the Author of the Fable of the Bees; and the Ideas of Moral Good and Evil are established according to the Sentiments of the Ancient Moralists: with an Attempt to introduce a Mathematical Calculation in subjects of Morality.* The somewhat ludicrous attempt to introduce mathematics into morality was quickly dropped in later editions.[2]

Anthony Ashley Cooper, the 3rd Earl of Shaftesbury, was the grandson of the Restoration statesman, the protagonist of the Whig and Protestant forces unleashed at the time of the Exclusion crisis. His early nurture had been under the care of John Locke, his grandfather's trusted adviser. Locke, indeed, had chosen his father's wife, attended her as physician in her confinement, and acted as tutor to the child. As far as was humanly possible, the young Shaftesbury was a Locke product. Nevertheless, he later diverged from Locke's views and openly criticized them. Forced to abandon politics for literature by his delicate health (he suffered much from asthma), he retained his political interests and never ceased to be aware of his Whig inheritance.[3]

At different periods he spent some time in the Netherlands, where, like Locke before him, he lodged in Amsterdam with the Quaker merchant Benjamin Furly, a key figure in the Anglo-Dutch network of independently-minded thinkers. Through Furly he met the influential French Huguenot exiles Bayle and Le Clerc. Shaftesbury's first work, *An Inquiry concerning Virtue*, was published surreptitiously by the ubiquitous freethinker John Toland, not altogether to Shaftesbury's pleasure. However, he became a patron to Toland for a while, as he was to Collins and other freethinkers.[4]

A series of Shaftesbury's essays, written between 1708 and 1710, were expanded and published together in 1711 under the title *Characteristicks of Men, Manners, Opinions and Times*, and it was this work which had so profound an effect on the young Glasgow students of Hutcheson's generation. Its appeal was as much literary as philosophical. Shaftesbury's style, though high-flown and convoluted, attracted the intelligent general reader, and was devoid of the worst obscurities of philosophical treatises. It consisted more of reflections than deep thought, and offered a theory of aesthetics which was elegant and patrician. The prevailing tone was one of religious scepticism, though this was hinted rather than expressed, and Shaftesbury himself continued throughout his life to take the Anglican sacrament. There was, however, no doubt at all about his robust anti-clericalism. As a consequence he was vigorously attacked as a Deist or worse.

Nevertheless the *Characteristicks* had an immediate success, and was reprinted many times. To this day Shaftesbury is a neglected English writer, but his influence has been greater on the Continent, especially in France and Germany. One of Denis Diderot's first publications was a free translation of the *Inquiry*, and Diderot was also very interested in Hutcheson's early writings.

Hutcheson's decision to acknowledge his indebtedness to Shaftesbury and Molesworth in the dedications to his *Inquiry* was courageous, and one of his objects in the work was to purge Shaftesbury's teaching of its sardonic references to Christianity. That he thanks Molesworth for a modification of one of his arguments is a further indication that some kind of philosophical club met regularly under his aegis.[5]

Arbuckle's connection with Molesworth seems to have begun early in 1722, when he wrote to ask his advice about the petition which the students wished to have presented in the House of Commons. In the letter he asks whether Molesworth has written anything else besides the *Account of Denmark* and the preface to *Franco-Gallia*.

I have lately been reading the writings of a noble friend of Your Lordship's, I mean the late Lord Shaftesbury. I had read them some time ago, when I was very young, and so had no other taste of them, than of a piece of genteel and easy writing. I need not tell Your Lordship what my sentiments of them now are. But there is one circumstance in them I cannot help taking notice of, as what gives me a good deal of pleasure, which is an imagination they raise in me, of My Lord Molesworth being the same person with Palemon in the Rhapsody.[6]

Whether or not because of this piece of flattery, Molesworth became Arbuckle's patron. It is almost certain that he was responsible for the launch of the *Dublin Weekly Journal,* and for establishing Arbuckle as its editor and chief contributor. The periodical published six of Hutcheson's early philosophical essays. Many of the other papers were by Arbuckle, and there were at least two articles by Samuel Boyse, the scapegrace son of one of the Dublin ministers, the Rev. Joseph Boyse. Boyse, who made a small literary reputation on the wider scene, and was the friend of Samuel Johnson, must be regarded as one of the Molesworth coterie at this time. For the rest, the pages of the *Dublin Weekly Journal* were filled up with pieces by anonymous contributors, gathered by Arbuckle as editor. A selection of the essays was published in two volumes by John Smith in 1729, and has generally become known as *Hibernicus's Letters*.

Arbuckle seems to have lived for a while in Molesworth's house at Breckenstown, where some of the papers were written, and when Molesworth died in 1725 he was left £10 in his will.[7] One of Molesworth's prevailing principles was the encouragement of ideas of liberty and truth, as the Whigs understood them, across the denominational divisions of Protestantism. It is not too fanciful, therefore, to assume that he made his residence in his retirement the centre for a coterie of like-minded young scholars and writers, including the Anglican Edward Synge, who was to become Bishop of Clonfert at an early age.

They may have formed some kind of philosophical and political club (there are shreds of evidence which would suggest this), and it is certain that the Molesworth connection was vital to Hutcheson's development through the links it provided with thinkers outside his own Church.

Synge belonged to a distinguished family of Protestant prelates. His father was the Archbishop of Tuam, and his grandfather had been Bishop of Cork, Cloyne and Ross. His uncles had been bishops, and he and his brother Nicholas were to move rapidly and smoothly to the episcopal bench. But Synge's father, the Archbishop, had written a popular work called *A Gentleman's Religion*, 'designed to explain Christianity both to the rational philosopher and to men of mediocre intelligence', and the young Synge was a disciple of Shaftesbury and Molesworth. It seems likely that he encountered Hutcheson at Breckenstown. Hutcheson admits that Synge had 'fallen into the same way of thinking before him',[8] and his influence on Synge is perhaps to be seen in the latter's support for toleration for the Dissenters. Synge was to preach a sermon to Parliament on the subject, and to be attacked by his fellow-clergy for his pains. It was another of his sermons, however, that caused the greatest outcry.

For over a century after the Irish Rebellion of 1641, the Church of Ireland held an annual service of Thanksgiving on 23 October for the deliverance of Protestants. On that day in 1725, Synge preached a sermon on the text 'Compel them to come in'. It was an impassioned plea for the relaxation of the penal laws. Synge took up the argument for the poorer Catholics of Ireland which Molesworth had advanced in his *Considerations for Promoting Agriculture* in 1723, attacking the actions of ecclesiastical courts in enforcing the collection of tithes, and suggesting that the Catholic clergy should be paid by the State. No one had a right to persecute, he argued, and to admit that right was to legitimize Catholic persecution of Protestants in countries like France and Poland. Coercion made hypocrites, and the proper conduct for Protestants was to set a good example. Molesworth argued that children should be given a non-sectarian education, and, while Synge obviously could not approve of this, he emphasized that the duties of citizenship should always be put before denominational loyalties.[9]

Throughout his life Hutcheson was singularly favoured by fortune. At the very moment when Molesworth died, he was taken up by a much more influential patron, though of very different principles – no less a person than the Lord Lieutenant, Lord Carteret. Ireland was then still in the grip of the extraordinary agitation over the affair of 'Wood's Halfpence'. The Duke of Grafton had been recalled, and Lord Carteret was sent over to try to placate opinion. Carteret was a powerful minister, and a dangerous rival to Walpole, who sought to neutralize him in the time-honoured way by sending him to Ireland. Carteret was an unusual Lord Lieutenant, and an untypical aristocrat, being highly intelligent, a scholar and linguist as well as a skilled diplomatist.

He had, in the words of another of his protégés, Jonathan Swift, come down from Oxford with more Latin and Greek than properly became a man of his station. The story goes that Carteret was so impressed by Hutcheson's *Inquiry* that he sent his private secretary to ask for the author at the bookseller's, and when he could not find out his name, he left a letter to be conveyed to him. One can only guess at Hutcheson's feelings on receiving such a letter. He came forward, and soon he was being received as a guest at the Castle, where Carteret liked to surround himself with scholars and men of wit as an occasional relief from the politicians he was obliged to receive.[10]

All the time he was in government, Carteret treated Hutcheson 'with the most distinguishing marks of familiarity and esteem', and it seems that overtures were made to him promising substantial advancement if he conformed to the Church of Ireland. It is even said that he might have been offered the Provostship of Trinity College, but that tale lacks credibility. No doubt Hutcheson was sorely tempted. At length these rumours reached the quiet manse at Armagh, and caused predictable consternation. His father wrote him an anxious letter.

Hutcheson's long reply is extant, dated 4 August 1726 and beginning 'Honoured and dear sir'. It is a most curious document, not so much a letter from son to father, as an essay on Church government. 'I would sooner have wrote you on this subject', he began,

had I apprehended you were uneasy about it. I knew there was such a rumour, but reports of that kind are so common, and so industriously spread by those who are fond of converts, upon any Dissenter's meeting with civility from persons of distinction, that I did not imagine they would make any impression upon my friends.

To summarize, Hutcheson defines at length his attitude to the Established Church, but on what would appear at first to be singular grounds for a Presbyterian.

As to the separation from the Church, I will own to you what I scarce ever owned to anyone else, that it seems to me only a point of prudence. I do not imagine that either the government or the externals of worship are so determined in the Gospel as to oblige men to one particular way in either . . . all societies may, according to their own prudence, choose such a form of government in the church, and agree upon such an external order of worship as they think will do most good, to promote the true need of all real piety and virtue, but without any right of forcing others into it.

As his biographer says, this letter does not indicate a startling deviation from the sincerity which gave him a character for moral honesty. But clearly he was preparing to rationalize his conforming to the Church of Ireland, should he finally decide on this step. 'I have kept my mind pretty much to myself', he confides,

and resolve to do so. I assure you if I should ever take contrary resolutions of which I have no present presumption, I will let you know it, and consult you on everything, which appears difficult to me; and pray, if you have leisure, let me know what you think faulty in what I write to you.

There is a postscript.

Pray write to me further on this subject, and assure yourself that there is no ground for your uneasiness. Were I disposed in that way, there is nothing to be got worth acceptance, without some vile compliance to which I would not submit.[11]

He did not conform, but the importance of his contacts with intellectuals of the Established Church, and with men of rank, in moulding his outlook and opinions, and those of his friends, can scarcely be overestimated. The circumstances were fortuitous, but the ripples from these events were to spread very widely. New avenues of knowledge were opened up for Hutcheson. He already held New Light views imbibed as a student of Simson at Glasgow, in contrast to those of his father, who was indeed shortly to become a champion of the Old Light doctrine. The experience of discussing theology and politics with men of the calibre of Edward Synge and William King (the future Archbishop of Dublin) was broadening, and it was for Hutcheson, as for them, a conscious effort to apply the Molesworthian principles of indifference to the divisions of Protestantism.

All this time, Hutcheson's reputation as an author had been growing. No doubt the Lord Lieutenant's patronage had not been a disadvantage, but the major reason was the steady demand for his book in

England. A second edition had been printed within six months of the first, and a considerable controversy had sprung up. A debate with Gilbert Burnet (the son of Bishop Burnet) in the columns of the *London Journal* was amicable, but Hutcheson was attacked on all sides by theological dogmatists who regarded him as virtually a free thinker.

To have placed Shaftesbury's name on the title-page was a bold act, since in some circles Shaftesbury was regarded as a Deist and a dangerous enemy of religion.[12] In 1728 Hutcheson published *An Essay on the Passions*, and an Irish edition was brought out by his friends John Smith and William Bruce 'with the errors of the London edition emended'. In 1729 a third edition of the *Inquiry* was printed in London, and the letters which Hutcheson contributed to the *Dublin Journal* were reprinted in a collected edition by James Arbuckle.[13]

The year 1729 was the turning-point in Hutcheson's life. His father, 'the best friend he had in the world', died in February, and in the same winter he lost one of his children. This double loss preyed on his spirits for a long time. On his visits to Armagh, to wind up his father's affairs, he made the acquaintance of yet another influential churchman, none other than the Primate, Archbishop Hugh Boulter. Later, through Hutcheson, Boulter was to give a sum of money to Glasgow University to provide bursaries for deserving students.[14]

In 1729, too, the Regent Gershom Carmichael died. Three candidates were thought of for the vacant chair – Carmichael's son Frederick, a Mr Warner, and Hutcheson. From the outset the election was seen as a contest between adherents of the old spirit and the new within the University. According to the Faculty minutes of 19 December 1729,

after several of the members had discoursed about a fit person, the question was put, who shall be elected to the vacant profession of Philosophy? And the clerk having called the roll, it was carried by the majority that Mr Francis Hutcheson of Dublin should be elected.[15]

After his election Hutcheson remained in Dublin and continued the work of the Academy until the beginning of the next academic year in October 1730. On the 30th, he gave his inaugural lecture, *De Naturali Hominum Socialitate*, defending the principle of benevolence, but according to one who was there, 'owing to his delivering it very fast and low, being a modest man, it was not well understood'! It was the custom to welcome a new professor over a glass of wine. On this occasion the wine flowed freely; a bill was subsequently presented for £5 for wine, and others followed for more wine, fruit and 'biskets'.[16]

Whatever diffidence Hutcheson may have shown in his inaugural address soon evaporated as he settled down to a new honour in familiar and congenial surroundings. The thirteen years of his absence from Glasgow had seen the academic body plunged into turmoil, and many reforms had been carried through. The relationship of the University to the Presbyterian Church (in Scotland, it must be remembered, it was the *Established* Church) remained unresolved. Hutcheson did not shrink from the challenge implicit in his appointment. He identified the West of Scotland ministers, some of whom looked upon all culture and intellectual refinement with suspicion, with the Old Light party of the recent broils in the General Synod of Ulster, and he at once declared for the more modern and progressive element. He opposed the conservatives not only from the whole cast of his thinking, but from resentment at the treatment of some of his friends, Abernethy, Haliday and Michael Bruce, during the Nonsubscription controversy.

Such a stance might easily have precipitated Hutcheson into the kind of heresy trials experienced by some of his predecessors. He was, however, a man of considerable tact and diplomatic skill who took readily to university politics. This, combined with a natural caution, kept him out of serious trouble, such as had befallen his old teacher, John Simson. Wodrow, whose sympathy was entirely with the old school, reported in the autumn of 1730 that he was 'well spoken of' and by the end of the year that 'he was much commended'.[17]

It was in the purely academic sphere, however, that Hutcheson appeared most revolutionary. Instead of the usual commentary in Latin upon a scholastic textbook, he inaugurated a new method, lecturing in English, and covering the whole field of natural religion, morals, jurisprudence and government in the five lectures he gave each week. At first he kept strictly to the familiar texts of Samuel Pufendorf and the *Compend* of his predecessor, Gershom Carmichael, but he soon began to deliver his own lectures, which proved to be very popular. At the same time he gradually built up over the years, with many digressions and additions, his *System of Moral Philosophy*, which was not published until after his death, but on which his reputation largely rests.

His students give ample testimony to the value of his teaching and the attractiveness of his personality. They included a great many men who would achieve distinction in later years, and spread Hutcheson's influence widely. Adam Smith, perhaps the most famous, speaks of the 'never to be forgotten' Hutcheson. Dugald Stewart, who was to become a friend of William Drennan, mentions among his students the Earl of Selkirk, Dr Archibald Maclaine, the translator of Mosheim's *Ecclesiastical History*, and his own father, Matthew Stewart, who became Professor of Mathematics at Edinburgh. Among his pupils, too, was Francis Allison, who was to exert enormous influence in the New World through his own students. He emigrated from Co. Donegal to Chester County in Pennsylvania, where he 'taught, undiluted, the Hutchesonian doctrine'.[18]

A tract written in 1772 with the express purpose of drawing attention to *The Defects of an University Education* makes an exception for Hutcheson.

If ever a Professor had the art of communicating knowledge and of raising an esteem and desire of it in the minds of his scholars; if ever one had the magical power to inspire the noblest sentiments and to warm the hearts of youth with an admiration and love of virtue; if ever one had the art to create an esteem for Liberty and a contempt for tyranny and tyrants, he was the man![19]

Nor was Hutcheson's influence confined to the lecture room. The undergraduates' perennial complaint about the aloofness of their professors was justifiably strong at Glasgow at that time. Hutcheson not only took the keenest interest in their welfare but made himself useful to students of all faculties when they needed his help. In particular, he acted as banker, guardian and friend of the students from the North of Ireland, many of them the sons and nephews of his friends. Some of these gave him a good deal of anxiety.

We learn something about them from his letters to Tom Drennan. Once away from parental and congregational control, these Ulster students were apt to kick their heels. As one might expect, they were both 'backward' (in the colloquial and not the intellectual sense) and unbearably arrogant and vain. 'They are left with little check or control over them', as one Moderator of the Synod complained, 'they seldom brought letters of introduction; they had no acquaintance, and they kept almost entirely to themselves; even in the Divinity Hall, they generally sat in a back place by themselves, and formed little acquaintance with the other students.' Yet, as Hutcheson himself observed,

'Our countrymen generally have such an affectation of being men and gentlemen immediately, and of despising everything in Scotland, that they neglect a great deal of good wise instruction that they might have here.'[20]

Hutcheson had a shrewd business sense, and his increasing involvement with the day-to-day running of the University helps to explain his failure to publish much of note during his last decade at Glasgow. In 1735 he published *Considerations on Patronage addressed to the Gentlemen of Scotland*, a document of some importance to historians of the Scottish Enlightenment, and in 1741 translated the *Meditations* of Marcus Aurelius with one of the colleagues, James Moor.

On Christmas Day 1745 the army of Prince Charles Edward occupied the city of Glasgow, and the University was thrown into panic. There is a tradition that it narrowly escaped being burnt by the Highlanders, though the Prince had promised to take it under his special protection. Obviously some of the professors of outspoken anti-Jacobite sympathies had an uncomfortable time. But, as every teacher knows, some pupils continue to cherish kindly thoughts of their early mentors, even when they become figures of consequence in the real world. The Jacobite cavalry was commanded by Hutcheson's old pupil, now the Earl of Kilmarnock. No doubt this was very welcome insurance, but all the evidence indicates that Hutcheson and Moor were more anxious about Kilmarnock's fate than their own, and though later they tried to repay his kindness, they could not save him from the axe. 'We have had a dull winter,' Hutcheson wrote to Drennan on St Patrick's Day, 1746, 'more so after the departure of the vagabonds than before.'[21]

In that spring Hutcheson had some of his Wilson relatives staying with him in Glasgow, and ominously they were all brought down with fever, and for a while were dangerously ill. In his last letter to Drennan he writes that he intends to take them back to Ireland in the summer, but that he is obliged to hang on in Glasgow 'for a most intricate business on which the soul of the College depends, and all may be ruined by the want of one vote'.[22] That business was in fact to ensure that James Moor was elected Professor of Greek as Dunlop's successor. Hutcheson then went to Dublin, and at once contracted fever. He died on 8 August, his birthday, at the age of fifty-two, and was buried in St Mary's churchyard in Dublin.

To determine Hutcheson's place in the history of philosophy is not within the scope of the present work. Even if he was not one of the great original thinkers, and if his whole system of ethics now seems outmoded, it is still true that he 'struck out very great lights, and made very considerable discoveries by the way'.[23] His influence has been remarkably wide – on the political views which led to the American Declaration of Independence, and on the debate on slavery half a century later; on the economic ideas of his pupil Adam Smith, and on the philosophy of Diderot and the *Encylopédistes*.

The political content of Hutcheson's teaching was startlingly modern. He taught that slavery in any form was a totally unnatural state and could not descend a generation. Nine-tenths of nations had been enslaved because men had been 'a great deal too tame and tractable', and civil war might be a lesser evil than subjection to a bad government. Hutcheson wholeheartedly endorsed the right of resistance to private and public tyranny. Servants have the right to leave unjust masters; wives have rights against husbands; even children are not obliged to obey their parents for ever.

As in the family, so it was in the State. The criterion of virtue in a trust or delegation of power was the well-being of the whole people, and of any failure to achieve this, the people must be the judge. Office should not go by inherited favour. Not even superior wisdom gave a right to rule. Government must be so planned as to prevent mischief even if it fell into bad hands. A popular elected assembly and a senate with a limited term would provide security against tyranny – essentially a republican form of government. Hutcheson believed a wide reform of representation was necessary, and he endorsed the idea of a ballot and frequent elections. He was an early advocate of the reform of Parliament and the simplification of the laws of the realm. He showed enthusiasm for the idea of a citizen army. Sixty years later, most of these views would appear verbatim in the columns of the *Northern Star*, the organ of the Belfast United Irishmen.[24]

# 12

# Ministers of Grace

Some special quality attaches to the Dublin ministers, setting them apart from the rest of the Presbyterian body, yet connecting them to obscure Dissenting congregations in the English Fenlands, to Rotterdam and Leyden, and to Roxbury and Boston in Massachusetts. What this quality is precisely, is not at first easy to identify, since there are several strands to it, and they have been the subject of little or no research. The essential clue does not present itself in conventional summaries, and it is not difficult to be led on false trails, but once it is found, most of the other pieces of the jigsaw fall into place. It is exemplified in the history of the Wood Street Congregation.

One consequence of the Cromwellian period in Ireland was that congregations of Independents and Baptists were established in some of the Southern towns and these in time became Presbyterian. This was true of several of the Dublin congregations, though one, Bull Alley, was founded by Northern Presbyterians. A congregation was already in existence at Wood Street in Cromwell's time. In 1647 its pastor was the Puritan divine, John Owen. To describe this Welshman simply as the pastor of Wood Street is in the highest degree misleading. He was later to be Vice-Chancellor of Oxford University, appointed so by Cromwell, and chosen by him as his chaplain in Ireland. Cromwell entrusted him with the task of remodelling the entire religious Establishment in Ireland, and one of his first acts was to appoint six salaried Parliamentary preachers for the city of Dublin.

Owen was a polymath, equally at home in the classics, mathematics, philosophy , theology, Hebrew and rabbinical lore. As if this was not enough, he was also a very accomplished flautist. Expelled from his first living by Archbishop Laud in 1637, he had published many weighty attacks on Arminianism, and had experimented with Presbyterian and Congregationalist forms of Church government. He preached before Parliament on the day after the King's execution, and his sermon was published along with a defence of private judgement in religion. After his spell in Ireland he was appointed official preacher to the Council of State, and rose high in the esteem of the Lord Protector. When a royalist rising was anticipated in 1654, he made himself responsible for the security of Oxford, and 'was frequently to be seen riding at the head of a troop of horse, well mounted and armed with a sword and pistol'.

An intellectual and physical giant, Owen lived almost to the end of Charles II's reign. Clarendon offered him high preferment if he would return to the Anglican fold, but he remained true to his principles. He had the reputation of being no persecutor, and, surprisingly, was held in high regard at the Restoration Court. He even spent hours arguing the rights and wrongs of Nonconformity with the Duke of York, the future James II. Owen died in 1683 and was buried in Bunhill Fields, that great necropolis of English Dissent.[1]

Owen's immediate successor in Dublin in the 1650s was another eminent Puritan theologian, Stephen Charnock. Charnock was chaplain in the household of Henry Cromwell, who was sent by his father to Ireland as Lord Lieutenant. Charnock resided with the Lord Lieutenant's family, and preached in Wood Street on Sundays 'having persons of the greatest distinction in Dublin for his auditors'.[2] The next pastor at Wood Street was the Rev. Daniel Williams, another Welshman, born at Wrexham in 1643. Williams was licensed as a Dissenting preacher at the age of nineteen, but after the Restoration life was made difficult for the preachers, and when an opportunity arose for him to become chaplain to the Countess of Meath in Ireland, he accepted with alacrity, and in 1667 he received an invitation to be the minister of Wood Street.

He was a Presbyterian minister in Dublin for the next twenty years, during which time he married a lady of considerable wealth. On the succession of James II, Williams's 'attachment . . . to Protestant principles was too well known to make it safe for him to reside in Dublin' and he removed himself to London, where he exercised much influence among the Dissenting ministers, prevailing on them not to vote an address to James approving of the toleration granted to them by the exercise of the King's prerogative. He preferred, he said, that they should be exposed to all their former hardships rather than give public approbation to a dispensing power destructive of the liberties of their country.

In 1688 Williams became the pastor of the congregation in Hand

Alley, in Bishopsgate Street. He was the friend of Richard Baxter, and it is said that King William III sought his advice on Irish affairs. Williams died in 1716 at the age of seventy-two and was buried, like Owen, at Bunhill Fields. He devoted much of his wealth to various charities, and he left his library of theological works to a foundation which is today the great Dr Williams Library in London. It is particularly rich in rare works by the Puritan divines of the Civil War and Commonwealth period. Williams was the first patron of that enigmatic character John Toland, who exercised an incalculable influence on Voltaire and some of the other French *philosophes*. Through Toland, Williams was brought into contact with the Huguenot publicist Jean Le Clerc in the Netherlands.[3]

Williams's successor was Boyse, who hailed from Leeds. His father was a Puritan who had lived for many years in the New England colonies but returned home on the setting-up of the Commonwealth. At some time about 1680, when he was twenty, Joseph Boyse became chaplain to the Countess of Donegall and came into contact with Ireland for the first time. But for a short while he officiated as minister of the English congregation in Amsterdam, before joining Williams as his colleague at Wood Street in 1683. Boyse was a prolific author of controversial pamphlets, one of which, on *The Office of a Scriptural Bishop*, the Irish House of Lords ordered to be burned by the common hangman.[4]

Boyse was the father of Samuel Boyse, whose literary career began with the articles he contributed to Arbuckle's *Dublin Weekly Journal*. Born in 1708, Samuel was educated in Dublin, and was possibly Hutcheson's pupil before going to Glasgow. While still an undergraduate, he married a Miss Atcheson and, without adopting a career, brought her home to live in Dublin on the slender resources of his father, the minister of Wood Street. Boyse was one of those unfortunate individuals who are dismissed in reference books with a single sentence of disapproval. For the stern Witherow, he was 'a fool and a profligate' who brought down his father's grey hairs with sorrow to the grave. Bonamy Dobrée, in his *English Literature in the Early Eighteenth Century*, records that 'he took no degree, entered no profession, and, bungling all his opportunities, died in poverty'.

Boyse was indeed not a model which any man would recommend to his son. When the minister died in 1728, he stayed on in Dublin for two years but was eventually forced to decamp to Edinburgh, where, remarkably, he gained the favour of many influential figures. They provided him with introductions, any one of which might have assisted him to embark on a successful career. The Duchess of Gordon gave him an introduction for a post in the Customs, but, as it rained heavily on the day of his interview, he decided to stay at home. He was given a letter of introduction to Pope, but the poet being away from home when he called, he never bothered to call again. Yet Boyse had won these favours by the recognition of his undoubted ability. He had printed a letter on 'Liberty' in the *Dublin Journal* in 1726, and in Edinburgh he had published 'The Tears of the Muses', and in London his best work, 'The Deity'. Unfortunately, as Dobrée remarks, his prayer in that work, 'O grant me Wisdom – and I ask no more', was not altogether answered.[5]

Boyse's genius was, however, recognized by Pope, by Fielding (who quotes him in *Tom Jones*) and by Samuel Johnson, who in his youth had shared some of the rigours of his poverty at St John's Gate. Boyse was a regular client of the local pawnbroker, and on one of these occasions the young Johnson collected a sum of money to redeem his friend's clothes, which two days later were pawned again. 'The sum', reflected Johnson sadly, 'was collected by sixpences, at a time when to me sixpence was a serious consideration.'[6]

Boyse's poverty became legendary, even in the annals of Bohemia. He is credited with the invention of paper collars, which he was driven to cut from strips of white paper, when his last shirt was pawned. When his entire wardrobe went, he was obliged to take to his bed, but having still some employment in writing verses for the magazines, 'he sat up in bed with a blanket wrapped about him, through which he had cut a hole large enough to admit his arm, and placing the paper upon his knee, scribbled, in the best manner he could, the verses he was obliged to make'.[7]

Another of Boyse's techniques for survival was to have his wife put affecting notices of his demise in the newspapers, so that the couple could live for a while from his friends' charity to the widow. The opportunities for repeating this ruse were of course limited.

In the pastorate of the first four ministers of Wood Street there is a theme of continuity. It is their connection with the Commonwealth, and the survival in muted form of some of its political and religious ideals, which in the seventeenth century had been but opposite sides of the same coin, as they are to a large extent in Ireland to this day.

There was another, and related, connection which was of considerable significance. Some of the Dublin ministers were the sons of Puritans who had fled to America, and left their mark on the early history of New England. Matthew Boyse had been an elder in the congregation at Rowley and had lived for eighteen years in Boston.[8]

The most interesting example, however, is that of the Rev. Nathaniel Weld, minister of the neighbouring congregation of New Row. The Welds were a distinguished English Catholic family residing at Lulworth Castle in Dorset, who in the nineteenth century would produce a cardinal. Thomas Weld, the minister's grandfather, became a Protestant and entered Holy Orders in the Church of England. In 1632, when Archbishop Laud began to enforce conformity of worship, he emigrated to the North American colonies where he was pastor of the Independent church at Roxbury. In 1638 he became overseer of Harvard College, and with Richard Mather and John Eliot prepared the Bay Psalm Book , the first book to be printed in English North America. He returned to England as the Bay Colony's agent to negotiate with the English Parliament. He did not return to America, but became rector of Gateshead.

The minister's father, Edmund, was a Harvard graduate who came to England and became chaplain to Cromwell when he was Lord Protector. He died at Cork at the age of thirty-nine. Nathaniel Weld was also a close friend of Sir Isaac Newton, and christened his son Isaac in his honour. Such was the background of a man who was a friend and colleague of Hutcheson and Drennan.[9] When, in 1784, William Drennan told his mother that he had dined with Mr and Mrs Isaac Weld, then an elderly couple, she reminded him that Nathaniel Weld had been 'your father's friend'.[10]

Two of Nathaniel Weld's predecessors at New Row were Samuel and Nathaniel Mather, who were the uncles of the Rev. Cotton Mather. There is no need to stress the importance of the Mather family in the early history of Massachusetts. This was a period which saw the beginning of a massive exodus of Irish Protestants to North America, by far the greatest proportion of them Presbyterians from the Bann and Foyle Valleys, and Cotton Mather was an ardent advocate of the settlement of the 'Scotch-Irish' in New England. He also had close connections with Glasgow University, which awarded him the degree of Doctor of Divinity in 1710.[11]

The linking of these themes can also be seen in the family of the

Rev. Robert Craighead, who was minister of Capel Street, Dublin. He had been educated at Glasgow, Edinburgh and Leyden, was a Nonsubscriber, Moderator of the Synod in 1719, and one of those ministers responsible for bringing Hutcheson to Dublin. Craighead's father had been a Puritan pastor appointed at Donoughmore in Co. Donegal, and subsequently Presbyterian minister there. His brother, the Rev. Thomas Craighead, and his brother-in-law, the Rev. William Homes, were among the first Ulster ministers to arrive in Boston, in October 1714, armed with testimonials from the Dublin ministers, including Boyse.[12]

Long before the days of Haliday and Drennan, circumstance had woven connections between the affairs of the Old Congregation of Belfast and the wider forms of Dissent known in Dublin. The congregation had its distant origin in the activities of the five military chaplains who accompanied General Monroe's Scottish army to Ulster in 1642. One of them, the Rev. John Baird, was appointed to preach in Belfast 'every third Sunday'. And it was the action of the 'Belfast presbytery' in lamenting the execution of Charles I which provoked Milton into some very impolite observations on the people of the North of Ireland. At the Restoration the bishops hardly waited for the sanction of Parliament to begin ousting the pastors. Thus, in the words of Patrick Adair, one of the ejected brethren, 'there came a black cloud over this poor Church'.[13]

The survival of the original Belfast congregation was owed to a curious circumstance. Arthur Chichester, 1st Earl of Donegall, who died in 1675, married, as his third wife, Letitia Hicks, the daughter of Sir William Hicks of Knockholt in Essex. The Countess of Donegall was, unusually, an English Presbyterian, and the Rev. William Keyes, the first of the uninterrupted succession of ministers at Belfast, was an English divine under her patronage. During the Commonwealth he held the rectory of Heswell in Cheshire, moving at some time before 1660 to become minister at Glaslough, Co. Monaghan. From there he transferred first to Carrickfergus and then to Belfast.[14]

Thanks to Letitia Hicks, the Belfast congregation was able to enjoy a kind of grudging patronage from the staunchly Anglican Donegall family, which owned the town and all the ground it stood on. This was to be important throughout its history. Equally important was the fact that at this critical stage, along with the Dublin congregations, it came under the influence of English Presbyterianism, which was distinct both in history and in outlook from the Scottish Presbyterianism established elsewhere in Eastern Ulster. It was markedly more tolerant, and freer in doctrine and discipline. In 1668 the Earl of Donegall gave the Belfast congregation a small piece of land near the North Gate, on which it built its first meeting-house.[15]

Both Lady Donegall and the congregation were displeased when in 1673 Keyes accepted a call to the pastorate at Bull Alley in Dublin. After vainly trying to prevent his removal, the elders chose as his successor the Rev. Patrick Adair of Galloway. Adair had been present in Edinburgh High Kirk on that memorable day in 1637 when there was a riot in protest against the introduction of the Scottish Prayer Book. Ordained minister of Cairncastle in Co. Antrim in 1646, he had led a stormy existence throughout the years of the Commonwealth and Protectorate, representing his co-religionists in almost every meeting with the Cromwellian authorities. Later in his life he sat down to write a *True Narrative of the Rise and Progress of the Presbyterian Government in the North of Ireland*, a valuable source of Nonconformist history for this period.

Adair's translation to Belfast was met with some opposition from the Chichester family. Henceforth the Countess of Donegall would have nothing to do with him or the congregation. She trusted her spiritual care instead to her chaplain, the Rev. Samuel Bryan, who had been a Fellow of Peterhouse and vicar of Allesley in Warwickshire. Ejected from his living in 1662, Bryan had spent six months in Warwick gaol for preaching at Birmingham, before obtaining the post of chaplain in the Donegall household.

In 1683 the Countess, now widowed, appointed Thomas Emlyn as domestic chaplain in her London house at Lincoln's Inn Fields. From its windows that July he watched the execution of the Whig 'Patriot', Lord Russell. In the following year he accompanied Lady Donegall to Belfast and continued to act as her chaplain even after she was married again, to Sir William Franklyn, an English gentlemen, who took up residence at the Castle in Belfast. Emlyn's situation was an ambiguous one. He attended the parish church of St Anne's and was even permitted to officiate there 'in a clergyman's habit'. On Sunday evenings when he preached in the Donegall household, the vicar of Belfast attended his sermons. With Adair he had no communication at all.[16]

Emlyn's engagement lasted until 1688 when the dynastic crisis and 'domestic difficulties' forced the household to break up. Franklyn was obliged to take his part with the other Protestant gentlemen in raising and commanding a regiment of Volunteers in the Williamite cause. According to Benn, the historian of Belfast, Franklyn was not enthusiastic about this, and 'his military ardour being perhaps not very great, he had expressed an intention of going to England'. However, when this design came to the knowledge of his soldiers 'they forced him to remain'.[17]

By this time Emlyn had received overtures from the congregation at Wood Street, Dublin, but he was determined to return to England where, in May 1689, he became chaplain to Sir Robert Rich of Beccles in Suffolk. Rich was a Lord of the Admiralty, and a leading member of a Presbyterian congregation which met in a barn in Blue Anchor Lane in Lowestoft. Emlyn ministered to them for eighteen months. The Wood Street call was then renewed and this time he accepted it, being ordained as the colleague of Joseph Boyse in May 1691. The consequences were to be momentous, not only for Irish Presbyterianism, but for Dissent in the British Isles as a whole.

For the next eleven years Emlyn continued as pastor to the Wood Street congregation without ever disclosing to them that he no longer believed in the divinity of Christ. At length a medical doctor in the congregation, one Duncan Cumming, noticed the odd fact that Emlyn never referred to the doctrine of the Trinity, even by accident, in his sermons or prayers, and suspected the true reason. He consulted Boyse and the two waited upon Emlyn in June 1702 and requested an explanation. Emlyn at once admitted candidly that he held Arian views and offered to resign without causing any strife.[18]

However, Boyse felt it necessary to bring the matter to the notice of his brethren in Dublin – Weld, Travers, Sinclare, Iredell and Tate. They further examined Emlyn and, finding him unrepentant in his opinions, assumed presbyterial powers and agreed to depose him from his office. Even at this stage it might have been possible to hush the whole matter up, but Emlyn insisted on taking the congregation into his confidence and asking its advice. No doubt there were some in the congregation who secretly sympathized with him, though later orthodox historians like Witherow do not dwell on this. Whatever the truth, his flock advised him to go to England for a few weeks, to give time for reflection on all sides. The ministers agreed, but enjoined him not to preach in the meantime.

Emlyn set out for England the very next day and stayed in London for ten weeks, during which, with more sincerity than prudence, he published *A Short Account* of his case, making the affair one of public debate. On his return to Dublin he was astonished to find that 'a great clamour against himself and his opinions was raging in the religious circles of that city'.[19]

He had been quite explicit in his defence of his position. 'I see no reason', he had written,

there will be to oppose those Unitarians who think him [Jesus Christ] to be a sufficient Saviour and Prince, tho' he be not the only supreme God; ... I may ... safely say thus much, that the blessed Jesus had declared himself not to be the supreme God, or equal to the Father, as plainly as words could speak, or in brief express.[20]

Emlyn had now placed himself in great danger. Publicly to deny the doctrine of the Trinity was, and remained until well into the nineteenth century, the crime of blasphemy, punishable by the law of the land. One Caleb Thomas, a Baptist, took out a warrant from the Lord Chief Justice, Sir Richard Pyne, to seize Emlyn and his books. Emlyn was obliged to put up bail and stand trial on a charge of blasphemous libel. The case was fixed for 14 June 1703. The trial excited enormous interest in the city and far beyond. At least six bishops, including the Archbishops of Armagh and Dublin, were on the bench, 'the very place', says Witherow, 'where they of all others should not have been.' Emlyn declined to help the prosecution by admitting authorship, to the indignation of the Chief Justice, and it was necessary to prove that he had, in private conversation, avowed the same opinions. No proof of blasphemy in the strict sense was offered; it was assumed that the expression of erroneous opinions was the equivalent. Counsel boldly asserted, and the Chief Justice confirmed, that 'presumption was as good as evidence'.[21]

It was all but impossible to find lawyers willing to plead for the accused, and those who did so were interrupted and contradicted and so browbeaten by the court, that they eventually withdrew. The defendant then offered to speak for himself, but was forbidden to do so. He was told that he must address the court through his counsel. Summing up, the Chief Justice repeated to the jury that *presumption was as good as evidence,* and told them that *if they acquitted the defendant, my lords the bishops were there.* Witherow, writing in

1879, observed that if any judge then dared to threaten a jury in this way, it would infallibly secure the acquittal of the prisoner. 'But the cravens in the box did not resent the insult and did as they were bidden.'

Emlyn was sentenced to a year's imprisonment and a fine of £1,000, 'or to lie in gaol till it was paid and to find security for good behaviour during life'. The Lord Chief Justice assured him that it was only because he was a man of letters that he had escaped the pillory, and congratulated him on his good fortune in living in Ireland. Had his lot been cast in Spain or Portugal, he would undoubtedly have been burned at the stake.

A paper was then attached to his breast, indicating his crime and the sentence pronounced upon him and he was led round the Four Courts like a captured wild beast, to be exposed to the rude gaze and insults of the populace. Such was religious liberty and such was the administration of justice in Ireland, in the reign of Queen Anne.

Witherow was unsympathetic to Emlyn's Unitarianism, but his sardonic comments show the extent to which Emlyn was regarded as a victim of the Establishment and a martyr for liberty of conscience, in the eyes of the entire Presbyterian community.[22]

It was felt by Nonconformists in England, too, and not only by Nonconformists. A caustic review of the *cause célèbre*, published by Sir Robert Steele, but actually written by the Whig Bishop, Benjamin Hoadly, concluded: 'The nonconformists accused him, the conformists condemned him, the secular power was called in and the cause ended in an imprisonment and a very great fine; two methods of conviction about which the Gospel is silent.'[23]

Emlyn was, of course, quite unable to pay the enormous fine, and he remained in prison for two years, preaching occasionally to the debtors and to some of his Wood Street congregation who came to visit him. He reflected that none of the bishops who had taken such a great interest in his trial ever came to the prison during those melancholy months to show him the error of his ways. But by now Boyse and his elders were suffering acute pangs of remorse, though Boyse had published a vindication of orthodox principles and Emlyn was busy composing a reply. Boyse alone of the ministers visited him frequently and worked actively for his release, eventually securing the intervention of the Duke of Ormond in his favour. The fine was reduced to £70 and in July 1705 Emlyn was set free, though even then the Archbishop of Armagh demanded his statutory share of one shilling in the pound on the original fine. He received £20 of it.

Emlyn's trial had a considerable impact on the thought of the Irish Dissenters and in retrospect it can be seen as the trigger of the Nonsubscription crisis. At its meeting in Antrim in June 1705 the Synod imposed subscription to the Westminster Confession on all new licentiates. And it is not a coincidence that 1705 saw the birth of the Belfast Society. Though one would hardly guess it from the authorized version of Presbyterian history, these developments were part of a much wider debate on cardinal points of Christian doctrine affecting the whole of the British Isles and dividing not only Dissenting Protestants, but the Church of England as well. In turn this was part of an even wider challenge and ferment in the whole of Western Europe, one which was most apparent in the Netherlands and in particular in the University of Leyden.

# 13

# *Tom Drennan and His Friends*

Thomas Drennan's Dublin friends did not neglect him when he returned to the North, though they frequently chided him for neglecting them. In 1736 Will Bruce writes to give him news of all their friends in Dublin, Glasgow and Edinburgh, where 'Will Wishart is made Principal'. In passing, he says, 'our subscript[ion] to Harrington goes on apace. It will be the prettyest and the cheapest Book that has been printed in Ireland.' And Bruce sends his best wishes to Haliday 'and all his agreeable family'.[1]

During the following summer Arbuckle sends some verses for his criticism, since 'I know no man upon whose Judgement I can better rely for that Purpose.' Drennan is not to be easy on him for the sake of old friendship, 'for I protest I am grown greatly indifferent about any Reputation resulting from Performances of this Kind, and I begin to look upon love of the Muse as an unseemly Passion at these years. And yet . . . the old Horse is apt to find Musick in the crack of the whip.' The letter ends with an affectionate recollection of their early days in Belfast.

I talk as if I were walking with you on the long-Bridge, or the Cave Hill. Indeed, when I think on subjects of this Nature, the Memory of those Places always occurs to me, by a very natural association of Ideas. You will pardon me if, upon such occasions, you constantly occupy a Place in the Landskip.[2]

In the 1730s Drennan's married friends regarded him as a confirmed bachelor, and it seems that he teased them about their lost freedom. But in 1741 he suddenly married. According to family tradition, Miss Anne Lennox had some occasion to visit Dublin, and her relations, well-to-do members of Belfast's Presbyterian community, were concerned to find a suitable chaperone. Her parents were both dead, and someone suggested the minister, who travelled regularly to see his friends or to preach to one of the Dublin congregations. The story goes that before the coach had reached Swords, on the outskirts of

Dublin, he had proposed to her and been accepted. He was forty-five and she twenty-three.[3]

Hutcheson's rather premature letter of good wishes suggests a more considered, not to say calculated, wooing.

Dear Thom,

Tho' I have often heard the rumour of your courtship without believing it, as I never thought your Talent lay in Fortune hunting; yet of late I have had such assurances that you're actually married, as I could not question it any longer. My wife and I congratulate you most heartily and wish you all the joys of that new Relation and wish the same to Mrs Drennan, who shows a more valuable Turn of Mind by her conduct than most young Ladies in such circumstances.

Remembering Drennan's indignation 'at the foolish metamorphoses of your comerads by marriage', he begs him now to set them all an example.

Away to Dublin every quarter; leave the wife behind you, or, if you take her along, don't mind her; stay at the Walshe's head till 2 in the morning; saunter in Jack's shop all day among books; dine abroad, and then to the Walshe's head again . . . I am sure you cannot be so foolishly fond, or so stupid, as to quit all comerads and sacrifice all merry conversation for one woman![4]

Thomas Drennan was married to Anne Lennox on 8 August 1741. According to Mrs McTier, Anne Lennox's mother was a member of the Hamilton family, descendants of the original Scottish Hamilton who persuaded James I to grant him the O'Neill lands in North Down. Teasing her brother in 1797 that he did not even know the name of his grandmother, 'on whom all the false pride of the family is built', she says that it just shows how little he has had to do with his cousin, Miss Martha Young, 'who feels great resentment at Hamilton of Mount Collier passing over his own relations' and thinks that Drennan should have inherited a small property at Gransha in Co. Down. But his trial in 1794 had 'stopped all attention from that quarter'. Drennan in fact did inherit the estate on Miss Young's death in 1807.[5]

The elder Drennan did not, it seems, answer Hutcheson's letter of congratulation. 'You are such a lazy wretch', Hutcheson complains in the following April,

that I should never write you more. Not a word of answer to my congratula-tory epistle, you got six weeks before you were married! Not one word of godly admonitions about spending an evening with friends at the Walshe's

Head and other pious sentiments about the vanity and folly of staying at home in the evenings.[6]

In his earlier letter, he struck the same note as Arbuckle: 'Dear Thom, I just write to you as I would talk to you if we were walking in Hackmer [Ballyhackamore] or on the Long Bridge, where I hope before I am many years older to have some pleasant walks with you and Mrs Drennan.'

It is an indication of the high esteem in which Hutcheson held Drennan that he took him into his confidence about his writing, and in particular the *System of Moral Philosophy*. As early as 1737, he writes:

I hope before it will be very long to let you see in print what has employed my leisure hours for several summers past; but I am at a loss how to get a right printer to employ, being a stranger in London. I don't incline to put my name to what I print or give any proofs of the Author to any wasps in this country. 'Tis a 'System of Morality' in English, larger than both my former books. You need not talk of this.[7]

Further correspondence in 1738 shows that Hutcheson sent the first draft also to Bruce, Abernethy, Synge and Dr Thomas Rundle, the Bishop of Derry, another admirer of Shaftesbury, and one whom Pope described to Swift as a 'benefactor of your unfriended and unbenefited nation'.[8]

In the following year there was news of Swift from another of the circle. 'But would you believe it?' wrote Arbuckle on 10 April 1739,

Dean Swift hath sent me a message, that a visit from me would be acceptable to him. My answer was, that whenever he pleased to appoint me a Day, I would do myself the Honour to wait upon him. . . . The only reason I can find for this unexpected favour is a Paper not long since published in Faulkner's Journal, entitled the Annals of a Travelling Gentleman of Ireland. As I never made a secret of it, I have been pointed out as the Author. This Paper hath hit the Dean's taste so much that I am now the only Man of Wit and Humour, and the best judge of Style in Ireland. I forget a hundred other fine things I have been told he says of me. So you see, it is more than one and a half to a hundred and fifty thousand, that I may be a great Man, whenever I shall turn Tory, or the Pre–r be King of G.B., both of which are Incidents very likely to happen in the same year.[9]

Arbuckle died in 1742, and Hutcheson in 1746. Thereafter Drennan's links with Dublin were largely through his colleagues in the ministry. One particular correspondent was the Rev. James Duchal. Thirty-three of his letters to Drennan survive for the period between 1738 and 1758. Duchal, who has been described as the most consider-able mind among the Nonsubscribers, was born, probably in Antrim, in 1697, and was therefore almost an exact contemporary of Drennan. He was educated partly by Abernethy whose close friend he became. In the Glasgow matriculation book he is described as *Scoto-Hibernus*, and he entered the Moral Philosophy class in 1710. Early in 1721 he became the minister of the small Dissenting congregation at Green Street in Cambridge. It had been an Independent congregation until 1696, but was now Presbyterian. At Cambridge Duchal had much leisure for study, and spent most of his time among his books. This, he later declared, was the happiest time of his life.

In 1730, when Abernethy was called to Dublin, Duchal succeeded him at Antrim. Abernethy's death on 1 December 1740 was followed early in 1741 by that of Richard Choppin, his senior colleague in the ministry of Wood Street, and the sole charge as their successor was offered to Thomas Drennan. Drennan declined it, and recommended Duchal in his place. Duchal remained at Wood Street until his death in 1761. According to the *Dictionary of National Biography*, his delicate health and shy disposition kept him out of society. He believed that 'a man if possible should have no enemies and very few friends'. Among those friends, however, were William Bruce and Thomas Dren-nan. Duchal was an indefatigable writer of sermons, and is reputed to have left 700 from his ministry at Dublin alone. The University of Glasgow conferred the degree of Doctor of Divinity on him in 1753.[10]

In the summer of 1743 he is lending sermons to Drennan, concerned to find him 'so much in the Vapours', and in November of the same year he condoles with him on the loss of a son.[11] The extent to which the Presbyterians still regarded themselves as vulnerable to charges of disaffection, despite their anti-Jacobite sentiments, is reflected in a letter at the end of 1745. Duchal reports that government is

fully satisfied with our loyalty. But it is the desire of many friends here that an exact account be sent up from every congregation [of how] many men fit to bear arms in each. This may be safely and speedily done and will best show the importance of the Dissenting Interest in a time of Danger. I hope you will put the Brethren on all sides of you with this, without delay and let us know the Result.[12]

There were other friendships and connections which went back to the days of the Nonsubscription controversy, back to the time when they had been young Glasgow graduates, imbued with new ideas, and all of them enthusiastic disciples of Shaftesbury. Arbuckle, Hutcheson, Drennan and the two Smiths had been much influenced by New Light theology – in the cases of Hutcheson and William Smith, at least, in direct opposition to parental views. To this list may be added the Bruces.

When the Nonsubscribing ministers were eventually herded together in the Presbytery of Antrim, they chose as their first secretary the Rev. Michael Bruce of Holywood, a prominent member of the Belfast Society. He was the elder brother of William Bruce the publisher, and both were sons of the Rev. James Bruce who founded the academy at Killyleagh in which Hutcheson received his early education. The Bruces, who were Hutcheson's cousins, their mothers being sisters,[13] claimed a distinguished lineage. James Bruce's father and mother were respectively the grand-nephew and grand-daughter of the Rev. Robert Bruce who had crowned Anne of Denmark as James I's Queen at Holyrood in 1590. He in turn was a descendant of the royal Bruces.[14]

In 1738 William Bruce became tutor to the son of Hugh Henry, a Dublin banker who had been an MP for Antrim in 1715, and travelled with his pupil to Oxford, Cambridge and Glasgow. In the 1740s he was an elder in Wood Street, his nephew Samuel's congregation, and in 1750 the Synod gave its approval to his plan for a fund which became the Presbyterian Widows' Fund. Bruce was a warm supporter of the Nonsubscribers and was generally held to be an Arian. The independence of his religious opinions was more than matched by that of his political views, which seem to have been fairly radical.

Bruce died, unmarried, in 1755 and was buried in Hutcheson's tomb. Shortly after his death one of his friends, Gabriel Cornwall, published anonymously 'An Essay on the Character of the late Mr William Bruce' in which he says that those of 'power, fame and high rank, courted his friendship'.[15]

The executor of Bruce's will was another friend, Alexander Stewart, and this connection is not without interest because of his family's subsequent history. Stewart was born at Ballylawn near Moville in Co. Donegal in 1700, the descendant of a Scots planter of modest origins who obtained a small portion of land in the Ulster settlement of the early seventeenth century. Set to a business career, he served his apprenticeship in Belfast before entering into partnership with two or three other merchants trading with the Baltic and the Netherlands. His business letters reveal extensive contacts with the ports of Holland and France, where his correspondents included John Black of Bordeaux. Stewart was an elder in the First Belfast Congregation, and a dedicated Whig in politics.

When, on the death of his brother, Stewart succeeded to the Ballylawn estate, he retired from business, and in 1737 he married his cousin, Mary Cowan, who had inherited a very large fortune from her half-brother, Sir Robert Cowan, a retired Governor of Bombay. With this inheritance Stewart bought his way into the landed gentry by the purchase in 1743, of estates at Newtownards and Comber. His son Robert became Marquis of Londonderry, and he also married a heiress. His grandson was Lord Castlereagh. By the late eighteenth century the Stewarts had ceased to be Presbyterians and had gone over to the Established Church; and Robert Stewart, having begun his political career as the champion of the radical Dissenters, gravitated by 1790 into the camp of the government. It fell to his son to play a leading role in suppressing the 1798 rebellion in the North, in which many of his radical Presbyterian tenants were involved, and in bringing about the Act of Union two years later. Alexander Stewart, however, remained a Dissenter, and held to liberal principles in politics, for which he was much admired in the circles he had once frequented.

When for a brief while he represented Derry in the Irish House of Commons, Stewart acquired a fine town house, which 'he filled with the best china, plate, wine, pictures and books'. He built up a collection of about a hundred paintings, including a large Nativity by Rubens and a Transfiguration by Carlo Muratti. Despite this affluence the inventory of his library bears witness to his unaltered principles. Beside the works of Shaftesbury and Hutcheson in different editions, his books included Harrington's *Oceana*, Ludlow's *Memoirs*, Molesworth's *Denmark*, Bayle's *Dictionary*, Hoadley's *Sermons*, and the unbound memoirs of Emlyn. In the 1780s the Presbyterians of Belfast and Co. Down placed high political hopes on the Stewart family, as has been seen, and they felt a correspondingly deep sense of betrayal at the later political actions of Robert Stewart and his son.[16]

Very little can be discovered about Gabriel Cornwall, who is mentioned several times in Hutcheson's letters. The Latin epitaph for the tomb of Hutcheson and Bruce, sometimes attributed to him, was in fact written by Drennan. It seems likely that he was the descendant, probably grandson, of the Rev. Gabriel Cornwall whose name appears as one of the fourteen ministers receiving grants from the Commonwealth government in 1655. Like so many others, he was ejected in 1661, and eventually became the Presbyterian minister at Ballywillan. Both his sons were ministers.[17] On 8 February 1784 the *Belfast Mercury* recorded the death of Mr Gabriel Cornwall, surgeon. The Cornwalls owned land in Co. Tyrone, and his funeral 'was the largest ever seen in that country'. The Stewartstown company of Volunteers, 'to which he belonged, in military mourning, and with bosoms bursting with sorrow' preceded the hearse, and four companies of the 1st Tyrone Regiment brought up the rear.[18]

At the time of the food shortages in 1756, Drennan's name appears among those trying to organize relief in Belfast. One would like to know something of his political attitudes, but the evidence is all but non-existent. In 1753, during the Money Bill disputes, Patriot clubs sprang into being all over Ireland to support the stand taken by the Speaker of the House of Commons, Henry Boyle. 'The people at large were by this means warmed in the cause of liberty,' runs a note in the Joy MSS, 'and taught to know their own consequence as electors and members of the State. The principles inculcated on this occasion were true Whig ones; love of the Revolution of 1688, of the Hanoverian succession and of the constitutional rights of the people.' The Patriot Club of Antrim, with Arthur Upton in the chair, drew up an 'Address to the Rt. Hon. Henry Boyle, Esq., from the free and independent inhabitants of Belfast'. The second name on the list of subscribers is that of Thomas Drennan.[19]

The Patriot clubs of Belfast and the surrounding area continued to flourish even after the infamous defection from the cause by their hero, Boyle. Chiefly they drank endless toasts 'to the memory of John Hampden, of Lord Russell and the Exclusioners, of the incorruptible Andrew Marvell' and, indeed, to the entire pantheon of Whig notables past and present. By 1757 and the war with France they were pledging: 'May the Protestants of Ireland have it in their power, by being *properly armed* and disciplined, to defend His Majesty's and *their rights* and possessions against *all* invaders.'[20]

# 14
## Fathers and Sons

Samuel Haliday, the urbane disturber of the ecclesiastical peace, had died in 1738.[1] James Duchal wrote to Drennan on 8 March of that year:

From Dr Kirkpatrick, last week, I had the first particular account of Mr Haliday's being in so desperate a condition with respect to his health, and wrote to the Doctor a letter, which I supposed he would communicate to Mr Haliday. But with what amazement am I struck to find that the eventual letter came too late. I left him, indeed, with very painful apprehensions concerning him, but none at all of his being removed so soon. Where in such surprise can the restless mind find any quiet but in the strong Assurances our Reason and Bibles give us, that the Supreme Arbiter of all things does nothing but what is the very best that can be done?[2]

Duchal's is the authentic voice of Pangloss.

On the Sunday following, Drennan preached the funeral sermon on a text from I Thessalonians 4:13, 'But I would not have you to be ignorant, brethren, concerning them which are asleep, that ye sorrow not, even as others which have no hope'. There is evidence that the circle of friends rallied round to assist the widow – not that Mrs Haliday needed financial support, for her husband left her £500 'and the £200 pr annum she possessed as the relict of the late Arthur Maxwell, Esq.', also all his plate and furniture in proof of his affection, and the leases of the fields on the road to Shankill.[3] But there were two sons to be educated at Glasgow.

In 1741 Robert, the elder, began to give Hutcheson considerable anxiety. On 1 June Hutcheson wrote to Drennan:

Dear Thom,
I must next write to you about an affair which gives me a great deal of trouble. Bob Haliday is not in right way as to his conduct. I gave him several of the strongest admonitions I could, I had many fine promises, I confined him in his expenses, and he seemed to take all well and to promise diligence. . . . The boy has a good genius but that is the poorest satisfaction to me, about anyone

I wish well to. He is conceity, thinks himself a wit and scorns advice from Gabriel Cornwall or Mr McMeehan, and trifles away money and time for nothing.

I know not how to write to Mrs Haliday, but as matters appear to me at present, there is little hope of his succeeding in any learned profession, and consequently he can have no business here. . . . I am disturbed about Mrs Haliday, whom I used to encourage with the best accounts of things.

Clearly Hutcheson considered that Mrs Haliday might take all this better from her minister, and be reconciled to Robert's coming down from the University. 'I would not send him home suddenly, till she were in some way prepared for it.' There is much more in this vein, and Hutcheson concludes with a reference to the last resort:

I have said a great deal against the Army, as the last of all good shifts to men who have no interest of shires or votes in Parliament. But I fear nothing else will suite his turn of temper, unless he alters a good deal.[4]

A year later, on 12 April 1742, Hutcheson is still asking Drennan to give Mrs Haliday what advice he could about her son.

He has not yet got habits of vice in the sense of the world. But I fear he is conceited, pert and self-willed. I have often told him my mind very freely. He was in hast to be a man, and thought the company in taverns mighty genteel and could rally the folly of bookish, studious lads.[5]

Alexander Haliday, who matriculated at Glasgow in 1743, seems to have had a more exemplary undergraduate career. On finishing his medical studies he set up in practice in Belfast, and rapidly became a very respected doctor and over the years an influential citizen. In 1770 the Hearts of Steel, a body of Co. Antrim tenants rebelling against their landlords, marched into Belfast and attempted to burn the house of Waddell Cunningham, who had arrested one of their number for maiming cattle. Dr Haliday tried to mediate, and later, when they attacked the military barracks, he intervened to persuade the soldiers to stop firing on them.[6] By the 1780s it was rare not to find Haliday's name associated with any forward-looking project in the town, from the opening of the new Poor-house to the founding of the Belfast Academy, today the city's oldest grammar school.[7]

On his death, William Drennan was to describe him as

a Genuine Whig . . . nurtured under the philosophy of Hutcheson, and early inspired by the poetry of Akenside; the study of the former gave him that chastity of the moral sense which binds political and personal duty in the same strict tie of honesty and honour; and the divine muse of the latter threw that sacred flame of liberty into his breast, which burned while he continued to exist. In the principles of civil and religious liberty he lived and in them he died ... these were ... the principles of the venerable Camden, and the amiable Charlemont, of the untitled Stewart, and the unpensioned Burke.[8]

The fact that Mark Akenside was Haliday's favourite author is illuminating. Not only was the Tyneside poet also a physician, and a graduate of Leyden; his best known work, *The Pleasures of Imagination*, is an attempt to put Shaftesbury and Hutcheson into verse. Akenside made no secret of his sources. He describes Shaftesbury as 'the most perfect of modern poets', who had applied the epistolary manner of Horace 'to the noblest parts of philosophy'. Hutcheson he calls Shaftesbury's 'most ingenious disciple'. Akenside's first poem, *The Virtuoso*, published when he was sixteen, was a satire on the figure described in Shaftesbury's *Characteristicks*. In his most ambitious poem, he versifies Shaftesbury's notion that God is revealed in nature, and that human reason, unaided by revelation or the Scriptures, 'is equal to framing a satisfying concept of God'. His argument is that the purpose of man is 'to enlarge his soul with the contemplation of the grand and sublime objects of nature, and thus rise in the scale of being to that point where limitations disappear and infinite perfection is discerned', an idea drawn directly from Shaftesbury.[9]

Haliday was not himself devoid of literary ambition. He wrote a tragedy, but it was never published. He sent it to Edmund Burke, who transmitted it to Sheridan. They both thought it 'excellent'. Sheridan offered to make some suggestions for its improvement, 'from his theatrical experience', and said he would 'bring it on next winter'. However, Burke warned Haliday that men of great genius were as prone to laziness and procrastination as men of no genius, and added this equivocal comment: 'The merit of the piece will, I dare say, ensure its success, in spite of its spirit and principles, which are wholly alien to those which prevail at this time, and in this kingdom.' Charlemont also read the play, and praised it, and from time to time he thanks Haliday for 'pleasing verses' and an 'incomparable epic ballad'.[10]

Haliday was apparently much put out by not being chosen Captain of the Blue Company in 1778, as he had been a lieutenant in the old Belfast company of Stewart Banks, but he more than made up for this slight by becoming Charlemont's right-hand man in all his dealings

with the Belfast Volunteers. When the General came to the town to
review his troops, Dr Haliday's house in Castle Street became his
headquarters.[11]

Dr Haliday was immensely charmed by his new acquaintance, which
enhanced his standing with his fellow-citizens, and he began to bom-
bard Charlemont with long letters on politics, crammed with literary
and classical allusions which he thought would appeal to the recipient.
Two years later, and not long after the triumph of Dungannon, he felt
sufficiently confident to ask a favour of Charlemont. It was on behalf
of the prodigal brother who had given such anxiety to Hutcheson,
forty years earlier. He had been, Haliday explained, 'through the
whole of his life a most unlucky fellow'. He had ended up as a collector
of revenue in South Carolina, where he had, from a high sense of duty,
opposed the rebellious colonists.

He was the only collector, my lord, in the vast line of our colonies who had
the firmness to get the obnoxious teas stored, instead of being sent back or
destroyed: while from a sense of official duty, he opposed the powers which
then took the lead in the province; with so much manliness and ability, as
nothing could have rendered safe, but the singular favour he had previously
acquired among them.

Now he was back in London, on a miserable pension, and with a
family to support. If Charlemont could with propriety interpose on
his behalf, 'you would be acting in your own chosen and blessed line
of doing good, and you would confer a most essential favour and
obligation on one who has the very best claim in the world on your
lordship, that of having been already very highly favoured and
obliged'.[12]

Charlemont wrote back immediately, though he claimed that he
dreaded writing because he could not comply with his friend's request.

What can I say, how can I express my disagreeable sensation . . . ? To refuse
favours for ourselves is no self-denial, but to deny ourselves the pleasure of
asking for friends 'hoc opus, hic labor est'; yet such is at present my situation.
I have for myself disclaimed the acceptance of office, and am so circumstanced
that it is impossible, because it would be highly improper at this time, to ask
any favour whatsoever.[13]

Haliday took the rebuff well, and begged Charlemont to think no
more of his letter, 'only do me the justice to admit that I could not

well decline the office'.[14] Neither man allowed the incident to disturb the harmony of their relationship.

As time went on, and Haliday's politics became more Charlemontean, he found a young ally in Dr William Bruce, the son of the Rev. Samuel Bruce of Wood Street, and the nephew of Hutcheson's publisher. The younger Bruce and the younger Drennan were friends from childhood, and in the 1780s they were exchanging letters which ranged over all their interests and youthful ambitions. Bruce had, very unusually for a Presbyterian, studied at Trinity College, Dublin, and been allowed to graduate with a BA. He had also attended the Dissenting academy at Warrington, where he had studied theology under Dr John Aiken, the father of Mrs Barbauld. He began his ministry in Lisburn, and in 1783 he was a Volunteer delegate at the National Convention, where he drew the unfavourable attention of Charlemont (see page 48).[15]

A sheaf of letters from Bruce to Henry Joy, preserved in the Joy MSS, throws some light on Bruce's intellectual and political development at this time. He had a cooler temperament, and in some ways a better judgement, than Drennan. It is clear that from an early stage he much admired Grattan, and the Renunciation issue threw him into a state of ambivalence. He privately thought that Grattan was right, and that if Flood had not disturbed the settlement, all would have been well. But he did not want to offend Joy and his 'judicious neighbours' such as Bryson, Drennan, and Joy's father, who was then still alive. At one point, in September 1782, he tells Joy that he has sent Drennan an account of the changes his political opinions have undergone. Ultimately the Drennan family would come to regard him, though still a friend, as one who had developed the habit of sitting on the fence into an art.[16]

Bruce further advanced his political education (something he was very anxious to do) by an extended tour of Britain in 1784 that took in Edinburgh, Oxford, Cambridge, London and Brighton. At Brighton he listened with great interest to a sermon by the radical Dr Price, collecting a respectable abstract 'by means of stenography'. His memorandum book was filling up with evidence of wide cultural interests. He now had experience of bad universities 'destitute of learning', and 'learned universities destitute of decent accommodation'.

Not surprisingly, while he is away he begins to take a more Olympian view of Irish problems.

I am a little out of humour with the progress of Irish politics. I hear the multitude are as base as their rulers and I cannot find any directing or supervising wisdom in our tumultuous, chaotic world of thoughtless faction and interested villany. Where is there a man, in whom the nation reposes perfect confidence? It makes me sick to read the newspapers, and sorry to behold the approaching Disunion, a disagreement among Protestants, or rather the irreconcilable animosity of Protestants and Patriots: for nothing will be done for the RCs, and their conduct at present satisfies me that the consequences of the disappointment will be deadly and *rerum novarum cupido*.[17]

Bruce was to make a political ally of Joy, to whom he was distantly related through his mother, a Rainey from Magherafelt. In the 1790s they would form the rearguard of the more cautious Belfast Presbyterians on the issue of Catholic emancipation, and in 1794 they jointly edited a collection of all the important Volunteer resolutions, along with Bruce's thoughts on the British Constitution and his strictures on Drennan's United Irish Test. They called the book *Belfast Politics* and dedicated it to Dr Haliday. After an argumentative evening in McTier's home in 1791, Wolfe Tone confided to his diary that he found Bruce 'an intolerant high priest'.[18]

# III

# A STABLE UNSEEN POWER

# 15
## *Orellana*

The year 1784 witnessed a distinct change in the political climate of Ireland. In the frustration which followed the failure of the National Convention, a scheme was widely canvassed, especially in Ulster, for bringing Catholics into the Volunteer ranks, and in various centres practical steps were taken towards this end. In Strabane the reformers called for the training of Catholic Volunteers. In Belfast the First Company opened its ranks on 13 May to people of every religious persuasion, 'firmly convinced that a general Union of *all* the inhabitants of Ireland is necessary to the freedom and prosperity of this kingdom'. On 26 May the Blue Company followed its example and on 30 May both companies paraded to attend Mass at Belfast's first Catholic church, in the town's most celebrated act of ecumenism. Many other Protestants attended besides those in Volunteer uniform, and a collection towards the cost of the building was taken up, amounting to £84. The Catholic congregation expressed their warm appreciation of this generosity, and said that they would gratefully receive (through the Rev. O'Donnell) any further benefactions that 'the liberality of their brother Christians may prompt'.[1]

In Downpatrick a new company of Volunteers was formed, consisting of thirty-seven Catholics and twenty-five Protestants, under the name of the Down Union. Its commander was a Church of Ireland clergyman, whose ensigns were a Presbyterian and a Catholic, and the Catholic Bishop of Down and Connor presented the company with new colours, bearing the appropriate motto: *Tria juncta in uno*. In Newry during the summer of 1784, probably in imitation of Downpatrick, companies of Protestant and Catholic Volunteers united to form the Newry Union.[2]

On his arrival in Newry, Drennan had become a Volunteer again, and without doubt he played a part in bringing the new corps into being. Thirty years later, when he was helping to edit the radical *Belfast Monthly Magazine*, he quietly slipped into its pages, without editorial comment, some of the papers which he had kept from that momentous decade. They included the declaration of the Newry Union in 1784:

We associate as volunteer soldiers, in order to maintain our rights as citizens. We are all sensible of the value of liberty and we all desire to possess the power of preserving it. We associate in order to form part of that Volunteer army, whose institution we venerate, whose principles we adopt as our own, and in whose cause we are ready to lay down our lives. We associate, although differing in religious opinions, because we wish to create that union of power, and to cultivate that brotherhood of affection among all the inhabitants of this Island, which is the interest as well as the duty of all. We are all IRISH-MEN. We rejoice and glory in that common title which binds us together: and we associate, in order to do everything, that the union of our hearts, and the strength of our hands, can effectuate, to render the name of IRISHMAN honourable to ourselves, serviceable to our beloved country, and formidable to its foes. We shall ever think that an association deserves well of our native land, whose chief object is *to unite the different descriptions of religion in the cause of our common country*, and although we cannot lay claim to the honour of having first taken up arms, there is still a glorious ambition left – not be among the last in laying them down![3]

The style marks this as unmistakably Drennan's, and a copy of the original draft in his handwriting is among the Drennan papers in the Public Record Office of Northern Ireland.[4]

Lecky records that the fashion for 'united' companies had begun in Dublin, when the 'Liberty' corps (so-called because it was recruited in the Earl of Meath's liberties, where the woollen manufacturers lived) thought fit, without consulting any other Volunteers, to advertise for recruits, 'and enlisted about two hundred of the lowest class, who were chiefly Roman Catholics'. This was wholly contrary to the wishes of Charlemont and defied the law which forbade Catholics to carry arms without licence, and 'at a time when the spirit of outrage was so rife in Dublin it was peculiarly dangerous'. Neither the serious rioting which broke out in Dublin, nor the marked downward social shift in the Volunteer movement, however, was specifically connected with Catholics joining the Volunteer companies. The riots seem to have been provoked by economic grievances, and the change in the social character of the Volunteers reflected the descending curve of the movement's political fortunes.

After the dissolution of the Convention, says Lecky, a great portion of the more respectable men connected with the movement retired from the ranks. They were replaced by another and wholly different class.

The taste for combining, arming, and drilling had spread, and had descended to the lower strata of society. Demagogues had arisen who sought by arming and organizing volunteers to win political power, and who gathered around them men who desired for very doubtful purposes to obtain arms.

In the House of Commons Grattan declared that the original Volunteers had been the armed property of Ireland. Were they, he asked, now to become the armed beggary?

The year was one of rumour and panic. The change in the character of the Volunteers was most marked in Dublin and the South of Ireland, and there was a growing fear among the Protestant gentry that, under the colour of Volunteering, 'an extensive and indiscriminate arming of Catholics was going on'. The Lord Lieutenant, the Duke of Rutland, complained that great quantities of arms were being scattered through the very lowest section of the population. In Ulster the Volunteers preserved much of their primitive character, but their radical sentiments made them still an object of suspicion to the government.[5]

Three years later, in the journal of his vice-regal tour of Ireland, Rutland was to observe that

the province of Ulster is filled with Dissenters, who are in general very factious – great levellers and republicans. There are many sects – Old Light, New Light, Seceders, etc. The former are the old Scotch Presbyterians, who agree with the Church of England in articles of faith, but oppose Church discipline. The second deny the divinity of Christ, and the last I know nothing about. There are some Moravians, who are a neat industrious people, quiet in their living, and of principles amenable to Government. The dissenting ministers are for the most part very seditious, and have great sway over their flocks, but they are cunning enough not to show their teeth but when they can bite, so that I found no interruption from them, nor were they troublesome to me in the course of my tour, though I know they have an essential point to carry with Government.

Politics aside, Rutland was clearly impressed by the growing economic prosperity of the North. Lisburn he found 'a large town about which the linen manufacture is in its greatest glory'. It was also, however, 'the seat of discontent and faction and sedition'. There a society had been formed to overthrow every establishment, 'calling themselves, by a prostitution of the term, the *Constitutional* Society'.

In Belfast he was received with great politeness and given the freedom of the borough, though Dr Haliday refused to attend the reception. 'Belfast is a giant of a town', the Lord Lieutenant recorded, 'flourishing in everything . . . Their trade is immense. They go to the West Indies, and to almost every quarter of the globe.' Nevertheless, it was full of Presbyterians, and 'much connected with the Americans during the calamitous contest . . . This is the town where the spirit of Volunteering has fixed its throne.'[6]

Certainly that spirit had not died. There were many who felt like Drennan that if Flood had marched to Parliament with 60,000 Volunteers at his heels, his Bill would not have been rejected with such scorn. On 8 July 1784 a town meeting convened in Belfast 'to take into consideration the Dublin resolutions in favour of Roman Catholic suffrage'. The chair was taken by Gilbert McIlveen, and among the town liberals who signed the request for the meeting were Dr Haliday, Robert Simms, William Sinclair, John Brown, Amyas Griffith and Patrick Gaw.[7] It is worth noting that at least three of these – McIlveen, Simms and Sinclair – were to be among the founders of the first Society of United Irishmen.

They were responding to the actions of their Dublin counterpart, the 'aggregate' meeting. Since the early spring a series of these aggregate meetings had tried to set up the machinery for another National Convention. A committee was elected, which wrote to the high sheriffs of the counties, but the replies which the committee received were mixed. Some sheriffs were willing to convene their counties, others replied guardedly that they would when requested by a majority of the freeholders. A few refused point-blank. As the summer went on, the response of the Northern counties was watched with particular interest.[8]

The Convention at last assembled on 25 October 1784 in the Exchange Rooms in Dublin, and sat for three days. A hostile newspaper described the delegates as persons 'at whose character and situations in life the pride of a gentleman would revolt', but the description was wildly unfair. They included 'a much respected peer, Lord Powerscourt, four baronets . . . several volunteer colonels, an archdeacon and respectable country gentlemen'. This might have been expected to a sufficient counterweight to the radicalism of some of the other delegates, and especially the dangerous men from the North. The list of the Northern delegates included the names of the Rev. William Bruce, the Presbyterian minister of Lisburn, and the Rev. Sinclair Kelburn, the minister of Belfast's Third Congregation and a new arrival on the radical scene. It also included the name of William Drennan.[9]

Drennan's move from Belfast to Newry had not proved wise. It had not brought him the professional success he had hoped for, and his efforts to enter local society, and to gain the patronage of the Patriotic MP Isaac Corry, had been indifferently successful. He had considered that it would be difficult to set up a practice in Belfast against the competition of well-established and much respected physicians like Haliday and Mattear, but the Newry doctors were just as formidable, and apt to close ranks against the newcomer. He had a number of good patients, who thought well of him, so the real reason for his lack of more general support was probably his growing notoriety in radical politics.

Drennan found Newry intolerably dreary, felt isolated from the mainstream of politics in Belfast and Dublin, and resolved to move to the metropolis as soon as he could afford to do so. In letters to his friend Bruce he poured out his frustration and his plans to set the world to rights. At first he tried to interest Bruce in founding 'a society for the purpose of propagating Constitutional Information similar to the one in England'. He thought that Bruce ought to have written the 'History of Modern Ireland' (in other words, the history of the Volunteers) before Crawford 'who botched it'. Drennan was really toying with the idea himself, reading Tacitus and writing down any sentences that made a deep impression on him. He noted 'how beautifully Gibbon has fitted them in the similar situations of his own history'.[10]

In June 1783 he was suddenly struck down by typhus and almost died of it. His illness precipitated a crisis for the Drennan family. Matty had gone to Bristol with Nancy. Sam McTier, who had recently had to endure much criticism from his wife and brother-in-law over the Fencible affair, at once travelled down to Newry with old Mrs Drennan, and for five weeks tenderly nursed Drennan back to health, restraining him in his delirium, spoon-feeding him and holding the chamber-pot. Drennan's lodgings were uncomfortable, and the landlady unsympathetic. For the first few nights Anne Drennan slept on the floor in the next room. Sam was embarrassed by the sick man's indecent raving, and innocently surprised to hear the minister's widow laughing. On the third day Dr Haliday arrived, and sat with the patient while Sam snatched some sleep.[11]

Drennan recovered slowly, 'very cross and positive' at first, accusing them of trying to starve him. He tearfully remembered how his mother had read *Robinson Crusoe* to him when he had been ill as a boy. Later he told Bruce that Sam had looked after him with the anxiety of a brother.[12] Sam's kindness was all the more creditable because his financial affairs were in confusion, and he and Matty had been reduced to real, if genteel, poverty. Matty's pride was hurt, and to escape from the claustrophobic atmosphere of the family home in Donegall Street, she persuaded Sam to take a small cottage just outside Belfast on the road to Newtownards. They refurbished it and called it 'Cabin Hill'. The site is now in the grounds of a well-known public school, Campbell College, and its preparatory department still bears the cottage's name. McTier's friends rallied round him and he considered a number of not very congenial projects before he achieved relative security by being appointed the first Ballast Master of the port of Belfast in 1785.[13]

The attempts to organize a second National Convention spurred Drennan to literary activity (he had had occasional pieces printed in the *Belfast Newsletter*), and now for the first time his writing began to attract widespread attention. A series of three powerfully expressed letters, castigating the defection of some of the Northern counties from the Volunteer cause, appeared anonymously in the *Belfast Newsletter* in November and December 1784. They were at once reprinted as a pamphlet by the Constitution Society of Dublin under the title of *Orellana, or An Irish Helot*, and Drennan eventually wrote another four letters.[14]

No discussion of the Helot Letters known to the present author attempts to explain the curious pseudonym. It seems probable that it is merely a play on the title of Mrs Aphra Behn's *Oroonoka, or the Royal Slave*, which Drennan would have read and admired. In eighteenth-century atlases, the river which we now call the Amazon was marked as the Orellana, in honour of the Spanish explorer who discovered it, Francisco de Orellana. Thus the two great rivers of South America were the Orellana and the Orinoco. In Mrs Behn's novel (published in 1678) Oroonoka was the grandson of an African king, captured by the master of an English slave-trading vessel, and

carried off to Surinam, then an English colony. There he stirs up the
other slaves to revolt and escape from their miserable condition. The
novel is remarkable as the first expression in English literature of
sympathy for the oppressed negroes, and it was directly based on the
author's memories of her early days in Surinam.[15]

The Helot Letters were a rousing call for Ireland to recover from
the lethargy she had fallen into in 1784. 'Fellow-slaves!' the first letter
began. 'A short time will discover whether the people of Ireland be the
most magnanimous, or the meanest of mankind.' The story was soon
told.

About six years ago the honest gentlewoman awaked from a trance; drest
herself by way of frolic in regimentals, entered as a volunteer into the English
service to supply the place of the invalids that were sent to guard our coasts,
marched up to the *Mons sacer* of Dungannon, marched down again, became
a strolling player, went to 'enact Brutus in the capitol', totally forgot her part,
threw off her warlike attire, and sunk down again – a wretched woman.[16]

In rhetoric which has an almost Swiftian power, Drennan goes on
to warn the people of Ireland that at this critical point in their history,
'if they sleep, they die'. But the first letter at once reveals a very
interesting shift of emphasis.

Your boyhood and your youth were led astray by false associations, and
blinded by the refined delusion of history: you claimed relationship with the
Saxon *Alfred* . . . with *Hampden*; Sidney, who shook the gallows with his
undaunted tread, was, *to be sure*, one of your great progenitors! 'Tis all the
fairy tale of infancy. You are all *native Irish*, under the controul of an *English
pale* . . . [17]

Drennan's Real Whig inheritance was being elbowed out by an urgent
patriotism, and one which included the Catholics, the adherents of
democracy's putative enemy.

The third letter begins with an attack on Charlemont and the Whigs.
'Persevere,' says the venerable Charlemont,

while the grand climacteric, like a sharp pointed sword, hangs dangling over
his head; *persevere* my dear countrymen, and by patience, prudence and the
possible intervention of fortunate contingencies, we shall attain, *in process of
time*, to the summit of our desires. In what time, my good Lord, in what time?
– for our yoke is heavy and in a little time we shall not, as it appears, be
allowed even to *groan* beneath the burden.

It is hardly surprising that Drennan is by now heartily sick of resolutions. 'Resolutions! Resolutions! Shall we never have done with resolutions? Resolution that stalks like a giant before, while the dwarf Performance comes lagging behind him.'[18]

With the Helot Letters Drennan makes the most open statement of his radicalism on the reform question and appears to part company with the Whigs and even with the Commonwealthmen. The only hope for the reform of Parliament lies in the Volunteers and their ability to overawe it in the name of the people's rights; and Drennan deliberately turns from constitutional politics to a doctrine which preaches the unity of all Irishmen in a common patriotism. This is, in one way, an older sense of Irish identity and one which will become paramount after 1800, the patriotism of Catholic Ireland. He is perhaps the first republican to embrace it.

But all will be lost if the critical moment is allowed to pass. 'The Arch of Liberty is nearly finished; one stone hangs upon another. Each supports and is supported. The *key stone* is just ready to be put in – without it all must give way.' Drennan goes on to admit that he considered the aggregate meeting of Dublin as 'a coarse stone in the arch which juts out a little from the rest'. Nevertheless, it had filled up the vacancy when a better was not to be had.[19]

The fifth of the Helot Letters is a plea for the unity of the sects. 'I call upon you, Churchmen, Presbyterians and Catholics to embrace each other in the mild spirit of Christianity, and to unite as a sacred compact in the cause of your sinking country. For you are ALL IRISH-MEN – you are nurtured by the same maternal earth.' If ever there was a time not to stir up sectarian discord it was now, when 'the enemy has forced open the gates, when they are within the walls', and just about to lay sacrilegious hands upon the ark of the Constitution. It was a time for zeal in politics and moderation in religion. Blessed is the man who in such times falls, like an affectionate Joseph, on the neck of his brethren and says: 'I AM THY BROTHER.'[20]

The question of reform must be considered strictly as a *political* question. Anyone who mixes religion with it, is an enemy of his country. Drennan goes on to paint a Utopian picture of an Ireland in which the Catholic, soothed by hopes of affluence, 'would melt into the citizen'; the Presbyterian would admit that all sects when in possession of power have abused it; and the Churchman would find a better security for his church than the abuses of the Constitution. In passing, he piously hopes that the time when Catholics have to be patient and resign themselves to fate will be made short by their own laudable exertions.

May the light of true science illuminate their minds and soften their hearts! May the gradual diffusion of property, while it engrafts their affection upon the soil which supports them, communicate at the same time the spirit to maintain what their industry has acquired; give them self-estimation, conscious dignity, and in short that republicanism of soul, which will announce to the world, that the people who possess it are stamped by the hand of Heaven, heirs of independence![21]

It was a prayer which time was amply to fulfil, though, as Drennan himself admitted elsewhere, not necessarily to the comfort of New Light Dissenters.

Drennan was eager to give some practical effect to this rhetoric. As early as February 1784 he had written to Bruce:

I should like to see the institution of a society as secret as the Free-masons, whose object might be by every practicable means to put into execution plans for the complete liberation of the country. The secrecy would surround the proceedings of such a society with a certain awe and majesty, and the oath of admission would inspire enthusiasm into its members. Patriotism is too general and on that account weak. We want to be condensed into the fervent enthusiasm of sectaries, and a few active spirits could, I should hope, in this manner greatly multiply their power for promoting public good. The laws and institutes of such a society would require ample consideration: but it might accomplish much.[22]

In May 1785, when Bruce had written to him about the formation of a Whig Reform Club which was to have a blue uniform with silver buttons and the motto *Persevere*, Drennan replied scornfully that the projected club was too large to achieve anything effectual:

Ten or twelve conspirators for constitutional freedom would do more in a day than they would do in ten. I should like to see a constitutional convenant drawn up, solemnly recapitulating our political creed, and every man who chose should subscribe his name to it. This would be a breaking down club – yours is but a switch, a rattan. . . . For my own part I am more eager than ever in the reform business. . . . I can't find men that would form a serious association, a sacred compact about the matter. I would sign such a confederation of my compatriots with my blood.[23]

In August he was telling Bruce that he had been twice to Belfast, once to see Mrs Siddons act, and another time to watch the Volunteer review, to see 'the buried majesty of the people arise and cross the stage for the last time. The ghost of Volunteering was dressed in its habit as it lived, and shook in vain its visionary sword.'

'I still think,' he continued,

that the segregation of the sincere and sanguine reformers from the rest into a holy and, as it were, religious brotherhood, knit together by some aweful formality, by the solemnity of abjuration, by something mysterious in its manner, like the freemason society, which would serve to stimulate the curiosity of others, and gratify our own pride; by a well-drawn association particular and precise in every article; by an insignia of an order, not external for public gaze and the vanity of a fine uniform, but internal and unostentatious, such as a broad ribbon with a suitable emblem to be worn next the skin and nearest the heart. I say, I still (however you may smile at such romantic boyisms) ever will think that such a constitutional conspiracy ought to take place as a means of perpetuating the best and noblest of political objects in the minds of the best and boldest men in the country; as a means of seizing opportunities that may occur, and of making them when they are tedious in their occurrence; as a means of strengthening a virtuous cause and giving lustre and a field of action for virtuous men that long to distinguish themselves by benefiting their country.[24]

Here in 1784 and 1785 Drennan outlined his entire scheme for a secret inner circle of dedicated radical reformers, within the Volunteer movement and directing its politics, six years before the United Irish Society was formed. What were the 'best and noblest political objects'? It is clear from Drennan's comments that they included the reform of Parliament and a cordial union of Dissenters and Catholics to break the political power of the Protestant Ascendancy. All his politics were now imbued with an ardent patriotism which led him to see that separation from Britain was Ireland's only opportunity for happiness. In the last letter quoted he says (in reference to the Commercial Propositions) that the only choices apart from a commercial treaty were Union or Disunion. 'And I hope in God that a short time will show the expediency, necessity and sublimity of the last choice, without which Ireland will never become a great or a happy people.'

The publication of *Orellana* brought Drennan the attention he so much craved. Soon after Christmas 1784 Mrs McTier was able to tell her brother that in Belfast he was generally known to be the author. 'You may consider what answer you will return if invited to represent your native town in Convention. I do not suppose you will or should refuse it, and as the "Helot" you will, I daresay, be received with respect.'[25]

Bruce's news in the summer of 1785 that a Reform Club had been established in Dublin 'which was likely to prove a formidable association', increased the rift between him and Drennan, who observed sarcastically:

Lord Charlemont and Stewart of Tyrone are to become members and Sharman has purchased his uniform, so that what the Volunteers could not do, what the genius which thundered and lightened exceedingly from the mount of Dungannon, what Pitt and Flood could not accomplish, is to be effected by a club, a switch, a rattan, a jovial crew that wear a blue coat with velvet cuffs, and capes of the same colour, and a gilt button with the motto 'Persevere'. I think the motto ought to be *Constitution, Revolution or Dissolution*.

It was a sorry sight to see all their efforts dwindle down into a Reform Club. The plan might have looked good seven years before, but it now seemed injurious to the Volunteer establishment 'by collecting all the gentlemen, the aristocracy, the chaff of volunteering, and leaving the yeomanry and the mechanics, who are the weighty grain, to themselves'. Bruce had said he meant to abjure politics on the breaking-up of the Assembly, but he was tempted to join a society which Drennan 'could not but think would be too numerous for any good end, and would hasten the oblivion into which that best Reform Club, the volunteers, were already sinking apace'.[26]

Of one thing Drennan was certain. He would not allow Charlemont to be a member, 'for I think it has been he who has given the signal to retreat, though our general, and the ghost of volunteering might now be made by the witchery of a master poet to rise and upbraid him'. Charlemont was not a man of nerve.[27]

Meanwhile in Belfast there was every sign that the old set was indeed abjuring politics and falling under the softer spell of Sarah Siddons. On 8 June Matty reported that 'Mrs Siddons is now here working wonders'. The effect of her Belvidera on the audience was devastating.

Haliday swelled, Mattear snivelled, Major Leslie cried and damned the play. W. Cunningham rubbed his legs and changed his posture, a Miss Aderton was ... taken out in convulsions, and Miss Lewis that was, now Mrs Britt, left the house and is at present in danger of a miscarriage ... Margaret Jones restrained her tears for a long time but at length they burst forth with an unwilling sob.[28]

In *The Unhappy Marriage* Siddons reached the height of her powers. Five ladies were carried out fainting, and hardly a man could stand it. Sam cried for half an hour after he went to bed. 'As for myself', wrote Matty, 'I can wonder, admire, be chilled, thrilled, etc., etc., but cannot cry, not that I *feel* too much for tears, but she does not melt me.'[29]

The account of Miss Margaret Jones's restrained tears was particularly affecting to Drennan, for he had fallen in love with this young lady and written poems to her. In August she fell desperately ill with fever. Haliday and Mattear attended her, but a third physician was called in. On learning from Haliday that she was suffering from typhus and likely to succumb, Drennan panicked, and, throwing medical etiquette to the winds, sent his advice. He rode hell-for-leather from Newry to Hillsborough to deliver the note. Then, realizing how he was likely to have offended Haliday, he told Matty, 'I shall write him a line tonight . . . to appease this Esculapian God.'[30]

Haliday, who knew how matters stood, was avuncularly kind. He wrote a note with the clinical details, adding that he had not taken Drennan's intervention in the case in the slightest amiss.

It would have been doing me a great injustice. . . . The lady's situation you will perceive is hopeful – I should be glad to add, and the gentleman's also – but I have some reason to think it is more friendly to be silent on that head.
With great and affectionate regard,
In haste, truly yours,
A. Haliday[31]

'I shall ever thank him for his kindness,' Drennan told his sister. But in fact Haliday had given him a new cause for worry. What did he mean by his hints? He would not think of asking him what his 'reason' was, but the puzzle gnawed at him, and of course he did.

Not surprisingly, Haliday's next communication was more frigid:

My dear Sir, the hint I gave you was surely well intended. I hope it was founded on a mistake. . . . It was, however, the office of a friend to put you on your guard against indulging a passion which he thought at the time likely to be disappointed. There could be no other objection to the one you cherish and I am happy to perceive that you think with the fairest prospects (a word or a meaning which, by the bye, I had never expressed). This is all I have to say on the subject. For the rest the convalescence goes on slowly. Fever gone, appetite returned, but still in bed. In great haste. Adieu. A Haliday.[32]

Matty's advice was down to earth. Propose to the girl as soon as she recovers. Drennan did so, at great length and in the most orotund prose. The lady's reply was shorter and unambiguous. She was sorry to have been the ignorant cause of uneasiness to him. She was obliged to him for his favourable opinion and concerned at his throwing it away on one who could not deserve it by feeling a return. 'I wish you happiness, but it is not nor ever will be in my power to do more.' She subsequently married Roger Bristow, who became sovereign of Belfast.[33]

With this, the tedium of his life in Newry closed in on Drennan. Isaac Corry asked him if he would not consider putting his talents at the service of a formed party, a perfectly honourable course of action, and one which might bring him the independence he so desired. Corry owned in confidence that he was himself 'attached to Mr Fox's party'. Drennan pretended to Mrs McTier that he thought it 'all fudge'. She strongly disagreed and urged him to take up the offer, which he was very tempted to do. But his obstinate republican honesty won the day. 'I think', he told his sister, 'I have within me an impregnable heart in politics.'[34]

Soon he was writing that 'politics are all dead and even I am uninterested', and later, 'How the noble enthusiasm of politics has failed. Alas! There is no spirit in Ireland or Irishmen.' Ennui was also engulfing Matty, who was dividing her time between her cabin and her mother's house in Belfast. Nearly fifty years of housekeeping had worn out most of what old Mrs Drennan possessed. She had replaced nothing for a very long time, and the house in Donegall Street now seemed 'antient'. Drennan had had his portrait painted by Home, and Nancy was fixing it up 'beside Dr Haliday and your Father over the parlour fireplace'. Matty's letters to Drennan become increasingly bitter at the inanity of her life, exacerbated by Sam's poverty, and at a time when Belfast seemed poised on the brink of booming prosperity. To cheer her up he recommends that she should read the new French novel, *Dangerous Connexions*, which everyone is talking about, assuring her that 'Mrs B., Mrs C., etc. all read it in public. It is a most masterly piece of dangerous seduction in stile and sentiment.'[35]

As for himself, 'I wish to Heaven there were some civil commotion that one might make their life and death of some service, but the day is spent in nauseous insipidity, the night in starting, and groaning, like Richard [III], even with a pure conscience.' There were two minor crises to disturb the flat calm of these years. In 1784 Pitt attempted to plug the gaps in the 'Constitution' of 1782 by putting a series of 'Commercial Propositions' before both Houses of Parliament – they amounted in reality to a kind of Anglo-Irish Treaty. But they were defeated by the protectionist jealousy of English manufacturers on the one hand, and by Irish national pride on the other. Then in 1788 George III's temporary lapse into insanity precipitated a constitutional crisis, in which it seemed for a while that the Irish Parliament would appoint the Prince of Wales as Regent without waiting for the government in England. A confrontation was avoided only by the King's recovery in health. 'I am now past my thirty-first year,' Drennan recorded, 'and all my life has been spent in preparing to live – perhaps five years longer – I almost wish there was a hearty rebellion.'[36]

# 16

# 'A Sketch by Raphael'

Into this stagnant pool in the summer of 1789 there was thrown a rock of such magnitude that the ripples from it are spreading still. The day came when the *Belfast Newsletter* was forced to omit an account of the Maze races to give the details of the remarkable convulsions in France. As Wolfe Tone was later to observe, the French Revolution changed the politics of Ireland in an instant, dividing society into Aristocrats and Democrats. The Aristocrats were those, of whatever station in life, who believed that the Constitution was like a living tree, to be reformed by gentle pruning, or left alone. The Democrats were those who, like the French, believed in taking an axe to the root and starting all over again. Within a year or so, the contrasting arguments were conveniently set out in Edmund Burke's *Reflections on the French Revolution* and Tom Paine's *The Rights of Man*.[1]

In the early months of 1790 the dormant reform movement began to show signs of returning life. 'Encouraged by the . . . glorious efforts of the French nation, the friends of liberty . . . renewed those efforts from which they had been so ingloriously compelled to desist in the year 1785.' The first appearance of this revival of public spirit in Belfast was on 6 March, when it was unanimously resolved at a meeting of the Belfast First Volunteer Company 'that this company do turn out in full uniform on the 17th inst. in order to celebrate our twelfth anniversary, and elect officers for the ensuing year'.[2]

Ten days later a town meeting was called, and a series of similar resolutions passed. An Address was voted to Grattan and he made a graceful reply. Meanwhile Charlemont, 'from a just and probably well-founded dread of the increase of democratic principles in the town of Belfast', drew up plans for the formation of a Whig Club in the town, modelled on the Dublin Club. 'I think', he wrote to Haliday, 'that an institution of this kind, would by holding out a congregation to the true believers at Belfast be a means of fixing, and even recalling many who might otherwise wander from the faith.'[3]

Haliday responded with enthusiasm. 'People here are at length roused, and after teasing others, I am now teased, in turn, about the speedy establishment of a Whig Club. Five of us, good men and true, are to meet on Sunday for that purpose, and I have been urged to prepare something as a groundwork.' He enclosed a draft manifesto, the preamble to which outlined the stand for Whig principles taken by the inhabitants of Belfast from the Revolution of 1688 to the present. In some respects the views expressed were more advanced than those of the Dublin Club.

We declare that government is an original compact between the governors and the governed, instituted for the good of the whole community; that in a limited monarchy, or more properly speaking (respect being had to the constitution of these realms) a regal commonwealth, the majesty is in the people and though the person on the throne is superior to any individual, he is but the servant of the nation.

Electors ought to be free, the elected independent. Parliamentary influence by places and pensions was inconsistent with the virtue and safety of the public. Prosperity depended upon trade. The freedom of the press was the bulwark of religious and civil liberty, and 'as religion is of the utmost importance to every individual, no person ought to suffer civil hardships for his religious persuasion, unless the tenets of his religion lead him to subvert the state'. The signatories further declared, as Irishmen, that 'the subjects of this realm are of right free from, and independent of, the authority of any parliament or legislative whatsoever, save only the parliament of Ireland, that is to say, the king of Ireland, and the lords and commons of this realm'. Nevertheless, 'we will maintain as sacred and inviolable our connection with Great Britain, in its present form, as indispensably necessary for the freedom of this kingdom'. It was with grief of heart that they considered the Constitution of Ireland as labouring under manifold imperfections and pressures, 'from which that of Britain is free'.[4]

Charlemont was delighted. Haliday's sketch, as he had modestly called it, was 'like a sketch by Raphael, more valuable than the finished picture'. To attempt correction would be to spoil it. A week later, however, his mood had given way to one of impatience. 'Every Belfast paper that arrives raises and disappoints my hopes. Why do I not see your incomparable resolutions and declarations? Where is the expected summons for your Whig club?' The truth was that Haliday had run into some opposition. It was being suggested that there should be two clubs since 'very many good Whigs in this town would have declined becoming members of the club, on the score that many country gentlemen of superior rank and fortune are expected to join'.[5]

In order to satisfy the country gentlemen, Haliday's 'fine historical preamble' had to go, and to make matters worse, the printer had left out a paragraph, rendering the declaration 'whole nonsense and half treason'. Haliday blamed Joy. But by now Charlemont was demanding some omissions of his own, and he gave Haliday the kind of advice of which modern advertising agencies would wholeheartedly approve.

In all associations of this kind, whose efficacy in great measure depends upon their numbers, care should be taken that, while the principles which form their foundation are solid and vigorous, the expression should be modified in such a manner as to render the subscribers as numerous as possible, by affording no handle for misinterpretation, and by sedulously avoiding every phrase which, by its sound rather than its sense, may alarm the more timid. The phrase 'regal commonwealth' is, I fear, liable to both these objections . . . why not then content yourselves with 'limited monarchy' which cannot be misrepresented and means the same thing?

Charlemont then proceeds to make his views on parliamentary reform and Catholic emancipation crystal-clear.

Respecting parliamentary reform, my sentiments have been again and again declared; they are still the same, and I care not how often I repeat them. But why was religion made part of the system? On this head you know my sentiments. They also have been fully declared, and remain unvaried. Toleration is still my darling principle, but to participate (sic) legislation I can never consent to.[6]

Since Charlemont was writing after having seen the printed (and amended) version, Haliday took offence, and replied very stiffly to the letter, 'the first I ever received from your lordship that I have perused with more surprise than satisfaction'. He recalled that he had sent the manuscript 'sketch' to Charlemont for his corrections and amendments. 'Unfortunately, I was not favoured with either.' Why should Charlemont now find these passages objectionable? None of the people he had discussed them with had objected, though 'as averse as any man breathing from republican ideas and from popery'. Haliday stuck to his guns over 'regal commonwealth'. And as for emancipation. . . . 'You ask, my dear lord, why religion was made part of the system. How was it possible to omit it? Is there any right more important to man?'

On this matter he professed to be completely in agreement with Charlemont, and drew the same casuistical distinction. 'And how should this open the door of legislation to Catholics? Have they no tenets in their religion which lead to the subversion of the state? They have. If they had not, the doors of parliament should be as open to them as the gates of heaven.'[7] It was typical of Charlemont that he was completely and humbly contrite. He apologized for not reading the printed resolutions properly, blaming his eyes and the hurry of other business. But there can be no doubt that he felt an underlying disquiet about the radical element in Belfast politics. He had intimated that he could not sign the resolutions, and disappointment was the real cause of Haliday's strictures, since he had gone out on a limb by taking Charlemont's membership of the Northern Whig Club for granted. Charlemont now indicated that he would be happy to join it, if his interpretation of the Catholic resolution was clearly understood.[8]

On 15 June 1791, the anniversary of the signing of Magna Carta, the Northern Whig Club met with Haliday in the chair and Joy as secretary and began to organize the civic commemoration of the French Revolution to be staged on 14 July. In it they hoped that Whigs and Volunteers would combine to create the most spectacular celebration the town had ever witnessed, a demonstration to Ireland and the world of Belfast's belief in the sovereignty of the people.

They were not disappointed. 'In this eventful period', enthused the *Belfast Newsletter,*

which reflects new light on the general principles and science of government, the unexampled Revolution in France forms the most prominent and luminous object. Twenty-six millions of our fellow creatures (near one-sixth of the inhabitants of Europe) bursting their chains, and throwing off, almost in an instant, the degrading yoke of slavery – is a scene so new, interesting and sublime, that the heart which cannot participate in the triumph, must either have been vitiated by illiberal politics, or be naturally depraved.

At 2 o'clock on the afternoon of 14 July the parade formed up at the Exchange buildings in the town centre – the two Volunteer companies, a troop of Light Dragoons and two artillery corps with four brass six-pounders. At 3 o'clock the Dragoons led off, followed by the First Company's artillery and a large portrait of Benjamin

Franklin, borne aloft by two young Volunteers, and under it a scroll with the doctor's own words, *Where Liberty is – there is my country*. Then followed the First Belfast Company and the Belfast Volunteer Company with a portrait of Mirabeau and the slightly distracting motto, *Can the African slave trade, though morally wrong, be politically right?* Next came the great standard, elevated on a triumphal car drawn by four horses. One side of the enormous canvas depicted a 'very animated representation of *The Releasement of the Prisoners from the Bastille*'. The other side had a large figure of Hibernia in a reclining posture, one hand and one foot in shackles, a Volunteer presenting to her a figure of Liberty, supported by an artillery-man leaning on a piece of ordnance. The motto was, *For a people to be free, it is sufficient that they will it*. The Northern Whig Club, resplendent in their new uniforms, brought up the rear, with a huge concourse of citizens. 'A green cockade, the national colour of Ireland, was worn by the whole body.'

Thus constituted, the parade passed through 'every street of consequence' in the town, until it arrived at the White Linen Hall, where *feux de joie* were fired by the battalion companies, and answered by the artillery. The Volunteers formed up in a circle to cheer the declaration of their sentiments on the Revolution, which was subsequently transmitted to the Assemblée Nationale.

Three hundred and fifty-four persons then sat down to dinner at a single table in the south wing of the Hall and drank their way through a paralyzing list of patriotic and reforming toasts. Nevertheless, it was recorded that 'the whole [company] separated at an early hour, with the pleasing consciousness that they had been celebrating an event which deserves to be considered, not merely as the triumph of Frenchmen, but the triumph of Human Nature'.[9]

The French responded warmly to the address. At Bordeaux, the Friends of the Constitution saw it in the *Courier de l'Europe*, and had it read out at a meeting to repeated bursts of applause. In their reply, they looked forward to the day when all parts of the civilized world would, like Belfast, raise their voices to teach the people to recover their rights. A reply was also received from the Friends of the Constitution at Nantes.[10]

At some point during the summer of 1791 the revived Belfast First Company changed its uniform from scarlet to green. On 1 August twenty-seven corps of Volunteers were reviewed on the commons at

Armagh by Colonel James Stewart of Killymoon. Joy records that the Belfast companies attended on this occasion, 'viz., the Belfast Troop, uniform, *Blue and Silver* – 1st Company, *Green and Gold* – Volunteer Company, and Artillery, two six-pounders, *Blue and Gold*'. Certainly by 1791 the Belfast First Company was being referred to as 'the Green Company'. Two years later, when the political situation was much changed, and the revived Volunteers were calling themselves National Volunteers in imitation of the French National Guard, the *Newsletter* recorded that the First Belfast Regiment 'finally and unanimously determined on their uniform, which consists of a green jacket, faced with yellow, green waistcoat, white breeches, long black gaiters and a leather cap'.[11]

# 17

# A Plot for the People

In December 1790 Drennan had at last succeeded in moving to Dublin.[1] Almost at once he was writing home to Belfast his first impressions of the popular politicians of the day: Grattan, 'his eyes rolling with that fine enthusiasm without which it is impossible to be a great man'; Lord Edward Fitzgerald, 'a fine tall young fellow'; and Napper Tandy 'in all the surliness of republicanism, grinning most ghastly smiles'.[2] Drennan was himself now a republican, as he admitted to Sam McTier. By 1791 his opinions were more extreme than they had been during his twenties. He was foremost among those radicals who wished to reconstitute the Volunteer organization, but he also revived his idea of the secret 'interior circle' within its ranks.

It is my fixed opinion [he wrote to Bruce], that no reform in parliament, and consequently no freedom, will ever be attainable by this country but by a total separation from Britain; I think that this belief is making its way rapidly, but as yet silently, among both protestants and catholics, and I think that the four quarters of the kingdom are more unanimous in this opinion than they themselves imagine. It is for the collection of this opinion (the esoteric part, and nucleus of political Doctrine) that such a society, or interior circle, ought to be immediately established, around which another circle might be formed, whose opinions are still halting between, who are for temporizing expedients and patience, and partial reform.

The letter goes on to urge the necessity for revolution to throw off the incumbency of Irish political and civil grievances. The prosperity of the nation depended more on liberty than on peace. Reform to mean anything must be revolution.

I think that revolutions are not to be dreaded as such terrible extremes, and that it is the highest probability, it would be as peaceful here as in France, as in Poland, as in Ireland itself in the year '79, provided the great irresistible voice of the whole declared itself explicitly upon the subject. I believe a reform must lead rapidly to a separation, and a separation as certainly to a reform: both are means, and both are ends.[3]

There were many who shared Drennan's exasperation with the Whigs, and one of them was a young briefless barrister in Dublin called Theobald Wolfe Tone. Tone was, nominally at least, a Church of Ireland Protestant whom circumstance and a restless temperament combined to make highly critical of his own caste. As a young man he had a passion for military uniforms (not unrelated to the magical effect they had on women), and his consuming ambition was to be an officer in the British army. Almost everything which happened to him subsequently may have stemmed from the denial of this ambition. The only portraits which we have of him show him in the uniform of a Volunteer company and in the blue uniform of a French officer.[4] Had his father allowed him to become a professional soldier like his brother William, his politics would almost certainly have been of a different kind. But then, had William Pitt bothered to answer the letters Tone delivered by hand at 10 Downing Street, advocating the establishment of a British military colony on the recently discovered Sandwich Islands, we might today remember him as an imperialist; and had the Ponsonbys and the Whig party fulfilled their hints and promises, he might have become a colleague of Charlemont and Grattan.

Instead, Tone seemed to focus in himself all the classic discontents of the colonial outsider, resentful like his hero Swift of a status less than that of a true-born Englishman, yet unable to identify with any other body of the Irish population. His open and generous nature reacted to the slights. He was highly intelligent, and capable of the most penetrating analysis of the contemporary political situation. He had been a freshman at Trinity in the year of the great constitutional victory, but even then he had seen just how hollow it was. He saw that the key to Ireland's future was the restoration of rights to Catholics; the problem was to determine how Protestants would cope with it. Like Drennan he was personally ambitious, but, receiving discouragement, he saw no reason why he should not give the Establishment (though he had relatives and protectors in it) both barrels of his critical and literary abilities.

Unusually for so sanguine a temperament, Tone was at the core a realist. His memoirs, which must rank as the most entertaining of any Irish patriot, are illuminated by good nature and an infectious sense of humour, qualities quite absent from his apotheosis. In their pages he seems like a free spirit forever trying to escape from the terrible fate which history has in store for him.

By the late spring of 1791 Tone had grown as exasperated with the Whig dining clubs as Drennan. Drennan thought every Volunteer 'should blush to quit his uniform and buy one for the Whig Club, North or South'.[5] Tone's opinion was that the Whigs dreaded the people as much as the Castle did. Unlike Drennan, he was not a separatist at this stage, but both men ardently desired to see some kind of democratic organization to fight for the people's rights.

It was at this point that the general committee of Belfast Volunteers and Whigs who were planning the 14 July celebrations approached both men to supply a declaration and a set of resolutions suitable for the occasion. The circumstances of Tone's involvement with the Belfast radicals were as follows. Tone met Thomas Russell, *more hibernico*, as a result of falling into an argument with him in the Strangers' Gallery of the Irish House of Commons. Russell was then still an officer of the 64th Regiment of Foot, home on half-pay after several years' service in India. He spent much of the summer of 1790 with Tone and his young wife at 'the little box at Irishtown' (a village outside Dublin where Tone had taken his wife for her health), and Tone gives an idyllic description of this holiday by the sea. In the autumn Russell was recalled to his regiment, which was stationed, as it happened, in Belfast. There Russell 'found the people so much to his taste, and in return rendered himself so agreeable to them, that he was speedily admitted to their confidence and became a member of several of their clubs'.[6]

This is Tone's account of what followed:

The Catholic question was, at this period beginning to attract the public notice, and the Belfast Volunteers, on some public occasion, I know not precisely what, wished to come forward with a declaration in its favour. For this purpose Russell, who was by this time entirely in their confidence, wrote to me to draw up and transmit to him such a declaration as I thought proper, which I accordingly did. A meeting of the corps was held in consequence, but an opposition unexpectedly arising to that part of the declaration which alluded directly to the Catholic claims, that passage was for the sake of unanimity withdrawn for the present, and the declarations then passed unanimously. Russell wrote me an account of all this, and it immediately set me on thinking more seriously than I had yet done on the state of Ireland. I soon formed my theory, and on that theory I have unvaryingly acted ever since.

The paragraph which follows is the most quoted of all his writings, since it states the political credo which he afterwards adopted, and with which he is most associated:

To subvert the tyranny of our execrable government, to break the connection with England, the never-failing source of all our political evils, and to assert the independence of my country – these were my objects. To unite the whole people of Ireland, to abolish the memory of all past dissensions, and to substitute the common name of Irishman in place of the denominations of Protestant, Catholic and Dissenter – these were my means.[7]

We know that here he was rewriting history, several years later in France, when the means had become ends in themselves. In 1791 his political objectives were by no means as clear-cut, and it does seem disingenuous of him to affect not to remember what the precise occasion of the resolutions was.

In July 1791, against the background of renewed sectarian clashes between Peep O'Day Boys and Defenders in Co. Armagh, the Catholic question had become a very delicate one with the Volunteers, even in Belfast, and references to it in both Drennan's and Tone's resolutions were dropped. However, the resolutions were both immediately adopted by the Belfast First Volunteer Company.

Tone's immediate reaction was to vow 'to become a red-hot Catholic',[8] and he did this by writing at great speed a thirty-two page pamphlet entitled *An Argument on Behalf of the Catholics of Ireland*. It is a pamphlet more often mentioned than actually quoted, for it contains much which a devout Catholic might find offensive. Even those opponents of Catholic emancipation who so irritated Tone might have hesitated to describe Irish priests as 'men of low birth, low feelings, low habits, and no education'. He looks forward to the day when

The emancipated and liberal Irishman, like the emancipated and liberal Frenchman, may go to Mass, may tell his beads, or sprinkle his mistress with Holy Water; but neither the one nor the other will attend to the rusty and extinguished thunderbolts of the Vatican or the idle anathemas which, indeed, His Holiness is nowadays too prudent and cautious to issue.[9]

Tone the Deist and child of the Enlightenment is anxious to establish just how unsympathetic he is to the Roman Catholic Church. The point is that he believed that the Irish Catholic was at last being emancipated from the thraldom of priests. Able to think for himself, he was more likely to join hands with the Irish Protestant in the sacred cause of the Rights of Man and the rights of Ireland. It is a strange irony which has made Tone revered almost as a saint in thousands of Irish Catholic homes. The reason undoubtedly is that he presses beyond these crude debating points to an impassioned argument for principles of universal justice, and associates them with love of Ireland to a greater degree than any Protestant had previously done.

Tone's pamphlet had two consequences of importance. It brought him to the attention of the radical and more forward-looking elements of the Catholic Committee, and it enraptured the radical and pro-emancipation Dissenters of Belfast, coming as it did so close on the heels on the publication of Part One of Paine's *Rights of Man*.[10]

Few facts in Irish history seem more firmly established than this, that the Society of United Irishmen was founded in Belfast in October 1791 by Wolfe Tone. Yet this is not what Tone wrote in his memoirs. Instead he says explicitly that he attended the first meeting of the society as an invited guest, and that his being there was, to a large extent, the result of mere chance. Moreover, he declares with considerable candour that shortly after the founding of the second society in Dublin he ceased to have any influence on its proceedings.[11]

Tone's version of the sequence of events is as follows. After the publication of his pamphlet on the Catholic question in September, the Belfast Volunteers 'of the first or green company' elected him an honorary member of their corps. He was naturally proud of this distinction as it was a favour they were very delicate in bestowing. 'I believe I was the only person, except the great Henry Flood, who was ever honoured with that mark of their approbation.' They also invited him to come to Belfast 'in order to assist in framing the first club of United Irishmen'. He accepted the invitation because he wished to cultivate the acquaintance of men who he knew only by reputation.[12]

His diary for 12 October 1791, the day after his arrival in Belfast, records:

Introduced to McTier and Sinclair. A meeting between Russell, McTier, Macabe and me. Mode of doing business by a Secret Committee, who are not known or suspected of co-operating, but who, in fact, direct the movements of Belfast . . . settled to dine with the Secret Committee at Drew's on Saturday, when all the resolutions, & c . . . of the United Irish will be submitted.[13]

On Saturday 14 October Tone dined with the Secret Committee at

4 o'clock (not an unusual hour in the eighteenth century). Russell and he made declarations of secrecy, and then Russell made a long speech on the politics of the Catholic Committee, of which the Belfast people 'appeared to know nothing'. Resolutions prepared for the society by Tone were then accepted unanimously, and it was agreed that a copy should be sent to the celebrated Dublin radical, Napper Tandy, with a request for his cooperation. Tone continues:

Settled the mode of carrying the business through the club at large, on Tuesday next. McTier to be in the chair. Sinclair to move the resolutions. Simms to second him. Neilson to move their printing; and P.P. [Tone's nickname for Russell] and I to state the sentiments of the people of Dublin.

Tone adds that the members of the Secret Committee were 'all steady sensible, clear men, and, as I judge, extremely well-adapted for serious business', and he identifies them as William Sinclair, Samuel McTier, Samuel Neilson, William McCleery, the brothers William and Robert Simms, Thomas McCabe, Henry Haslett, William Tennent, John Campbell and Gilbert McIlveen. This is not how Tone spells their names. He gives versions like McLeary, Macabe, and McIlvaine, which further suggests that he did not know them very well. We know from other evidence that these were in fact the first United Irishmen. They were all Presbyterians; two at least were sons of the manse.[14]

Neilson, then a prosperous woollen draper in Belfast, was the third son of the Rev. Alexander Neilson, minister of Ballyroney, Co. Down. Tennent was the son of the Rev. John Tennent, minister of the Secession congregation of Roseyards, Co. Antrim. William Sinclair was a linen merchant who had been very active in the Volunteer reform campaign of 1784–5. William McCleery was a tanner, and the Simms brothers owned a paper mill at Ballyclare. Thomas McCabe was a radical watch-maker, famous because single-handedly he had shamed Waddell Cunningham and some of the other Belfast merchants from involving the town in the slave trade. (This had not deterred him, however, from assisting Robert Joy in installing machinery in the poorhouse to teach the orphans how to spin and weave cotton.)[15]

In the month before this meeting the Secret Committee had laid plans for launching a newspaper which would propagate its views. Neilson, with eleven other Belfast businessmen, founded the *Northern Star*. The twelve partners held forty shares of £50, amounting to capital of £2,000. They were all reasonably affluent, 'respectable' in the eighteenth-century meaning of that word, and all Presbyterians. Neilson, who contributed more than a quarter of the capital, and became the editor of the journal, owned the Irish Woollen Warehouse, then the largest in Belfast. Before he neglected his business for politics, he was said to possess property worth £8,000, a modest fortune at the time. His partners were: William Magee, printer and bookseller; William Tennent, merchant; Gilbert McIlveen, linen merchant; William McCleery, tanner; John Haslett, woollen draper; John Robb, clerk; William and Robert Simms, merchants; John Boyle, merchant; Robert Caldwell, banker; and Henry Haslett, merchant.[16]

Evidence for the activities of the Secret Committee before the autumn of 1791 is thin. This is hardly surprising, given that it was kept secret from the rest of the Volunteers. But there are indications that it began to meet in the early summer, and that it consisted of carefully selected members of both the Green and the Blue Companies. Various accounts of the genesis of the Society of United Irishmen have been given. Some of the radicals concerned were in the habit of meeting in one or other of the taverns off High Street in Belfast, Peggy Barclay's in Sugarhouse Entry or John Stewart's in Crown Entry. The proper name of the former was the 'Dr Franklin Tavern', and Benjamin's portrait, 'awful and pompous, stood in a swinging frame over the door'. Drennan speaks of meeting there with Kelburn and other liberals in 1785. 'We will call upon Mrs Barclay, that lady who distinguishes herself by having the geniuses of the Island at her levee, yet would like more substantial pleasures, etc., etc.' He describes Kelburn as 'that Epicurean cynic, that oily little man of God who has such a roguish twinkle in his eye, and laughs in his sleeve at politics and religion'. Kelburn was the son of the Rev. Ebenezer Kelburn, one of the Dublin ministers.[17]

The first meeting of the committee is supposed to have taken place on 1 April 1791 at Barclay's tavern, and a document has been cited which reads:

Resolved: – That we the undersigned do solemnly declare ourselves in favour of the proposal of Samuel Neilson, a merchant of this town whose name is firstly subscribed hereto, to form ourselves into an association to unite all Irishmen to pledge ourselves to our country, and by that cordial union maintain that balance of patriotism so essential for the restoration and preservation of our liberty, and the revival of our trade – Signed: Samuel Neilson, John Robb, Alexander Lowry, Thomas McCabe and Henry Joy McCracken.[18]

The document cannot now be authenticated, but it does not conflict with other evidence. Madden, the rambling and unreliable hagiographer of the United Irishmen in the nineteenth century, asserts that the club was originated by Neilson, and Mary Ann McCracken, the sister of the leader of the Co. Antrim insurgents in 1798, always insisted to Madden that her brother, Henry Joy McCracken, was one of the founders. But Henry was only twenty-four at the time, and his name does not appear elsewhere in the early records. Edna Fitzhenry, his biographer, on the evidence of the Russell and Madden papers gives Barclay's as the meeting place, and says that it was to McCracken and Russell that Neilson 'in the summer of 1791' first suggested a club which should unite Irishmen of all creeds in an effort to secure a reformed or independent Parliament.[19]

All of these were friends and political associates of Sam McTier, and well known to Drennan. Neilson was a close friend of the Drennan family. It is possible that quite a number of the radicals had the same idea at about the same time. It has recently been claimed that the society 'was not entirely a Belfast initiative', on the grounds that correspondence had taken place over the summer between Dublin radicals, members of the Catholic Committee and Belfast men 'like McTier, Sinclair and McCabe'. The name of the society and its prospectus had already been decided. Tone's 14 July resolutions were to be remodelled, printed and distributed, and a special United Irish edition of the *Argument* was being printed in Dublin before Tone and Russell set out for Belfast.[20]

It was precisely because Tone's *Argument* was so well received in the North, however, that these developments took place at all. Tone was immensely proud of the fact that this edition would be so widely distributed there, and this was the reason for inaugurating the new society in Belfast rather than in Dublin. The men of the Green Company were once again the most advanced of the radicals, and Drennan's correspondence throws more light on the process from the early summer.

On 21 May 1791 Drennan had outlined to McTier, in the fullest detail so far, his plan for a quasi-Masonic secret society within the Volunteers:

I should much desire that a Society were instituted in this city [i.e. Dublin] having much of the secrecy and somewhat of the ceremonial of Freemasonry, so much secrecy as might communicate curiosity, uncertainty, expectation to the minds of surrounding men, so much impressive and affecting ceremony in its internal economy as without impeding real business might strike the soul through the senses. A benevolent conspiracy – a plot for the people – no Whig Club – no party title – the Brotherhood its name – the Rights of Man and the Greatest Happiness of the Greatest Number its end – its general end Real Independence to Ireland, and Republicanism its particular purpose – its business every means to accomplish these ends as speedily as the prejudices and bigotry of the land we live in would permit, as speedily as to give us some enjoyment and not to protract anything too long in this short span of life. The means are manifold, publication always coming from one of the Brotherhood, and no other designation. Declaration, a solemn and religious compact with each other to be signed by every member, and its chief and leading principles to be conveyed into a symbol worn by every of them round their body next the heart. Communication with leading men in France, in England and America, so as to cement the scattered and shifting sand of republicanism into a body (as well as those malignant conspiracies which courts and classes of men have formed) and when thus cemented to sink it like a caisson in the dark and troubled waters, a stable unseen power.[21]

Drennan went on to explain the reasons for secrecy. It gave greater energy within, and greater influence without. It protected the identity of members whose professions made concealment expedient until the moment of trial came. Therefore, for the present, McTier should not mention it.

You are not, I believe a republican, but not many years will elapse till this persuasion will prevail, for nothing else but the public happiness as an end, and public will as the power and means of obtaining it, is good in politics. . . . Such schemes are not to be laughed at, for without enthusiasm nothing great was done, or will be done.[22]

Despite all the admonitions about secrecy, Drennan expanded his idea in a paper some seven pages long, which he sent first to Henry Joy, the proprietor and editor of the *Belfast Newsletter*, and then to McTier and his friends. He probably hoped that Joy would publish it, as he had published Drennan's earlier political pieces, but Joy thought it much too dangerous. On 2 July McTier wrote to Drennan:

I received yours and the enclosure which I had read several times and am highly pleased with it. I have showed it in confidence to several gentlemen here who all approve very much of it except Bruce, whom I found had seen it before by H. Joy. Bruce is against all appearance of secrecy, which point he says he has frequently argued with you. Indeed I think Bruce is guided too much by H. Joy who would not in my opinion risk the circulation of his newspaper for any political scheme whatever. He is one of your very prudent patriots . . .

We rejoice here at the King of France being taken, and are making great preparations for celebrating the 14th. At the meeting of the different Volunteer corps they named me as one of a committee to prepare some declaration or resolutions to be published from the Meeting on the 14th which I believe will be the most numerous ever was in Belfast. I know they appointed me in hopes they would get something from you and I will be much obliged to you if you'll do something for us, and let me know soon if I may expect it . . .

McTier added a significant postscript:

P.S. July the 2nd 1791. If your Club Brotherhood takes place we will immediately follow your example.[23]

This indicates that Drennan had hoped to establish his society in Dublin.

Drennan had already been approached on behalf of the Volunteers by Joy, however, partly perhaps to soften the blow of refusing his paper. On 3 July he wrote to Sam McTier:

I enclosed on Saturday to H. Joy, who had wrote to me on the subject, a declaration adapted to the occasion of the 14th, and desired him to show it to you and Bruce. As I think it a very proper opportunity to speak out, I wrote it with perhaps too much spirit for your assent. I hope not, however, for I cannot consent to have it all altered, and I am only sorry I had not room to express the necessity of conciliating the interests of Catholics and Protestants at present.[24]

On 9 July McTier wrote: 'Last night we had a meeting of the Committee for preparing matters for the 14th, when I laid your paper before them, which was received with unanimous approbation.' On the following morning Colonel William Sharman, a prominent Volunteer who had agreed to take the chair on the 14th, told Sam that he had received 'a blank cover with two or three papers that he did not rightly understand', and that he had given one of them to George Black. (Black was another son of the wine importer of Bordeaux and had been the town sovereign in 1782 and 1785.)

'Afterwards I met G. B. and asked him for a sight of the paper Mr S. had given him. He asked his son for it, who said that Captain McNevin had not returned it. McN, he said, had behaved very ungenteely, for he only desired him to get a reading of it. By this time I doubt not it is in the Secretary of State's hands at the Castle of Dublin. Upon my enquiring at G. B. what kind of paper it was, he said it was something like Freemasonry, but contained a Cataline conspiracy, that it was devilish well-written and in strong nervous language. I advised him to get it, be cautious of shewing for fear of its getting abroad as it might do mischief in the hands of hot-headed people; he agreed. I send this by Neilson, and this night your declaration is to be adopted by the Committee. What would you think of some printed copies dispersed on Thursday morning that country people, who join, and the townsmen, might know beforehand what they were going to declare?[25]

McTier's apprehensions were all too well founded. Two days later Drennan ruefully reported:

The paper on the Brotherhood was read publicly by Sheridan in the Four Courts the day after I had sent it to three in confidence, and he was not one of the number, so that, seeing it public, I sent it to all I liked. It will neither damp nor destroy the business. Another name may be taken and all will be the same . . . [26]

The full text of Drennan's prospectus for the new society can be read in the appendices of the House of Commons Committee of Secrecy's Report on the United Irish conspiracy, published in 1798. The accompanying note declares that the paper was circulating in Dublin in June 1791, and that it contained the original design of the association which became the Society of United Irishmen. There is no indication that Drennan was suspected of being the author, and it is only since the publication of extracts from the Drennan letters in 1931 that historians have noticed that under the bold headline IDEM SENTIRE, DICERE, AGERE, the preamble is in the same words used in the letter to McTier of 21 May.

The name of the society was to be the IRISH BROTHERHOOD; its object was to be the promotion of 'the Rights of Man in Ireland' and 'the greatest happiness of the greatest number'. Every member was to wear, day and night, an amulet around his neck

containing the great principle which unites the Brotherhood, in letters of gold, on a ribbon, striped with all the original colours and enclosed in a sheath of white silk, to represent the pure union of all the mingled rays, and the abolition of all superficial distinctions, all colours and shades of difference, for the sake of one illustrious end.

More importantly, the Brotherhood was to have as its fundamental principle Hutcheson's 'greatest happiness of the greatest number', and was to determine such questions as:

What is the plan of reform most suited to this country?
Who are the people?
What are the rights of Roman Catholics, and what are the immediate duties of Protestants respecting these rights?
Is the Independence of Ireland nominal or real . . ?
Is there any middle state between the extremes of union with Britain and total separation, in which the rights of the People can be fully established and rest in security?[27]

Drennan regretted that in his first declaration he had 'found no room to express the need for conciliating the Catholics'. He had suggested to McTier that the Belfast Presbyterians should draw up articles for the basis of a political alliance between them and the Catholic Committee. He urged that these articles should be ready for publication on 14 July. There was no time to be lost, because some of the Catholic leaders, notably Lords Kenmare and Fingall, were already in negotiation with the government. McTier agreed and on Drennan's letter, in his hand, are the toasts he suggested for the 14th. They included 'May the Catholics and Protestants of Ireland be of one mind in ascertaining their rights as Men, and establishing the independence of their country' and 'May honest Catholic and Protestant be ever united'.[28]

The critical point was reached when the rejected resolutions in favour of Catholic emancipation were adopted by the First Company. On the last day of August, Drennan was able to write that William Sinclair had received two addresses to the Belfast Volunteers from two meetings of Catholics at Elphin and Leitrim. He thought it prudent not to publish these at once 'lest it draw down the aristocratical part of the R. Catholics to damp all such proceedings by their united influence and power, but rather to wait until the system of conciliation and consequent unity of council and action should be farther completed'.[29]

An organized Catholic political structure had been in existence since 1759 when a group of Catholic gentlemen met at the Elephant Inn in Dublin, to discuss what steps they might take to bring about the mitigation of the Penal Laws. A committee was appointed, and by the end of the year its members had drawn up an address to the Lord

Lieutenant expressing their loyalty and the earnest hope that the legislature would find means of 'rendering them useful members of the community'. This circumspect beginning marked the revival of Catholic political organization, which had virtually ceased to exist since the reign of James II.[30]

From 1760 there was in existence a Catholic Committee, which was, in its earlier years, dominated by the Catholic aristocracy and clergy. On the outbreak of the American war, Catholics acted quickly to assure the Crown of their loyalty, and in 1777 the Lord Lieutenant promised that the government would do something to meet their requests. A Bill introduced in the Irish Commons by Luke Gardiner in 1778 repealed a great part of the Popery Act of 1704, in so far as it related to land. The motives of the government were partly economic, but even so, the Bill passed only because it was supported by the Patriot members.

When the French Revolution began in 1789, the initial reaction of most Catholics was hostile. The treatment of the Church by the revolutionaries evoked horror and alienated the clergy and upper classes represented on the Catholic Committee. But there was a democratic element among the Catholic merchants and traders of Dublin which was determined to pursue the campaign for emancipation, if necessary by novel means, setting the question in the context of the Rights of Man, and seizing the opportunity presented by the challenge of France. By 1791 they had begun to work out a strategy of appealing directly to the Crown, short-circuiting the Ascendancy-dominated Irish Parliament, and at the same time implicitly threatening to join hands with the radical Presbyterian Dissenters should their petitions be unavailing. In July 1791 Westmorland, the Lord Lieutenant, was to write to Henry Dundas that 'the language of these dissenters is to unite with the Catholics and their union would be very formidable. That union is not yet made, and I believe and hope it never could be.' But by the summer of 1791 it had been made.[31]

It would appear that Tone was responsible for suggesting that the society's name should be changed to 'the United Irishmen'. In a letter to Russell in July, enclosing the draft of his resolutions, he writes: 'I have left, as you see, a blank for the name, which, I am clearly of opinion, should be "The Society of United Irishmen".'[32]

That Drennan considered himself to be the real father of the United

Irish Society is indicated in a letter written to McTier during the
following winter:

You may keep my letters, as they will show what has been done, or the news
of the day, if one should wish to make out any historical sketch of the business
from the Belfast address until now. Perhaps my little paper was the first seed
of the coalition, I mean that of the Brotherhood, and, if so, I shall ever deem
myself very happy – it appeared in June, and the address to the French, 14
July, the amendment to which was, I think, the first motion to Union on our
part, answered by the Catholics at Elphin and Jamestown, and promoted by
the establishment of the United Irishmen at Belfast and Dublin.[33]

Three weeks after the founding of the Belfast Club, Tandy gathered
together in Doyle's tavern eighteen Protestant and Catholic radicals,
including Drennan, to form a similar club in the capital. They balloted
for each other, Drennan recorded, and then called themselves the
Dublin Society of United Irishmen. A further eighteen members were
elected to membership in their absence, including Tone and Russell.[34]
The first chairman was Simon Butler, the barrister brother of Lord
Mountgarret, but he was soon to be succeeded by Drennan, much to
Matty's alarm. One of the Society's first actions was to adopt a 'Test'
composed by Drennan and designed to impress on each initiate what
he was undertaking.

I, A. B., in the presence of God, do pledge myself to my country that I will use
all my abilities and influence in the attainment of an impartial and adequate
representation of the Irish nation in Parliament, and, as a means of absolute
and immediate necessity in accomplishing this chief good of Ireland, I shall
do whatever lies in my power to forward a brotherhood of affection, an
identity of interests, a communion of rights, and an union of power among
Irishmen of all religious persuasions, without which any reform must be
partial, not national, inadequate to the wants, delusive to the wishes and
insufficient for the freedom and happiness of this country.[35]

The test was opposed by Tone 'with curious bitterness' both at his
first attendance at the society and in a letter to Belfast. He wished
everything to be followed from the Belfast Society by adoption, but
Drennan's view prevailed. Soon afterwards Tone lost his chief ally in
the society when Russell obtained the post of stipendiary magistrate
in Dungannon, through the influence of the Knox family.

Contrary to popular belief, the United Irish movement did not at
once spread like wildfire throughout the country. In fact it never at

any time affected more than a small part of Ireland. The founding of the first society in Belfast was followed a few weeks later by the establishment of societies at Templepatrick, Doagh, Randalstown, Killead and Muckamore in the radical areas of Co. Antrim. The first society in Co. Down was formed at Saintfield on 16 January 1792 by the Presbyterian minister there, the Rev. Thomas Ledlie Birch, who was a prominent radical and a Freemason. Soon afterwards, three more societies were formed in Belfast. During the constitutional phase of its history there was no branch of any importance outside the North except the Dublin Society, which was also the only one to have a large and religiously mixed membership. It achieved its maximum numbers towards the end of 1792. Its regular place of meeting was a building which two centuries earlier had been a Jesuit chapel. It was at this time the Hall of the Tailors' Guild. It was also the headquarters of the Grand Lodge of Freemasons.[36]

# 18

# The Company and the Lodge

The arch is nearly finished. As Drennan wrote, one stone hangs upon another, and the keystone is ready to be put in.

In 1896, when the old White Linen Hall of Belfast was being demolished and the site cleared for the erection of the present City Hall, the workmen discovered the original foundation-stone of the building. In a cavity within the stone was a glass tube, which was found to contain some coins and three rolled-up documents.[1] The first paper was an account of the meeting of the Volunteers at Dungannon on 15 February 1782. The second was a cutting from the *Belfast Newsletter* of 25 April 1783 concerning the Renunciation Act. The third read as follows:

Belfast, 28 April 1783. These papers were deposited underneath this building by John McClean and Robert Bradshaw, with the intent that if they should hereafter be found, they may be an authentic information to posterity that by the firmness and unanimity of the Irish Volunteers, this Kingdom (long oppressed) was fully and completely emancipated.

If in future times there should be an attempt to encroach upon the liberties of this country, let our posterity look up with admiration to the glorious example of their forefathers, who at this time formed an army, independent of Government, unpaid and self-appointed, of eighty thousand men. The discipline, order and regularity of which army was looked upon by all Europe with wonder and astonishment.[2]

As it happens, the laying of the foundation-stone is well documented, but the circumstances are singular, and not perhaps what might be expected. The engraved copper plate on the stone bore this inscription:

The first stone of the Belfast White Linen Hall was laid the 28th April AD 1783, in the year of Masonry 5783, by John Brown Esq, Worshipful Master of the 'Orange Lodge' of Belfast, No 257 (High Sheriff of the County of Antrim and Major of the Belfast Battalion of Volunteers) assisted by the Wardens and Brethren of the other Lodges, the Sovereign, Burgesses and principal inhabitants of the town. In aid of which building the Orange lodge presented the managers with the sum of £100.

The 'Orange Lodge' here referred to had nothing to do with Orangeism or Orange lodges, a much later phenomenon. The Orange Order did not come into existence until 1795 and the only connection is that it so obviously emulated the Masonic form of organization and the significance attached to emblems and regalia. The unfortunate assonance has nevertheless misled some historians, including even George Benn.[3]

The 'Orange Lodge' was not the only Masonic lodge to be present at the foundation ceremony. Lodge 272, 'New Blues', was also there in strength. On 29 April 1783 the *Belfast Newsletter* recorded that 'in the procession at laying the first stone of the Belfast White Linen Hall last Monday, Joseph Clotworthy, High Priest of Lodge No. 272, an old man who had attended every publick matter of the sort for upwards of sixty years, dropped dead just behind the deacons of the "Orange" lodge.' The newspaper report went on to say that it was remarkable that the deceased had frequently been heard to pray that his dissolution might be in the very midst of his brethren, 'and indeed it so happened, in the very centre of some hundreds'.[4]

Examination of the known membership of these lodges reveals some interesting connections. John Brown, Worshipful Master of the Orange Lodge, was the captain of the Blue Company, and reputed to be the wealthiest man in Belfast. He was later to be a pillar of the conservative faction and four times sovereign of the town at the turn of the century. One of the Lodge chaplains was the Rev. Matthew Garnet, the vicar of Carnmony, who had been Constable of Belfast Castle and the headmaster of the little classical school set up in Church Lane by Lord Donegall, in which William Drennan received his earliest lessons. Another was the Rev. James Bryson, minister of the Second Presbyterian Congregation in Rosemary Street. He had become a Mason in 1782.[5]

The highlight of the Masonic year is St John's Day, 24 June. In 1781 the Orange Lodge attended the parish church on that day, and the following year went to the Presbyterian meeting-house. In the eighteenth century it was still the custom for the Freemasons to parade publicly and in full regalia, headed by the Master in a red cloak and carrying the warrant; and we are told that the members all dressed with their aprons, gloves and jewels, and such as were Knights Templars with beautiful and embroider'd and set stars and garters, marched to Meeting, where they heard a most edifying and incomparable sermon upon the occasion from their Brother the Rev James Bryson, and also made a handsome collection for the Poor-house.[6]

In 1783 the ceremony took a different form, when the Orange Lodge organized a concert of sacred music in the parish church for the benefit of the poorhouse. The choristers of Hillsborough came to sing an anthem specially composed for the occasion. The following year the brethren 'marched in grand procession to church, preceded by the band of music belonging to the 49th regiment' and heard their chaplain, the Rev. Matthew Garnet, deliver an 'excellent and well adapted discourse'. Afterwards the Lodge dined at the Donegall Arms 'and entertained in a most elegant style their notable brethren the Earl of Hillsborough and Lord Kilwarlin, who walked to church in their procession'.[7]

It will be remembered that the First Company had held its initial church parade on 'the last Sunday in June' (St John's Day) in 1778. A substantial number of the original members can be identified as belonging to the Orange and True Blue Lodges, and it seems likely that the raising of the company was in part a Masonic initiative. It is sometimes said that Freemasonry had all but died out in Belfast before the arrival there of Amyas Griffith as an excise officer in 1780. This is not true, but it seems certain that he revitalized Lodge 257.

Born in Roscrea, Co. Tipperary, Griffith was an exotic who blazed a track through the Northern skies like Halley's comet and then disappeared again.[8] At the early age of sixteen he had decided to make a name for himself as an author, and in 1763 boldly published the complete *Works in Prose and Verse of A. Griffith*. He also composed a comedy, *The Swadler*, described as 'a vicious attack on Methodist lay preachers' and concerned with their 'chicanery, collusion, low cunning, canting deceit, vile hipocracy [sic] and evil doings'. Many young authors discover that the world receives their work with restrained enthusiasm, but Griffith was more fortunate. His early literary ventures brought him not only critical acclaim but financial success, a mixed blessing, since it encouraged in him habits of extravagance which were to prove his undoing. 'He expended the profits of those early publications in the purchase of an ensign's commission in the Queen's Regiment of Foot', but his military career was short and ten months later he sold his commission to pay his debts. 'He launched his slightly fraught bark on a sea of extravagance; he quitted the haven of prudence, and plunged into excess.'

He then obtained the position of 'supernumerary gauger' with the excise in Wexford, married there, and used his wife's dowry to set up in business as a shopkeeper. But 'mirth, wine and an actress, whom he had taken into keeping, filled every space of time his employment left him, save those moments he devoted to his muse' and his business failed. Fortunately he was promoted just at this time to be an excise officer at Fethard in Tipperary. There he seems to have been content and happy, and it was at this point that he began to write articles in the Dublin press, attacking the government. Despite the use of a wide variety of creative pseudonyms, he was recognized and became a popular figure with the radicals. He even put himself forward as a candidate for Lucas's Dublin seat on the latter's death in 1771, but he was persuaded to withdraw.

Further promotion in the excise took him to the capital, where he became for a while the owner and editor of a scandalous news-sheet called *The Public Monitor*, one of many put out of business by the passing of the Stamp Act. In spite of these activities (or perhaps because of them – the government was pleased with him for providing the pretext for censorship) Griffith advanced steadily in the service. Appointed Inspector-General of the Province of Munster at a salary of £1,500 a year all told, he 'made the advancement of the revenue his chief delight; wherever he went he made detections and seizures and discovered many capital frauds'.

In April 1780 Griffith was suddenly dismissed from his lucrative post. He had got himself into trouble over a married woman, and her husband, an Anglican clergyman, issued a writ against him for £5,000 damages, and began a suit in the ecclesiastical court for criminal conversation (that is, adultery).

Griffith decided that his only hope of avoiding prison lay in immediate flight. Fortunately the same evening that brought him this news brought also a letter from the revenue commissioners, offering him a humble post at Belfast, at a basic salary of £65 per annum, though emoluments might increase it to £400. He arrived in Belfast, penniless and alone, on 10 May 1780, followed some days later by his long-suffering wife and family. But as is usual with such temperaments, he

recovered his spirits quickly and within a few days he was writing to
his friend the Countess of Glandore:

The people here are not so affable as in Munster, but I dare say more sincere
in their friendships – when they form any. The common people speak broad
Scotch and the better sort differ vastly from us, both in accent and language.
They have indeed many peculiarities, but the men in general are well read,
shrewd and sensible. The better sort of women are all dressy, neat and
pretty. . . . The town is the fifth in size in Ireland, very extensive in trade, but
the people in general industrious and rich. You see no ragged wretches here,
as with you – no beggars of any kind. The poorest peasants here are tight,
clean and whole and the common labourers are all paid a shilling a day,
beside food.[9]

Griffith had been prominent in the Volunteer movement in Munster,
and he was also a very active Freemason. According to the records of
the Grand Lodge of Ireland he had been initiated in Lodge 244, a
military lodge within the 2nd Regiment of Foot, on 3 December 1764.
He later helped to found Lodge 71, Tralee, Lodge 484, Fethard, and
Lodge 504, Skibbereen, and he was a member of Lodge 96, Clonmel
and Lodge 492, Dublin. In 1780 there were only three lodges in Belfast,
one of which, 257, was dormant. Griffith at once determined to change
all that. With the assistance of James Stewart and Benjamin Edwards,
he revived Lodge 257 and called it the 'Orange' Lodge. While he was
in Belfast from 1780 until 1785 the membership increased to 170.
Nor was it simply a matter of numbers; Griffith succeeded in attracting
more men of wealth and social standing. He was a superb publicist
and the first reference to the Lodge in the *Belfast Newsletter* is a
theatre advertisement, which announced that

By the desire of the Right Worshipful the Master, Wardens and Brethren, of
the Ancient and Honourable Society of Free and Accepted Masons of the
Orange Lodge of Belfast, No. 257, on Wednesday evening, being the 9th of
May, will be presented a comedy called 'Wonder! A Woman keeps a Secret'.[10]

In 1781 Griffith edited the fifth edition of *Ahiman Rezon, Or Help
to a Brother*, a compilation of the laws and regulations of the Grand
Lodge of the 'Antients', first drawn up by Laurence Dermott in 1756.
The title was later adopted by Freemasons in Ireland and America
for their constitutions. Griffith's edition of *Ahiman Rezon* is chiefly
interesting for the details it gives about the Orange Lodge, No. 257,
the list of members and some of his Masonic poems. He continued to

be a very efficient revenue officer and he endeared himself to his adopted fellow-townsmen by strictly enforcing the provisions of an Act of Parliament which laid certain excise duties on malt liquors for the advantage of the Lagan Navigation (the canal from Belfast to Lisburn). He extended the levy of tax not only to imported malt liquors but to all British porter and ale, which so pleased the Belfast brewers that they presented him with an elegant silver cup.

Griffith took a very active part in the town's social life, founding in October 1781 the Belfast Knot of the Friendly Brothers of St Patrick, a club dedicated to 'good food, plenty of drink and the abolition of duelling'. He was the moving spirit in founding the Adelphi Club, a literary society, in 1782, and later the Belfast Amicable Society. Unfortunately for its founder, the Amicable Society dabbled much in politics, in particular supporting the campaign for the reform of parliamentary representation, and it was this which led to Griffith's downfall when he intervened so disastrously in the election at Carrick-fergus. He was dismissed from the excise service on 3 April 1785. After trying desperately to find another post, Griffith became bank-rupt, 'paying six shillings and eight pence in the pound'. The dividend was paid by his brethren in the Orange Lodge. At the end of 1785 he and his family left for Dublin. The rest of his career is obscure, apart from the publication of some pamphlets, including *A Narrative of the Misfortunes of the Author*. He was imprisoned for debt in 1791 and the Masons and the Friendly Brothers of St Patrick organized a benefit for him, which apparently did not bring in enough money for his release, for he remained in prison until 1795. He died in September 1801.[11]

That Freemasonry was moribund in Belfast until Griffith's arrival is very much open to doubt. The first recorded warrant was issued by the Grand Lodge on 5 October 1748 to the 'True Blue Lodge, No. 182' in Belfast. The exiguous list of its early members contains a number of familiar names, and these are taken to be the fathers of Belfast Masonry.[12] But it is certain that there were other lodges, whose warrants have not survived. Masonic activity was fairly widespread also in the countryside. We have seen how the Masons associated themselves with Wilson's parliamentary triumph in 1776.

There is evidence of the philanthropy of the 'True Blue' Lodge in the mid-century. For example, in 1753 the Society for the Relief of Protestant Strangers gratefully acknowledged donations from Belfast,

including one from the Lodge, remitted by the hand of Stewart Banks.[13]
Much more interesting, though, is the curious affair of the French
prisoners. Initially the officers and soldiers taken prisoner from Thurot's ships were treated less well than those left behind at Carrickfergus.
With several hundred other French prisoners they were lodged under
military guard in barracks in Belfast.

After some time, the English colonel-in-charge became uneasy at
the complaints which he was receiving from the prisoners' spokesmen.
They alleged that the bread they were given was half-baked, the meat
was frequently bad, the beer was in general thin and sour. Worse still,
they often had to sell or barter their rations for tobacco, soap and
candles, and other small necessities. In any event, these provisions
were invariably delivered three hours late, too late for the meat to be
dressed and cooked for the next day. They had no utensils to eat from,
except 'a dirty tub' supplied to each apartment. Not having a proper
supply of fresh straw, the Frenchmen had to sleep on the bare boards,
apart from a few who had managed to purchase beds, 'which beds are
intolerably bad'. The allowance of coal to heat four messes was barely
sufficient for one. In such conditions the men were miserable, and
several of them fell ill.

Colonel Higginson invited his fellow-officers to accompany him on
an inspection of the prisoners' quarters and was incensed at what he
found. The French had, indeed, out of civility, hesitated to make a
fuss to the military authorities until the situation became acute. The
commissary responsible for the welfare of the prisoners was a certain
Mr Stanton, who was a profiteer, and, as Higginson soon realized,
working in collusion with local contractors, hence the inferior meat
and bread, and the short supplies of coal and medicines. Though the
government allowed him sixpence per day for the support of each
prisoner, Stanton was feeding them at threepence three farthings or
less.

Higginson therefore wrote to the sovereign and burgesses of Belfast,
drawing their attention to Stanton's frauds and asking, 'Can the town
of Belfast thus suffer a man to make a fortune at the expense of such
objects, and the character which these Nations are so fully entitled to,
for their unparalleled humanity? I hope, Gentlemen, you will not . . .'
The sovereign acted with commendable dispatch. He visited the barracks with the Rev. James Mackay, Thomas Drennan's junior colleague in the First Congregation, to assure himself of the truth of the

allegations. Then he set up a committee of the townspeople to look after the welfare of the French prisoners. Proper supplies were provided at once, and the French benefited from a great deal of charity and goodwill during the rest of their enforced exile, for which they expressed their gratitude, and the town continued for some years to take great pride in the 'Committee for the support of the French prisoners'.

The details of these transactions are taken from the pages of a rare pamphlet, reproduced by the *Ulster Journal of Archaeology* in 1903 and 1904, which contains the affidavits of Higginson and his officers, various merchants and contractors, and others directly involved in the investigation.[14] The affidavit of one merchant, made to the sovereign, James Hamilton, in 1761, immediately invites attention:

William Haven of Belfast, in the county of Antrim, merchant, came before me and made oath, that on Saturday, the twenty-seventh day of December last, this deponent, being the Master of the TRUE-BLUE LODGE OF FREE AND ACCEPTED MASONS assembled to celebrate the Festival of St John . . . was addressed by the several gentlemen who composed the same . . .

They wished him to invite, in their names, the sovereign, Colonel Higginson, and some other gentlemen of the town to meet them in order to fall upon some scheme for the relief of the French prisoners 'which the said Lodge thought to be highly becoming, as two of the French officers were their brethren'.[15]

The pamphlet gives at one point a full list of the members of the committee. The very first name on the list is that of Samuel McTier. He was then described as Samuel McTier, Jnr, and his father's name is fifth on the list. From all this one might infer that the French officers who were Masons communicated their distress to fellow-Masons among the English officers, who in turn activated the Belfast Masons of Lodge 182.

The fact that some of the French officers were members of Masonic lodges would explain other curious aspects of the Thurot affair, for example, the ease with which men such as Flobert and Cavagnac were able to establish contact with the local aristocracy. As soon as he was mobile, Flobert went to stay with the Earl of Moira at Montalto in Co. Down. Francis Rawdon, Earl of Moira, was later to be Cornwallis's second-in-command during the American War of Independence. A decade later, he was acting Grand Master of the Grand Lodge of England.[16]

A word might be said here about the origins of the English Grand Lodge of Free and Accepted Masons, and its Irish counterpart. The subject is one which has produced some debate among historians. English Freemasonry traces its modern history from the setting-up of the Grand Lodge in London in 1717. The Craft, as Masons call it, was of course a great deal older, with roots running back to the guilds of operative (that is, actual) stone-masons who built the medieval cathedrals and churches. Speculative Masonry took hold in England in the seventeenth century, but, because of the constitutional upheavals of the end of that period, it had become virtually the covert arm of Jacobitism. The first recorded lodges in France, Spain and Italy, formed under British influence, were really Jacobite clubs. After 1714, how- ever, these Masonic lodges were successfully infiltrated by Hanoverian agents.

At the same time English Freemasons, who thus lay under the imputation of being secret Jacobites, made a deliberate effort to assure the Crown of their allegiance. They approached the King, saying in effect that their peculiar activities were quite innocuous and unpoliti- cal. The Grand Lodge was created as a Whig and Hanoverian attempt to break what had been a Jacobite monopoly. The initiative was taken by four lodges in London, and by 1723 there were fifty-two lodges under the Grand Lodge's protection. A new set of constitutions, or 'charges', for Freemasons was drawn up in 1723 by a Scottish Presby- terian minister, the Rev. James Anderson.[17]

The situation was greatly complicated by the continuing existence of 'old' Masonry, including all the higher degrees. The Craft of the 'Antients' remained important in Ireland. At some time in, or just before, 1725 a Grand Lodge of Ireland was formed in Dublin, presum- ably on the London model. In the thirteenth number of the *Dublin Weekly Journal*, James Arbuckle included a detailed description of the Grand Lodge's St John's Day procession. In one of his essays, on 'Man and his Honour', Arbuckle had made a passing reference to Freemasonry, and this has led to a claim that he was himself a Mason.[18] Neither of these entries proves this, of course, and in context they look like external comments on an interesting phenomenon.

It would be significant if elements of the Shaftesbury–Molesworth connection were Masonic, but it must be said that there is no clear evidence for this, at least from research to date. There are nevertheless some teasing parallels and similarities. The only portrait of Shaftesbury depicts him in the customary classical dress, but with an arch and keystone obvious in the background. There was some correlation between Freemasons and early Fellows of the Royal Society, and Molesworth was a Fellow. Moreover his supra-denominationalism is suggestive. Hutcheson was tutor to the Earl of Kilmarnock, and later to his three sons. Kilmarnock's name is very prominent in the history of Freemasonry. Apart from the painting which hangs in the University of Glasgow, the only other portrait of Hutcheson is the fine likeness on the medallion struck after his death by one of his pupils, the Earl of Selkirk. It conveys a remarkable sense of his confident and vivacious personality. The reverse depicts a woman mourning. She holds a sceptre in her right hand, and her left foot rests upon a cube, the symbol of stability. To an initiate it would immediately suggest the Masonic ashlar, the perfect cube of hewn stone.[19]

The early eighteenth century was a golden age of clubs and sodalities. Shaftesbury's protégé Toland, for example, was involved at one time or another with many secret societies. Mrs Margaret Jacob, on the strength of papers connecting him with a group centred on The Hague, calling themselves 'Les chevaliers de la jubilation', has argued that he was a key figure in archaic, radical, English Masonry, but this has been disputed by other scholars. Toland certainly knew some of the founders of Dutch Freemasonry. If Toland 'exported to the Continent a determinedly subversive Masonic organization', it leaned towards a materialistic cosmology which was abhorrent to the English Grand Lodge.[20] Even Anderson's Charges, however, included the ambiguous, and later controversial, instruction that a Mason need only acknowledge a belief in a Supreme Being and the religion that all men accept.

Whatever the truth of these matters, there can be no doubt about the influence of Freemasonry on Irish radicalism sixty years later. The extent to which it was involved in Volunteer politics has largely been ignored by historians of the period, though Fr. Patrick Rogers drew passing attention to it in his study of the Volunteers and Catholic Emancipation, written over fifty years ago.[21] Most of the Belfast pioneers were Masons – Stewart Banks, John Brown, Waddell Cunningham and Sam McTier among many others. When the Dungannon Convention met in February 1782, the chair was taken by Colonel

William Irvine, who was Provincial Grand Master of Ulster. He was the delegate of the 'Lowtherstown Masonick Volunteer Company', one of many formed directly from individual lodges. In portraits of Volunteers, Masonic emblems are clearly to be seen on their badges and equipment.[22]

Once the fact of Masonic involvement in the Volunteer movement is realized, its extent becomes staggering. To begin with, most of the companies which had 'Blue' or 'True Blue' in their title were largely Masonic. Sky-blue was the chosen colour of English Speculative Masonry.[23] The Union companies and battalions which appeared in 1784, with both Protestant and Catholic members, now appear to be entirely a Masonic initiative. This would explain why the Downpatrick Union adopted a Masonic motto, *Tria juncta in Uno*. The Newry Union was undoubtedly Masonic. It was founded in the year 1784, long after the older Newry companies, and it would account for Drennan's Masonic preoccupations just at that time. We are told that the Dromore Union 'is entirely composed of Freemasons, looking smart at the Review in their blue uniforms'. The brethren of Lodge 485, meeting at Aughnacloy in 1790, 'consist of Volunteers'. The Moy and Dungannon Company called themselves the Brotherly Union corps. It became common form in newspaper obituaries to say that the deceased Volunteer had been buried 'with military and Masonic honours'.[24]

Nor was the association the peculiarity of a province. Charlemont was a Mason, and so was Grattan. The importance of this for the conduct of Volunteer policy, and in particular its bearing on the Catholic question, should not be underestimated. It may even explain some rather mysterious comings and goings on the international stage.

From time to time the Masonic activities of Benjamin Franklin have attracted the attention of historians. There is a curious example of this during his visit to Ireland in 1771. In Dublin Franklin met Wills Hill, the Earl of Hillsborough, who had been bitterly critical of Franklin's public pronouncements on the gathering crisis with the colonies. Franklin expected the meeting to be frosty, but to his surprise Hillsborough greeted him with great warmth, and learning that he proposed to visit Belfast, pressed him to stay at Hillsborough Castle, which he must pass on his way. Franklin accepted the invitation, and was afterwards pleased he had done so. On his leaving for Belfast he was helped into the carriage by Hillsborough's son, Lord Kilwarlin, who placed his own warm coat around his shoulders.

Hillsborough and Kilwarlin were, rather surprisingly, prominent members of the Orange Lodge No. 257 in Belfast. Nothing is known of the last four days of Franklin's visit; he left for Scotland in stormy conditions and had a very uncomfortable crossing, but he says nothing at all about the people he met in Belfast. One would assume, however, that he wanted to meet some of the democratic Dissenters who were so supportive of the colonists' cause. No doubt he would also have been entertained by local Masons.[25]

In 1779, when he was living in Paris as virtual American ambassador, Franklin became the Master, or Vénérable, of the prestigious French lodge of Masons called 'Neuf Soeurs' (Nine Sisters) which included John Paul Jones and Voltaire among its members. At this time Franklin had made Paris the centre of the vast American spy network which he had built up in his capacity as Postmaster-General. In the late eighteenth century it was taken for granted (even in Belfast) that postmasters were controllers of espionage. This professional interest brought him into contact and friendship with Sir Francis Dashwood, his British counterpart. Dashwood had been appointed joint Postmaster-General in 1766, and his first colleague in the office was Hillsborough.

Dashwood was an indefatigable promoter of secret societies and as far back as 1732 had set up a quasi-Masonic society, the Dilettanti, of which, as we have seen, Lord Charlemont was a member. In 1746 he founded an irreverent 'Order of St Francis' in playful allusion to his name. Franklin became a 'Franciscan', and it has recently been alleged that this American 'paragon of moral rectitude at home' took part in lascivious orgies in the caves under Dashwood's estate at West Wycombe.[26]

Dashwood's name is often associated with the notorious Hell Fire Club, or 'Monks of Medmenham Abbey', but its founders were Hillsborough and the Duke of Wharton. There was founded in Ireland in 1779 a pale imitation of the Hell Fire Club, whose members dressed for their revels in monastic habits and called themselves 'Monks of the Screw'. Its members were very distinguished, and its rites seem to have been confined to over-indulgence in food and drink, with a lot of political discussion, laughter and good fellowship. The founder, or Prior, was the Patriot MP and later judge, Barry Yelverton, and the membership included Charlemont, Grattan and the advocate J. P. Curran. Such vaguely dubious societies abounded in the eighteenth century, and were not connected with Freemasonry except in the similarity of initiation rites. In this case, however, every one of the persons named was also a Freemason.[27]

In March 1780 a startling piece of intelligence reached Lord Stormont, the British ambassador in Paris. He learned that a secret Irish delegation, consisting of both Protestants and Catholics, had arrived in Paris in December 1779 and had been received by Louis XVI, to whom they outlined a plan for achieving the independence of Ireland.

They propose that Ireland shall be an Independent Kingdom, that there shall be a sort of Parlt, but no king, that the Protestant religion shall be the established religion . . . but that the Roman Catholics shall have the fullest Toleration. The Delegates are closely connected with Franklin who, my informer thinks, carries on a correspondence by means of His, Franklin's sister, a Mrs Johnstone now in London who has a small lodging in Fountain Court in the Strand.[28]

It would be hard to disagree with the conclusion that 'from these seeds, some twenty years later, a new quasi-Masonic organization was to spring, the Society of United Irishmen',[29] but a historian familiar with the Ireland of this period would find it difficult to identify who these 'Catholics and Independents' actually were. It is perhaps significant that the Earl-Bishop, who was in daily contact with Franklin, left Paris suddenly at this time and without explanation. What, if any, connection had the incident with the Volunteer movement? Was it perhaps a deputation from the 'Monks of the Screw', which had Catholic members? One thing is suggestive – the only framework within which Irish Catholics and Protestants were likely to be cooperating at that time was that of the Craft.

Drennan's sudden adoption of the language of Freemasonry in 1784 when developing the idea of his 'interior circle' is interesting, if inconclusive. To the non-Masonic eye there is little else in his entire correspondence to suggest that he was a Mason. But the evidence of the committee for the support of the French prisoners shows clearly that Sam McTier was a member, at least in 1761, and so were some of his relations. Was Drennan initiated in Newry in 1784? It seems just possible. There are a few sly references to Freemasonry in his poems from this period.[30] The imagery might even seem to be connected with the ceremonial of the higher degrees of Royal Arch Masonry, part of the ritual of the 'Antients' which continued to flourish in Irish

Freemasonry. Drennan's idea seems to be closer to that of the Illuminati in Bavaria, and it may be significant that 1784 was the year in which their secrets were exposed. However, the Illuminati, too, were merely a schismatic branch of European Freemasonry.[31]

In any event the cult of Freemasonry is to be found in almost every aspect of the Enlightenment. It is frequently an element in the many challenges to the status quo in State and Church. Montesquieu and Voltaire were Masons, as were Goethe and Mozart, Franklin and Washington. The United States was to have been the perfect Masonic state, and to this day the symbols of Masonry are openly displayed on the back of every dollar bill.

In Irish terms Freemasonry was important because it was almost the only sphere in which Catholics and Protestants could meet on equal terms. For Catholics it was a refuge from the penal laws, even after 1738, when Pope Clement XII's dramatic edict threatened excommunication to Catholics who became Masons. Since the eighteenth century, it has been easy to overlook this very important point. It explains what has always been seen as something of a mystery about Irish politics in the 1780s, why the old asperities between Protestants and Catholics seemed suddenly to melt, and both persuasions, especially in the North of Ireland, seemed eager to create a new Irish nationality, one more liberal than the 'Protestant nation' or a hypothetical theocracy dominated by the Catholic Church.

The evidence of this is taken to be the fraternal affection and assistance shown by the Volunteers in Belfast and Derry in 1784, and the ecumenical celebration of the centenary of the Siege of Derry in 1788. The coming together in a new sense of nationhood reached its highest point with the formation of the United Irishmen in 1791.

But in general the old asperities had not softened, as was ironically demonstrated when Wolfe Tone, on his way back to Dublin from his second visit to Belfast in July 1792, had to try to quell sectarian riots at Rathfriland in Co. Down.[32] Far from being smothered in 1791, the sectarian flame was just about to break out with a renewed ferocity, which has hardly abated since. Nationalists of the Catholic tradition lament what they see as the Protestant desertion of the ideal of brotherhood, and wish for its return. But when all is said and done, the radicals and republicans were a small segment of the population, susceptible to the Enlightenment influences specific to the eighteenth century. They never thought of themselves as honorary Catholics, as modern republicans would wish to portray them. If the idea of brotherhood was in fact largely a Masonic inspiration, then much of the history of Ireland in this period needs to be rewritten.

# 19

# The Last Convention

The year 1792 witnessed a revival of radical activity on the scale of that of the previous decade. A period of intense political excitement affecting the whole country lasted from the beginning of 1792 until the spring of 1793, when the government suddenly admitted Catholics to the elective franchise and smothered the radical agitation.

In January 1792 fifty-three citizens of Belfast requested a general meeting of the principal inhabitants at the Townhouse to consider the propriety of a petition to Parliament in favour of Catholic emancipation.

We anxiously wish to see the day when every Irishman shall be a citizen – when Catholics and Protestants, equally interested in their country's welfare, possessing equal freedom and equal privileges, shall be cordially united, and shall learn to look upon each other as brethren, the children of the same God, the natives of the same land . . .

The resulting assembly was the largest the town had ever seen, except for the Bastille celebrations of the previous year, and since the Townhouse was too small to accommodate it, the meeting was transferred, appropriately enough, to the Third Presbyterian church, and the minister, Sinclair Kelburn, was called to the chair.

A motion introduced by Bruce and Haliday for gradual emancipation, '*from time to time, and as speedily as the circumstances of the country, and the general welfare of the kingdom will admit*', was hotly attacked by the United Irishmen and overwhelmingly defeated. The temporizing clauses were struck out, and the petition, with over 600 signatures, went up to Parliament in February. The degree to which the United men had succeeded in persuading their fellow-citizens was indicated by the fact that Haliday and his friends felt obliged to issue a counter-declaration that their only objection had been to immediate enfranchisement.[1]

From this point onward we can trace two streams of Presbyterian opinion, both originating in Volunteer radicalism. One leads through the Society of United Irishmen to the Dissenters' part in the insurrection of 1798, to political defeat and the chastened liberalism of the nineteenth century; the other through a gradual rapprochement with the government to support of the Union, and even of the Orange Order, with which the Presbyterians had, at first, very little to do. As the radicals became more exasperated between 1792 and 1798, the cautious 'time-to-time' party retreated even farther from its original protestations.

The nature of the Presbyterian dilemma was soon apparent to all the interested parties. The Catholic Committee representatives hinted to the government their desire to refrain from political controversy if they were well received, which Drennan interpreted as an attempt to dissociate themselves from the Dissenting radicals, whose principal object remained the reform of Parliament. The United Irishmen saw the danger to their cause and tried to avert it in their propaganda. The government acted decisively on it in 1793.

The origin of the new Catholic strategy was to be found in the palace revolution in the Catholic Committee, in which the leadership had passed from the hands of aristocrats like Lord Kenmare to those of the young Dublin merchants, who were susceptible to the heady politics of France and ready to adopt a more secular and aggressive approach. Drennan accurately identified what they were about. 'The truth was, and is, the Catholics wish to have two strings to their bow – a *part* to treat with Government, a *part* to ally with us – and if one string cracks, why, try the other. This is good, and *perhaps* fair archery.'[2] To implement the strategy Tone was recruited as a paid agent of the committee, and a significant number of the Catholic Committee became members of the Dublin Society of United Irishmen.

In July Tone travelled again to Belfast to see the third anniversary of the Bastille celebrated by a Volunteer review of 800, and the firing of a triple *feu de joie*. After the parade, a meeting was convened in the Linen Hall, and two addresses were adopted, one to the people of France, composed by Drennan, and the other to the people of Ireland, composed by Tone. A delegation of Catholic representatives had arrived on the 13th, and had been warmly received. That evening the representatives were entertained to dinner by the United Irishmen, with Sam McTier in the chair. The radical majority in Belfast was now confident of swaying the opinion of the Volunteers the following day.

Success was critical for Tone, for the Catholics and for the Belfast United Irishmen. But there was still formidable opposition to be overcome from the 'time-to-time' party in the town, and the country detachments might well decide the issue. Tone's nervousness is vividly conveyed in his diary:

[July 13. Afraid for tomorrow in every way.... Dr Haliday's wig grows miraculously grey with fear of the Catholics.... Go at seven to meet the Jacobins. The time-to-time people say with great gravity that Mr Hutton [Tone] is come to force seditious papers down their throats.... Expect a sharp opposition tomorrow. Some of the country corps no better than Peep O'Day Boys. Antrim folks, good; Down, bad.[3]

It got worse as the night progressed:

A plot! a plot! Neilson comes to my bedside at one o'clock with orders to prepare for battle in the morning. Passing by a room at the inn, he heard Cunningham's voice very loud; the door being half open, he went in and found to his utter astonishment delegates from the country corps, with Waddell haranguing against the Catholics, and talking of some sedition to be broached the next day. Waddell taken aback by this apparition of Neilson. Neilson abuses him and reads the papers; the company breaks up without coming to any determination, but Neilson expects hot work in the morning.

Tone ends the entry by calling Cunningham a rude word.[4]

Next morning he was in a more cheerful mood, donning his regimentals and having breakfast with the Catholics, then to the parade ground. 'Drums beating, colours flying, and all the honours of war ... First and second companies far the best in all particulars. Green Company 102; Blue 90 ...' The radicals and the Catholics held a council of war in a potato field. Tone thought some of those present, including Tandy, 'frightened out of their wits', and was impatient at their defeatism.

We are undone; we shall be defeated; all the country corps decidedly against us, from the report of some seditious paper (the old story); better to adopt something moderate, that shall include all parties; danger of disunion; risk of credit if we should even succeed by a small majority which is the best that can be hoped.[5]

At 3 o'clock in the afternoon they marched back into the town, to be greeted by hundreds of citizens wearing green ribbons and laurel leaves in their hats. A group of people from the South Antrim parishes of Carnmony and Templepatrick was carrying a green flag, bearing the motto: 'Superstitious jealousy, the curse of the Irish Bastille; let us unite and destroy it'.[6] That evening in the Linen Hall, Drennan's address was accepted unanimously and with bursts of applause. Tone's address produced a debate which went on for hours. He had insisted (against Tandy's advice) on including the words 'that no reform, were such attainable, would answer our ideas of utility and justice, which should not equally include all sects and denominations of Irishmen'. Henry Joy at once moved the expunging of the whole paragraph, and the substitution of words 'welcoming the gradual enfranchisement of the Roman catholics', and ardently looking forward to the day when their complete enfranchisement should be 'a measure not only of safety but of expediency'. Nevertheless Joy found himself in a minority, and the address was carried, to Tone's elation.[7]

The divisions in Presbyterian politics were inevitably sharpened by the nightmare course of events in France during the autumn. The United Irishmen applauded the fall of the monarchy, and supported the new National Convention. At the end of October both the Belfast Volunteers and the Northern Whig Club dined in celebration of the defeat of the Duke of Brunswick.[8] On 3 December, the day on which the Convention decided to put Louis XVI on trial, the Catholic Committee met in Dublin and drew up a petition for emancipation which was to be presented, not to the Irish Parliament or administration, but directly to the King in London. The committee's delegates prudently declined to be waited on by a deputation from the Dublin Society of United Irishmen, but they arranged to travel to London via Belfast, where they were received with great enthusiasm. The populace unharnessed the horses from their carriage, and drew it in triumph through the streets.[9]

Some weeks earlier the Dublin radicals, led by Tandy, decided to form a new Volunteer organization modelled closely on the French National Guard. It was to be called the First National Battalion, and have a *sans-culotte* uniform of green coat and loose striped trousers, the device on the button a shamrock crowned with the cap of liberty. Almost at once the Privy Council, distinguishing between the old and the new Volunteers, issued a proclamation directing the magistrates to act against them if they paraded in arms. As if to provoke the government, the Dublin United Irishmen produced a counter-proclamation, signed by Drennan as chairman and Archibald Hamilton Rowan as secretary, calling on the citizen soldiers to stand to their arms. (For this Drennan had to stand trial on a charge of seditious libel in 1794, though he was acquitted.) Most of the old Volunteers, however, were reluctant to challenge the law, and from early 1793 Volunteering in Dublin ceased.

The Belfast radicals were contemptuous of this collapse, Sam McTier observing that if the Volunteers were to clash with the army in Belfast, within forty-eight hours there would be 10,000 armed men in the town. Several corps of the old Volunteers were formed into a single body, calling itself the 'First Belfast Regiment of National Guards'. On Sunday 3 February 1793 they paraded in uniform to the Second Congregation's meeting-house. Their uniform was green, faced with yellow, green waistcoat, white breeches, long black gaiters and a leather cap. At the same time some of the other Belfast companies were united into one regiment and took the name of the 'Belfast Battalion, Blue'.[10]

Another crowded town meeting had convened on Boxing Day 1792 to discuss a petition for the reform of Parliament, and one of the decisions taken was that a provincial convention on the old model should be held at Dungannon in the spring. The radicals began to organize it at once, and as time went on Drennan became almost obsessed with the conviction that only a revival of the conventions could force the government to concede their demands, though by now 'convention' was a word with very dubious connotations. Parochial and county meetings were held, and the Northern Star exhorted the delegates to go to Dungannon, 'an auspicious place, on 15 February, an auspicious date, and in the name of your country, in virtue of the constitution, never return until you have given the people of Ireland a firm assurance of obtaining an equal representation in Parliament'.[11]

The New Year opened, however, with an event which was inauspicious for the radicals, the execution of the King of France. Drennan expressed surprise at the horror excited by the King's fate, 'particularly among the women'. It revealed to him that there was 'more seeming than substantial republicanism, and that aristocracy is ready to lift its head'. Mrs McTier's reaction was more humane, and probably more typical. Although she had once written, 'I never liked kings, and Paine has said of them what I always suspected', she wished most ardently for the life of 'poor wretched Louis', and later the treatment of Marie Antoinette completed her loss of faith in the Revolution.[12]

In spite of some bickering, the Northern counties began to select their representatives, and on 27 January McTier considered that, with the calling of Armagh in a few days, the delegation to the provincial convention would be complete. He was too sanguine, for at the end of the month he reported that there was not to be a county meeting in Armagh. The defection of Armagh was the most significant event of the whole period, for that county had taken the initiative in calling the first Volunteer Convention of 1782. In the end only Antrim, Down, Derry, Tyrone and Donegal sent full delegations, and it is significant that these were the only counties which had substantial Presbyterian populations. When the representatives assembled in Dungannon Presbyterian church to hear a sermon from the Rev. William Steel Dickson, he chose his text, ominously, from Joseph's advice to his brethren, 'See that ye fall not out by the way'.[13]

In the end the Convention was a severe disappointment. The deterioration of the Revolution in France, and the fact that by the time the Convention met, France and Britain were at war, had pulled the carpet from under the United Irishmen. The resolutions, though they revealed deep dissensions, were studiously moderate. 'The meeting was rather led by aristocracy', Neilson admitted to Drennan afterwards, 'but the people's spirit was infused into their resolutions.' The *Northern Star* was guilty of more than hyperbole when it declared that the Convention had shown that the whole province was one great society of United Irishmen.[14]

But the Convention was interesting in other ways. The two most prominent speakers at the two-day meeting were Dr Caldwell and Dr Reynolds, and both were, like Neilson himself, Masons. Both had protested vehemently against the criticisms made of republican forms of government. Dr Reynolds was a member of the Dublin Society of United Irishmen and a friend of Tone. He was also Worshipful Master of Lodge 738 (Cookstown).

When the Volunteers were reconstituted after 1791, Masonic companies were very numerous and are well documented. Despite the strict Masonic injunction against any discussion of politics or religion, many of the Ulster lodges entered the frenzied debate on parliamentary reform and Catholic emancipation towards the end of 1792, and published their resolutions in the newspapers. The first of these appeared in the *Belfast Newsletter* on 11 December 1792, when Lodge 650 (Bellaghy) published a resolution calling for reform and virtually advocating passive resistance to government.[15]

At this time, as the reform movement was reaching its climax before the outbreak of war with France, whole clusters of lodges met together to discuss the political situation and pass such resolutions as 'The House of Commons must be freely and frequently chosen by *The People* and obedient to their instruction' and 'We love our brethren the Volunteers of Ireland'. On 7 January 1793 a meeting was held in Dungannon of no fewer than forty Masonic lodges, with Reynolds in the chair, a clear indication of Masonic determination to stage-manage the Convention, which was to meet a month later. The meeting agreed on the following pledge to be taken by every member:

I solemnly promise and declare that I will by all rational means promote the universal emancipation and adequate representation of *all* the people of Ireland, and will not be satisfied until all these objects are unequivocally obtained, and I entertain no desire of subverting the present form of government, consisting of King, Lords and Commons.

The assembled Masons also made this startling declaration: 'Let every lodge in the land become a company of citizen-soldiers – let every Volunteer company become a lodge of masons.'[16]

By then the Grand Lodge had taken action, reminding Masons of the origin and object of the Craft, and requiring them to refrain from all religious and political discussions and publications on these subjects. This injunction seems generally to have been obeyed, but there is a great deal of evidence that many lodges became little more than meeting-places for United Irish societies after the association was banned in 1794, and this pattern continued right up to the outbreak of the rising in 1798.[17]

The resolutions of the Dungannon Convention had scarcely reached the printers when the Volunteers were disbanded by proclamation of the Lord Lieutenant, and forbidden to parade in uniform. At once the organization which had for fifteen years provided an outlet for radical opinion was removed from the scene. This was a step which the government had not dared to take in 1782 or since, and although the country was at war, it was accomplished with hardly any resistance. At the same time troops were being quietly moved into Belfast – in January Mrs McTier had told her brother that the military 'were sliding in very fast'.[18] Incidents began to take place between the citizens and the soldiers. On 9 March there was a serious military riot, and the situation was defused only by the very diplomatic stance taken by the commander-in-chief and the townsfolk. The Society of United

Irishmen began to go underground. The Blue Battalion managed to hide two of its cannon, brass six-pounders, and they were not seen again until 7 June 1798, when one of them appeared in the main street of Antrim, and was fired on the British army. But that, as they say, is another story.

# Afterword

William Hazlitt, in his essay on 'Coffee-House Politicians', makes a sharp comment on the old radical clergy.

It is not very long ago that I saw two Dissenting Ministers (the *Ultima Thule* of the sanguine, visionary temperament in politics) stuffing their pipes with dried currant leaves, calling it Radical Tobacco, lighting it with a lens in the rays of the sun, and at every puff fancying that they undermined the Boroughmongers . . . They had *deceived the Senate*. Methinks I see them now, smiling as in scorn of Corruption.

> — —'Dream on, blest pair:
> Yet happier if you knew your happiness
> And knew to know no more!'

The world of Reform that you dote on, like Berkeley's material world, lives only in your own brain, and long may it live there! These same Dissenting ministers throughout the country (I mean the descendants of the old Puritans) are to this hour a sort of Fifth-monarchy men; very turbulent fellows, in my opinion altogether incorrigible, and according to the suggestions of others, should be hanged out of the way without judge or jury, for the safety of church and state.[1]

The charge is half-affectionate. Hazlitt knew whereof he spoke. His father, the Rev. William Hazlitt, was a Unitarian minister of strongly radical views. Interestingly, he was a graduate of Glasgow University, a pupil of Hutcheson, and the son of a Co. Antrim Presbyterian, who was distressed by his conversion to Unitarianism. In 1780 he became minister of the congregation at Bandon, in Co. Cork, having before that been Unitarian minister at Wisbech, Marchfield and Maidstone. But his Arian views caused controversy in his flock, and in 1783 he emigrated to Boston, where further disappointment awaited him. He returned to England and settled for the rest of his life as pastor of the Dissenting congregation at Wem, in Shropshire, where the young Hazlitt grew up. Hazlitt was a less docile son than William Drennan, but his emotions towards his father were similar. His abandonment of Dissenting piety while still at school upset the Rev. William Hazlitt, just as the latter's defection from orthodoxy had upset his father. But Hazlitt continued to hold his father and his father's politics in great affection.

At Wem, Hazlitt's closest friend was a youth called Joseph Swanwick. In 1800, when he was nearly fifty, Drennan married Sarah Swanwick of Wem, 'a singularly amiable woman who seems to have won the affections of all her relations'.[2] She was Joseph Swanwick's sister.

Charlemont and Haliday both lived to see some of their worst fears realized in the United Irish rising of 1798. The Volunteer Earl died in the following August, fourteen days short of his seventy-first birthday. The father of Maria Edgeworth, visiting Charlemont House soon afterwards, was moved at seeing his chair 'in its accustomed place, his gloves and snuff-box on the table, and *Practical Education*, which he had been reading, lying open on his chair'.[3]

Haliday died in 1802. Matty McTier told her brother:

Three nights before he died, Bruce and I played cards with him, and the very night that was his last, he played out the rubber. Now, said he, the game is finished, and the last act near a close; blessed the departing guest and sent his love to her sister; was helped up to bed, comforted his wife, spoke of the blessing her sister and William had been to them, the last gloomy winter – and the rest you know.[4]

Dr William Bruce became in time Belfast's best-known citizen and its leading intellectual in his day, pastor of the First Congregation and Headmaster of Belfast Academy, the doughty champion of many a theological and educational cause. He remained a convinced Unitarian. When he died in 1841, the Victorian age was well under way, and most Ulster Presbyterians had become loyalists, like Bruce himself.

In the summer of 1795 the McTiers went on a visit to the West of Scotland. As their carriage approached Carrickdool, 10 miles from Inveraray, Sam McTier suffered a massive stroke, and died a few hours later. It being a very wet day, the local apothecary refused to go out, and sent his apprentice instead, 'a youth in pantaloons'.[5] For Matty, nearly half a century of widowhood stretched ahead. She was ninety-five when she died, in the year of Queen Victoria's accession, and reputed to be the oldest woman in Belfast.

Drennan died in 1820. After his trial for seditious libel in 1794, he took no further part in United Irish affairs, though he never gave up his radicalism. For obvious reasons he kept very quiet, in the years after 1794, about his part in founding the United Irish Society, but in the new century he cautiously reiterated his claim to have been one of the founding fathers. He was buried in the old Clifton Street Burying Ground, where so many of the Dissenting radicals lie. A monument erected by his sons bears the lines:

> Pure, just, benign; thus filial love would trace
> The virtues hallowing this narrow place.
> The Emerald Isle may grant a wider claim,
> And link the Patriot with his Country's name.

For Drennan was the first person to coin the phrase 'the Emerald Isle'. As Richard Aldington wrote to Lawrence Durrell in 1959, 'the original W. Drennan has much to answer for'.[6]

# Notes and References

SHORT FORMS OF CITATION

Authorities are indicated in the Notes in short form. Full titles and bibliographical details are given in the Sources and Bibliography.

In references to the unpublished Drennan correspondence [PRONI D 531 and T 765] the following abbreviations are used: WD = William Drennan; MM = Martha McTier; SM = Samuel McTier; AD = Mrs Anne Drennan.

In addition, these abbreviations are used throughout:

| | |
|---|---|
| BM | *Belfast Mercury* |
| BNL | *Belfast Newsletter* |
| DNB | *Dictionary of National Biography* |
| HMC | Historical Manuscripts Commission |
| IHS | *Irish Historical Studies* |
| IMC | Irish Manuscripts Commission |
| IS | *Irish Sword* |
| [Joy] HC | [H. Joy] *Historical Collections relative to the Town of Belfast* |
| NS | *Northern Star* |
| PRONI | Public Record Office of Northern Ireland |
| RGSU | *Records of the General Synod of Ulster* |
| UJA | *Ulster Journal of Archaeology* |

## PROEM

1 Morison, *John Paul Jones*, p. 5. Jones's first attempt to cut out the *Drake* on 20 April was unsuccessful. He returned at daybreak on 24 April, having in the interval raided the English port of Whitehaven and the residence of the Earl of Selkirk on St Mary's Isle. Finding the Earl not at home, and the Countess having her breakfast, he carried away a quantity of valuables, including a silver teapot with the tea leaves still in it. He had a point to carry with the Earl about American prisoners. Some days later he returned all the loot, with a letter of apology to Lady Selkirk. The best account of these events is that of Admiral Morison.

2 ibid., p. 139.

3 ibid., p. 158.

4 Joy MSS, 4, pp. 176–8. 'Mr Dobbs, first lieutenant of the *Defence* man-of-war, happened to be in Belfast at that time, where he was only a few days before married.'

5 John Paul Jones to Lady Selkirk, 8 May 1778 (Morison, p. 148).

1 THE DAY APPROACHING

1 *BNL*, 28 April 1778.
2 Akenson, *Between Two Revolutions*, p. 16.
3 *Charlemont corres.*, I, p. 51.
4 'History of the Volunteers of Ulster originating in Belfast, 17 March 1778' (Joy MSS, 5, p. 56). The muster-roll is printed in Benn, *History of Belfast*, pp. 754–5.
5 [Joy] HC, p. 140.
6 MM to WD, 7 July 1778, Drennan corres. (PRONI D 591/31); Joy MSS, 5, p. 57.
7 The text of the letter is given in [Joy] HC, pp. 140–1 and MacNevin, *History of the Volunteers of 1782*, p. 72.
8 McDowell, *Ireland*, p. 255; Lecky, *History of Ireland*, II, pp. 223–7.
9 Lecky, op. cit., II, p. 220.
10 *Charlemont corres.*, I, pp. 52–3.
11 McDowell, *Irish Public Opinion*, p. 52; Beckett, *Making of Modern Ireland*, p. 211.
12 Lists of Volunteer companies, Joy MSS, 5; MacNevin, op. cit., pp. 220–36; Paterson, 'The Volunteer Companies of Ulster'.
13 Dickson, *Revolt in the North*, p. 76.
14 Joy MSS, 5, pp. 70–1.
15 Joy MSS, 9, and see McNeill, *Mary Ann McCracken*, p. 21.
16 McNeill, op cit., pp. 13–36.
17 Joy MSS, 4, p. 100.
18 ibid., p. 101.


2 IN THE HOUR OF DANGER

1 The account of the French landing at Carrickfergus which follows is based largely on Beresford, 'François Thurot and the French Attack on Carrickfergus, 1759–60'. Other sources used are the Joy MSS, 4, pp. 120–55; Bigger, 'The French Prisoners in Belfast', *UJA* (second series), 9 (1903), pp. 151–6; and 10 (1904), pp. 21–5, 69–72, 138–41, 187–91; Colles, *History of Ulster*, IV, 96–103; Kennedy, 'Thurot's Landing at Carrickfergus'.
2 Information from Benjamin Hall, 23 February 1760 (Joy MSS, 4, pp. 163 ff).
3 Beresford, art. cit., p. 255.
4 ibid., p. 257.
5 ibid., p. 271. (The regiments, with numbers present at the review, are listed in the French military archives as: *Gardes françoises et Gardes suisses (510); Artois (333); Cambis (232); Bourgognes (233); Voluntaires étrangères (250).*)
6 ibid., p. 259.
7 The full text of the articles of capitulation signed by du Soulier and Jennings is given in *UJA*, 10, pp. 70–1; and see Jennings's terms for surrender in Joy MSS, 4, p. 111.
8 [Joy] HC, p. 102.
9 ibid.
10 ibid., p. 103.
11 Beresford, art. cit., p. 266.

12 Lists of the Volunteer companies raised in 1760 are in Joy MSS, 5, pp. 82 ff.; [Joy] HC, pp. 105–9; and Sibbett, *On the Shining Bann*, pp. 74–5.

13 *Charlemont corres.*, I. p. 12.

14 ibid.

15 Beresford, art. cit., p. 274, n. 82.

16 Hardy, *Memoirs of Charlemont*, pp. 113–14; Craig, *The Volunteer Earl*, p. 111; *Charlemont corres.*, I, p. 13, no. 1.

17 John Wesley to E. Blackwell, 7 May 1760 (*Letters of John Wesley*, IV, pp. 95–6); Wesley, *Journal*, 5 May 1760, IV, pp. 380–3.

18 *Charlemont corres.*, I. p. 13, no. 1.

19 Smyth, 'Our Cloud-Cap't Grenadiers', p. 185.

20 *Charlemont corres.*, I. p. 12.

21 Smyth, art. cit., p. 192.

22 Smyth, art. cit., pp. 192–3.

23 ibid., p. 193.

24 Joy MSS, 5, pp. 58–9.

3 THE STORY OF THE INJURED LADY

1 McDowell, *Irish Public Opinion*, pp. 51–4.

2 *Charlemont corres.*, I, p. 51.

3 For the penal laws see Lecky, *History of Ireland*, I, *passim*; Moody and Vaughan, *A New History of Ireland*, IV, pp. 16–21; Johnston, *Eighteenth-Century Ireland*, pp. 17–52.

4 Beckett, *Making of Modern Ireland*, pp. 51, 79, 153–4, 221.

5 Simms, *William Molyneux*, pp. 102–19.

6 Molyneux, *Case of Ireland*, p. 148.

7 Curtis and McDowell, *Irish Historical Documents*, p. 186.

8 For discussion of Jonah Barrington's *Rise and Fall of the Irish Nation* see Beckett, *Anglo-Irish Tradition*, pp. 52–3. 'For him there was no break in continuity. England was the enemy in the eighteenth century as in the twelfth; and the Anglo-Irish gentry represented the Irish nation as fully and as truly as the ancient Gaelic monarchies.' William Drennan's draft of an unpublished History begins: 'It is now six hundred years since a cruel coward and odious fugitive, a tyrant, an adulterer, entered into a conspiracy, or, as it was called, a coalition, with a king and a pope for the conquest of his native country' (Drennan papers, D 531/6).

9 Simms, 'The making of a penal law'.

4 DUNGANNON

1 Smyth, 'The Volunteers and Parliament, 1779–84', in *Penal Era and Golden Age*, p. 122; Colles, *History of Ulster*, IV, p. 110.

2 For the quarrel with Piranesi see Wilton-Ely, *Piranesi*, pp. 48, 62–3 and Craig, *The Volunteer Earl*, pp. 85–97. The correspondence (in Italian) is in *Charlemont corres.*, I, pp. 231–48. Letters from Jane Hogarth (ibid., I, pp. 383, 385, 388).

3 Hardy, *Memoirs of Charlemont*, I, p. 57.

4 ibid., pp. 63–6.

5 Black MSS, 874/V/9–11, Joseph Black to John Black, 23 November 1754, 2

September 1755; 874/IV/4, Letter of Montesquieu to 'M. Jean Black, négociant anglois aux charterons à Bordeaux', and copies of two letters from Montesquieu to John Black. See also references to Montesquieu's friendship in John Black's letters (PRONI D 719).

6 *Charlemont corres.*, II, pp. 308–9.
7 ibid., I, p. 6.
8 ibid., p. 7.
9 ibid., pp. 8–9.
10 Boswell, *Life of Johnson*, pp. 1127–8.
11 *Charlemont corres.*, I, p. 38.
12 Lecky, *History of Ireland*, II, p. 282.
13 Hutchison, *Tyrone Precinct*, p. 98.
14 Henry Flood to Lord Charlemont, 7 January 1782 (*Charlemont corres.*, I, p. 392).
15 *Volunteer Resolutions*, printed as a broadsheet by Joseph Gordon in 1782.
16 Charles Sheridan to Richard Brinsley Sheridan, 27 March 1782 (Grattan, *Memoirs*, II, p. 214).
17 Gwynn, *Life of Grattan*, p. 122.
18 Lord Charlemont to the Marquis of Rockingham, 17 April 1782 (Grattan, op. cit., II, pp. 240–2).
19 Lord Charlemont to Charles Fox, 11 April 1782 (ibid., pp. 221–4).
20 ibid., p. 236.
21 Lecky op. cit., II, pp. 307–18.
22 Jupp, 'Earl Temple's Viceroyalty and the Renunciation Question, 1782–3', p. 500; *Lord Grenville*, p. 21.
23 Hutchison, op. cit., p. 100; *Charlemont corres.*, I, p. 413.
24 Belfast Address to Grattan and his reply ([Joy] HC, pp. 208–9).
25 ibid., pp. 209–10.
26 ibid., p. 211.
27 Smyth, art. cit., p. 126, n. 53.
28 [Joy] HC, pp. 214–15.
29 ibid., p. 215.
30 [Joy] HC, pp. 217–18; Smyth, op. cit., p. 129.

## 5  THE EDICTS OF ANOTHER ASSEMBLY

1 The correspondence, which also includes a number of letters from Henry Flood and Lord Charlemont, is in the Joy MSS, 11.
2 William Pitt to Henry Joy, Brighthelmstone, 11 August 1783 (Joy MSS, 11); MM to WD, ? September 1783 (D 591/96).
3 *Charlemont corres.*, I, p. 115.
4 McDowell, *Ireland*, p. 303; Hutchison, *Tyrone Precinct*, p. 101.
5 BNL, 3 October 1783; McDowell, *Ireland*, pp. 303–4.
6 *Charlemont corres.*, I, p. 124.
7 ibid., p. 122.
8 Lord Hervey to Sir William Hamilton, 2 June 1778, Childe-Pemberton, *Earl-Bishop*, I, p. 203.
9 Lord Hervey to Sir Edmund Pery, 15 May 1778 (ibid., I, p. 197).
10 Lord Hervey to Sir John Strange, 25 March 1778 (ibid., I, pp. 191–2).

11 Lecky, *History of Ireland*, II, p. 369.
12 ibid., p. 370; *Charlemont corres.*, I, p. 123.
13 *Charlemont corres.*, I, p. 124.
14 ibid.
15 ibid., p. 125.
16 ibid., p. 127.
17 Fisher, *End of the Irish Parliament*, p. 150.
18 Beckett, *Making of Modern Ireland*, p. 232.


6 TRUE OLD WHIG PRINCIPLES

1 Reid, *History of the Presbyterian Church in Ireland*, III, p. 341.
2 *BNL*, 17 February 1792.
3 The first decennial census of population was made in 1821, but it was not until 1861 that statistics of religious denomination were obtained. The census of 1834 was based on returns made by the clergy, on the framework of the official census of 1831. (See Report of the Census of Ireland on Religion and Education, pp. 4–5, 9.)
4 Lord Castlereagh to Henry Addington, 21 July 1802 (*Castlereagh corres.*, IV, p. 223).
5 [Joy] HC, pp. 131–2.
6 ibid., pp. 127–8.
7 ibid., pp. 134–6.
8 McDowell, *Irish Public Opinion*, p. 41; Beckett, *Making of Modern Ireland*, p. 207.
9 Caldwell MSS (D 1518/1/1).
10 *BM*, 5 October 1784.
11 Dickson, *Narrative of the Confinement and Exile of the Rev. William Steel Dickson, D. D.*, pp. 9–10, 19.
12 Bailie, 'William Steel Dickson, D. D.', p. 245; McClelland, 'Thomas Ledlie Birch'; Crombie, Rev. James, *The Experience and Utility of Volunteer Associations . . .* ; *Belfast Literary Society Centenary Volume*, p. 30; Kernohan, *Rosemary Street Presbyterian Church*, p. 32; Morrow, 'Rev. Samuel Barber', *UJA*, second series, XIV, pp. 105–19.
13 Reid, op. cit., III, p. 345.
14 Dickson, op. cit., pp. 17, 229.
15 McClelland, 'Thomas Ledlie Birch', p. 27; WD to MM, about September 1783 (D 591/95).
16 McClelland, 'Amyas Griffith', pp. 18–20.
17 Reid, op. cit., III, p. 354.
18 ibid., pp. 355–6.


7 THE BLUE COMPANY

1 WD to MM, 3 April 1776 (D 591/3).
2 WD to MM, 16 November 1777 (D 591/11). Drennan's admission cards to lectures are preserved in Edinburgh University Library.
3 WD to MM, 3 April 1776 (D 591/3).

4  WD to MM, 14 November 1777 (D 591/9A).

5  WD to MM, 13 December 1777 (D 591/17). The Rev. John Joachim Zubly, a
   Swiss who was minister of Savannah, Georgia, was one of the delegates to the
   Continental Congress. He later became very unpopular by changing sides, but in
   the nineteenth century two streets in Savannah were named after him – Joachim
   and Zubly (Sprague, *Annals of the American Pulpit*, III, pp. 219–21).

6  General Burgoyne with an army of 6,000 men surrendered to the Americans at
   Saratoga Springs, New York, on 17 October 1777.

7  WD to MM, 20 January 1778 (D 591/20).

8  WD to MM, 6 April 1778 (D 591/28).

9  MM to WD, 7 July 1778 (D 591/31).

10  WD to MM, 5 August 1778 (D 591/32).

11  William Drennan to William Bruce, 29 May 1782 (D 553/3).

12  Notes on the Drennan correspondence (typescript) by Ruth Duffin (T 765); [Joy]
    HC, pp. 215–17.

13  ibid., pp. 219–23.

14  MM to SM, 2 October 1782 (D 591/46).

15  William Drennan to William Bruce, 20 October 1782 (D 533/5).

16  ibid.

17  MM to SM, 2 October 1782 (D 591/46).

18  MM to WD, n.d. [1783] (D 591/65). 'Nancy has taken your Wardrobe into
    consideration and finds it wants variety, and that but one dress'd coat has a mean
    appearance.'

19  The theme is reiterated by Drennan, with more general application to his life, in
    lines written in 1806.

INDEPENDENCE shot past him in letters of light,
Then the scroll seemed to shrivel, and vanish in night;
And all the illumin'd horizon became,
In the shift of a moment, a darkness – a dream.
                ('w.d.' *Fugitive Pieces*, p. 124)

## 8  AN HONEST GHOST

1  'I remember my dear father, when I used to walk along with him . . .' WD to MM,
   3 April [1776?] (D 591/3); WD to MM, 20 November [1797] (D 591/684). See
   also Drennan's poem 'My Father', v. 5 (*Fugitive Pieces*, p. 121).

2  WD to SM, 1 December 1792 (D 591/353).

3  [W. Bruce], 'History of Nonsubscription', in *Christian Moderator*, I. p. 429 (1
   April 1827).

4  Drennan, 'My Father', vv. 8–10, *Fugitive Pieces*, p. 122.

5  William Drennan to William Bruce, ? August 1785 (D 553/45).

6  William Drennan to William Bruce, ? May 1785 (D 553/43); William Drennan to
   William Bruce, n.d. [1785] (D 553/50).

7  MM to WD, ? February 1801 (D 591/902).

8  Shakespeare *Hamlet*, I. ii. 132–4.

9  ibid., I.v. 135–8.

10  ibid., I.v. 95–101.

11  *Christian Moderator*, I, p. 430 (1 April 1827); page of sermon presented to H. Joy by Mrs McTier in 1817 in Joy MSS, 13.
12  MM to WD, 30 July 1805 (D 591/1166). Bruce was inaccurate in one particular. Thomas Drennan was not 'educated by' Hutcheson, except in the widest sense.
13  *Christian Moderator*, I, p. 429.
14  Drennan, 'Intended Defence on a trial for sedition in the year 1794'. *Fugitive Pieces*, pp. 192–3.
15  Scott, *Francis Hutcheson,*. pp. 4–7.
16  Witherow, *Historical and Literary Memorials*, I, p. 342.
17  Scott, op cit., p. 8; McCreery, *Presbyterian Ministers of Killyleagh*, p. 110.
18  Stuart, *Historical Memoirs of the City of Armagh*, pp. 488–9.
19  Scott, op. cit., p. 24.
20  *Christian Moderator*, I, p. 429.
21  [Gordon], *Historical Memorials*, p. 56.

9  THE BELFAST SOCIETY

1  Witherow, *Historical Literary Memorials*, I, pp. 192–9.
2  *RGSU*, I, p. 69.
3  [Kirkpatrick, J.], *Conclusion* of Appendix to Duchal's sermon on the death of Abernethy, pp. 49–52.
4  Reid, *History of the Presbyterian Church in Ireland*, III, p. 114.
5  ibid., p. 116; *DNB*, Abernethy, John and Hoadley, Benjamin.
6  *RGSU*, I, pp. 34, 100.
7  For the trial of Thomas Emlyn see *Christian Moderator*, I, pp. 33–5; Witherow, op. cit., I, pp. 130–42; [Gordon], *Historic Memorials*, pp. 26–9.
8  Reid, op. cit., II, pp. 118–19, and for the earlier use by 'The Presbytery of Belfast' see Hughes, M. Y., *Complete Prose Works of John Milton*, III, pp. 297–9.
9  Gebbie, *Ardstraw*, pp. 44, 53; *Christian Moderator*, I, pp. 271–2, 1 December 1826; Witherow, op. cit., I, pp. 266–7; [Gordon], op. cit., p. 56.
10  ibid., p. 56.
11  Reid, op. cit., III, pp. 124–5.
12  ibid., p. 127.
13  Haliday, *Reasons against the Imposition of Subscription to the Westminster Confession of Faith*; Witherow, op. cit., pp. 269–76; [Gordon], op. cit., pp. 30, 56.
14  Reid, op. cit., III, pp. 145–7; Empress Eugénie descended from Kirkpatrick, ibid., p. 42.
   Sarah Ferguson, Duchess of York, descended from Dr Victor Ferguson, The Macarthy Mor, 'The Fergusons of Belfast', *Familia*, vol. 2, no. 2 (1986), p. 15–21 and family tree p. 22. Tom Carson, 'Sarah Ferguson – the Belfast Connection' in the *Belfast Telegraph*, 25 April 1986. Dr Victor Ferguson was the son of Captain Ferguson listed in the 1669 Co. Antrim Hearth Money Roll. The Fergusons were cousins of the Edmonstone family of Co. Antrim.
15  *RGSU*, II, pp. 16–17, 33–4.
16  Reid, op. cit., III, pp. 157–8.
17  ibid, pp. 160–1.
18  ibid, pp. 165–6, 193.

10 'O DOMUS ANTIQUA'

1 James Arbuckle to Thomas Drennan, 10 April 1739 (D 531/2A/156–7).
2 *BNL*, 1 May 1739.
3 Murray, *Memories of the Old College of Glasgow*, p. 481.
4 James Arbuckle to Thomas Drennan, 10 May 1719 (D 531/2A/515).
5 Mackie, *The University of Glasgow*, p. 173.
6 [Smith and Arbuckle], *A Short Account of the Late Treatment of the Students of the University of G . . . w*, pp. 10, 13.
7 ibid., p. 4.
8 ibid., pp. 5–6.
9 ibid., p. 17.
10 Smithers, *Life of Joseph Addison*, pp. 277–8.
11 ibid., p. 156.
12 [Smith and Arbuckle], op. cit., p. 19.
13 ibid., pp. 20–1.
14 ibid., pp. 23–4.
15 ibid., pp. 7, 27.
16 ibid., p. 27.
17 Danaher, K. and Simms, J. G., *The Danish Force* (Irish MSS Commission, 1962), pp. 6–7, 9–12.
18 ibid., p. 10. It was alleged that Molesworth had poached game in the King's private coverts, and forced a passage on a road reserved for the royal carriage.
19 Murray, op. cit., p. 490; Scott, *Francis Hutcheson*, p. 33.
20 [Smith and Arbuckle], op. cit., p. 33.
21 ibid., p. 35.
22 James Arbuckle to Lord Molesworth, 31 October 1722 (HMC, VIII, p. 351).
23 William Stuart to Lord Molesworth, 5 March 1722 (ibid., p. 333).
24 George Turnbull to Lord Molesworth, 3 August 1722 (ibid., pp. 343–4).
25 William Wishart to Lord Moleworth (ibid., pp. 347–8).


11 'A CONTEMPT FOR TYRANNY'

1 *DNB*, Bernard Mandeville; Boswell, *Life of Johnson*, p. 948.
2 Scott, *Francis Hutcheson*, pp. 31–2.
3 Voitle, *Shaftesbury, passim*; Brett, *Shaftesbury*, pp. 33–58.
4 John Toland (1670–1722). Born a Catholic on the Inishowen Peninsula, Toland was sent to Glasgow University by the Protestant Bishop of Derry, Dr Ezekiel Hopkins. He soon quarrelled with the Archbishop of Glasgow, and was taken up by the Presbyterians, who secured a scholarship for him. When the Revolution came, Toland distinguished himself by haranguing the rabble at the barricades, and the Glasgow magistrates gave him a certificate declaring that he was 'ane trew Protestant and loyal subject'. An inveterate founder and joiner of secret societies, Toland was to become notorious as the author of *Christianity Not Mysterious* (1695). Among his patrons were Shaftesbury (see p. 92), the Rev. Daniel Williams (see p. 104) and Molesworth, who offered him 'bare necessaries'. 'These are but cold comfort to a man of your spirit and desert; but 'tis all I dare promise!' (D'Israeli *Calamities of Authors*, II, p. 153.) Toland is all but expunged from the

history of his native land, but his works occupy ten columns in the British Library Catalogue, and he is given more space than Berkeley in the *Biographie Universelle*. Voltaire called him 'a proud and independent soul'. For Toland's life see Sullivan, *John Toland and the Deist Controversy*, chapter 1, and Simms, 'A Donegal Heretic', *IHS*, vol. 16, no. 63 (March 1969).

5 Scott, op. cit., p. 31.
6 James Arbuckle to Lord Molesworth, 13 February 1722 (HMC, VIII, p. 355).
7 Scott, op. cit., p. 34.
8 ibid., p. 29.
9 Robbins, *Eighteenth-Century Commonwealthman*, pp. 165–6.
10 Scott, op. cit., pp. 37–40.
11 Hutcheson's letter is given in the *Christian Moderator*, II, pp. 350–3 (1 December 1827).
12 Scott, op. cit., p. 52.
13 ibid., p. 53.
14 ibid., p. 54.
15 ibid., pp. 54–5.
16 ibid., p. 56.
17 ibid., p. 62.
18 ibid., p. 64; Fitzpatrick, *God's Frontiersmen*, p. 89.
19 Scott, op. cit., pp. 74–5.
20 ibid., p. 69.
21 Francis Hutcheson to Thomas Drennan, 17 March 1746 (Mic. B/39).
22 Francis Hutcheson to Thomas Drennan, 15 April 1746 (Mic. B/39).
23 Dobrée, *English Literature*, p. 332, quoting Pope.
24 Cousin, V., *La Philosophie Ecossaise*, pp. 134–7; Robbins, 'When it is that the colonies may turn independent'.

12 MINISTERS OF GRACE

1 *DNB*, John Owen.
2 *DNB*, Stephen Charnock; Irwin, *A History of Presbyterianism in Dublin*, p. 313.
3 Witherow, *Historical and Literary Memorials*, I, pp. 60–3; For Williams and Toland see Sullivan, *John Toland and the Deist Controversy*, pp. 9–11.
4 Witherow, op. cit., I, pp. 79–87.
5 *DNB*, Samuel Boyse; Dobrée, *English Literature*, p. 508; Witherow, op. cit., I, p. 83.
6 Boswell, *Life of Johnson*, p. 1385.
7 *DNB*, Samuel Boyse.
8 Witherow, op. cit., I, p. 80; *DNB*.
9 *Dictionary of American Biography*, Thomas Weld; Irwin, op. cit., pp. 56, 325–6.
10 WD to AD, 17 May 1790 (D 531/292): 'Mrs Weld, a fine old lady of eighty, remembered my father when he was resident in Dublin.'
11 Bolton, *Scotch-Irish Pioneers*, pp. 16–17.
12 ibid., pp. 81–2.
13 Adair, *A True Narrative*, p. 252.
14 [Gordon], *Historic Memorials*, p. 53.
15 ibid.; Benn, *History of Belfast*, p. 389.

16  [Gordon], op. cit., pp. 53–4.
17  Benn, op. cit., p. 158n.
18  The Emlyn case: Witherow, op. cit., I, pp. 130–42; [Gordon], op. cit., pp. 26–29, 54.
19  Witherow, op. cit., I, p. 134.
20  [Gordon], op. cit., p. 26.
21  Witherow, op. cit., I, pp. 136–7.
22  ibid., p. 137.
23  [Gordon], op. cit., p. 29.


13  TOM DRENNAN AND HIS FRIENDS

1   William Bruce to Thomas Drennan, 13 July 1736 (T 1072/1).
2   James Arbuckle to Thomas Drennan, 12 August 1737 (D 531/2A/147).
3   Notes on family history by Ruth Duffin (T 765, vol. 1).
4   Francis Hutcheson to Thomas Drennan, 8 July 1741 (Mic. B/39).
5   MM to WD, 2 January 1797 (D 591/644).
6   Francis Hutcheson to Thomas Drennan, 12 April 1742 (Mic. B/39).
7   Francis Hutcheson to Thomas Drennan, 21 September 1737 (ibid.).
8   Francis Hutcheson to Thomas Drennan, 27 February 1738 (ibid.).
9   James Arbuckle to Thomas Drennan, 10 April 1739 (D 531/2A).
10  DNB, James Duchal; Sermon on the death of the late Rev. John Arbernethy, 1741 (with an appendix by Kirkpatrick); Posthumous Sermons (3 vols.), 1764–7.
11  James Duchal to Thomas Drennan, 23 August 1743 (Stewart transcript, T 1759/3B/6).
12  James Duchal to Thomas Drennan, 12 November 1745 (D 1759/3B/6). On 8 October he had reported that 'the Hurry at the Banks is pretty much over'.
13  Scott, Francis Hutcheson, p. 8; DNB, Hutcheson, Bruce.
14  Porter, The Seven Bruces, pp. 1, 23, 35.
15  DNB, William Bruce; The Dublin banker, Hugh Henry, was one of the trustees of Stewart's wife's fortune and property. It is likely, therefore, that Alexander Stewart had something to do with the appointment of William Bruce as tutor to the banker's son. When Bruce accepted it, his partnership with John Smith was dissolved. Smith continued in business as a bookseller for another twenty years. He announced his retirement in 1758, and held two auctions of his stock, before taking up a completely new career as agent for the Hibernian Silk Warehouse. He died in 1771. (Reid, op. cit., III, pp. 286, 534; Pollard, Dublin's Trade in Books, p. 198)
16  Commercial papers (D 654/B2/1–174). Catalogue of books belonging to Alexander Stewart, (D 654/51/2) (Londonderry papers); Hyde, Rise of Castlereagh, pp. 9–15.
17  Mullin, Julia E., The Presbytery of Coleraine, pp. 27–8.
18  BM, 8 February 1784.
19  Joy MSS, 4, pp. 96–7; [Joy] HC, p. 95.
20  Joy MSS, 4, pp. 100, 103; [Joy] HC, p. 100.

14  FATHERS AND SONS

1  *BNL*, 9 March 1738. 'On Wednesday night last was interred in the Church-yard Mrs Dobbs who died the Tuesday before. At the same time was interred the corpse of the late Mr Samuel Haliday.'
2  James Duchal to Thomas Drennan, 8 March 1738 (D 1759/3B/6).
3  Benn, *History of Belfast*, p. 406, n. 1.
4  Francis Hutcheson to Thomas Drennan, 1 June 1741 (Mic. B/39).
5  Francis Hutcheson to Thomas Drennan, 12 April 1742 (ibid.).
6  Benn, op. cit., pp. 611–16; Maguire, 'Lord Donegall and the Hearts of Steel'.
7  Stewart, *Belfast Royal Academy*, pp. 3, 5, 9.
8  Drennan, 'Character of Alexander Henry Haliday, M.D.', *Fugitive Pieces*, p. 155.
9  Houpt, *Mark Akenside*, pp. 12–13, 71–2.
10  *Charlemont corres.*, II, pp. 193, 214.
11  MM to WD, 7 July 1778 (D 531/31).
12  Alexander Haliday to Lord Charlemont, 2 June 1782 (*Charlemont corres.*, I, pp. 404–5).
13  Lord Charlemont to Alexander Haliday, 6 June 1782 (ibid., p. 406).
14  Alexander Haliday to Lord Charlemont, 7 June 1782 (ibid., p. 407).
15  Porter, *The Seven Bruces*, pp. 35–6; *Belfast Literary Society*, pp. 29–34.
16  William Bruce to Henry Joy, 14 August and 8 September 1782 (Joy MSS, 14).
17  William Bruce to Henry Joy, 9 September 1784 (Joy MSS, 14).
18  Tone, *Autobiography*, I, p. 86.


15  ORELLANA

1  [Joy] HC, pp. 293–6.
2  Magee, J., 'Politics and Politicians, 1750–1850', in *Lecale: A Study in Local History*, p. 92; *BNL*, 4 June 1784.
3  'A Seed of Catholic and Protestant Union, Sown in 1784', signed 'X', *Belfast Monthly Magazine*, July 1812, p. 35.
4  Manuscript notes and memoranda on the Volunteers (PRONI D 531/6/51). I am grateful to Dr D. H. Smyth for drawing my attention to the draft in Drennan's hand.
5  Lecky, *History of Ireland*, II, pp. 394–8.
6  Journal of the Duke of Rutland's tour in the North of Ireland (HMC, 14th Report, III, pp. 419–23).
7  [Joy] HC, pp. 297–8.
8  McDowell, *Irish Public Opinion*, pp. 104–5.
9  ibid., pp. 106–7; [Joy] HC, p. 323; MM to WD, ? September 1784 and 14 October 1784 (D 531/109, 112).
10  William Drennan to William Bruce, 25 September and 30 October 1783 (D 553/15, 16). William Crawford's *History of Ireland* was published in 1783.
11  Correspondence relating to Drennan's illness begins at D 591/84. It is omitted from Chart (ed.), *Drennan Letters*.
12  William Drennan to William Bruce, n.d. (D 553/25).
13  MM to WD, about October 1785 (D 591/170); Owen, *History of Belfast*, p. 19.
14  *Letters of an Irish Helot, signed Orellana*, republished by the Constitution Society

of the City of Dublin (1785); *Letters of Orellana, an Irish Helot, to the Seven Northern Counties not represented in the National Assembly of Delegates held at Dublin, October 1784, for obtaining a more equal representation of the People in the Parliament of Ireland* (1785).

15  *The Oxford Companion to English Literature*, 5th edition (ed. M. Drabble), pp. 81–2. William Drennan to William Bruce, n.d. [1785]: 'The name of Orellana I wished to get rid of as he was a slave that, not being able to accomplish his purpose in raising a mutiny, leaped with his companions into the sea . . .' (D 553/ 36).

16  Drennan, *Orellana*, p. 6.

17  ibid., pp. 7–8.

18  ibid., pp. 17–18.

19  ibid., pp. 28–9.

20  ibid., pp. 35–7.

21  ibid., p. 40.

22  William Drennan to William Bruce, 7 February 1784 (D 553/20).

23  William Drennan to William Bruce, 15 May 1785 (D 553/43).

24  William Drennan to William Bruce, August 1785 (D 553/45).

25  MM to WD, n.d. [1785] (D 553/124).

26  WD to MM, 20 May 1785 (D 553/161).

27  William Drennan to William Bruce, 15 May 1785 (D 531/43).

28  MM to WD, 8 June 1785 (D 591/163).

29  MM to WD, ?June 1785 (D 591/165).

30  WD to MM, August 1785 (D 591/184/185/187A).

31  Alexander Haliday to William Drennan, 10 August 1785 (enclosed with D 591/ 186).

32  WD to MM, 25 August 1785, with copy of Haliday's letter and copy of one from Bruce (D 591/190).

33  'The Gentleman's Epistle' and 'The Lady's Reply' in D 591/192; and see Chart (ed.), *Drennan Letters*, p. 37.

34  WD to MM, n.d. [1785] (D 591/196); MM to WD, n.d. [1785] (D 591/197).

35  D 591/200/201/204; *Les Liaisons Dangereuses*, the novel by Choderlos de Laclos, was published in 1782; WD to MM, n.d. [1786] (D 591/211).

36  WD to MM, n.d. (D 591/216A).


16  'A SKETCH BY RAPHAEL'

1  *BNL*, 28 July 1789; Tone, *Autobiography*, I, p. 39.

2  [Joy] HC, p. 330.

3  ibid., pp. 331–4; Lord Charlemont to Alexander Haliday, 4 December 1789 (*Charlemont corres.*, II, pp. 109–110).

4  Alexander Haliday to Lord Charlemont, 18 February 1790 (ibid., pp. 114–16).

5  Lord Charlemont to Alexander Haliday, 20 and 27 February 1790 (ibid., pp. 116–17).

6  Lord Charlemont to Alexander Haliday, 9 March 1790 (ibid., pp. 118–19).

7  Alexander Haliday to Lord Charlemont, 11 March 1790 (ibid., pp. 119–20).

8  Lord Charlemont to Alexander Haliday, 15 March 1790 (ibid., pp. 120–1).

9  *BNL*, 14 July 1791; [Joy] HC, pp. 348–55.

10 [Joy] HC, pp. 355–7.
11 ibid., p. 357; *BNL*, 4 July 1792.

17 A PLOT FOR THE PEOPLE

1 WD to MM, 1 February 1790 (D 591/289).
2 WD to SM, 3 May 1790 (D 591/290).
3 William Drennan to William Bruce, n.d. [1790] (D 553/70).
4 The portraits may conveniently be compared in MacDermot, *Wolfe Tone*, facing p. 13. Both are reproduced also in Elliott, *Wolfe Tone*, frontispiece and fig. 11. The portrait of Tone in Volunteer uniform is in the National Gallery of Ireland. The corps is unidentified. Since the uniform is dark blue with red facings and silver epaulettes, it cannot be the Belfast First Volunteer Company, of which he was so proud to be a member. (See Van Brock, 'A Proposed Irish Regiment and Standard, 1796' in *IS*, vol. 11, No. 45 [1974] p. 226 and note on plate 5.)
5 WD to SM, 5 February 1791 (D 591/299).
6 Tone, *Autobiography*, I, pp. 28–30, 50.
7 ibid., pp. 50–1.
8 ibid., p. 76.
9 Tone, *An Argument*; MacDermot, op. cit., pp. 80–1; Elliott, *Wolfe Tone*, p. 127, McDowell, *Ireland*, pp. 368.
10 The first part of Paine's *Rights of Man* was published in March 1791, and the second in February 1792 (McDowell, op. cit., p. 352).
11 Tone, *Autobiography*, I, pp. 55–6. The paragraphs which follow are based on my article ' "A Stable, Unseen Power": Dr William Drennan and the Origins of the United Irishmen'.
12 Tone, op. cit., p. 53.
13 ibid., pp. 76–7.
14 ibid., p. 78.
15 Dickson, *Revolt in the North*, pp. 192–4; Stewart, *Seceders in Ireland*, p. 268; McNeill, *Mary Ann McCracken*, pp. 29–30, 48; O'Byrne, *As I Roved Out*, pp. 11–14.
16 McDowell, *Ireland*, pp. 384–5; Dickson, op. cit., pp. 88, 105.
17 Peggy Barclay's Inn (The Franklin Tavern), O'Byrne, op. cit., pp. 39–42; Stewart's Tavern in Crown Entry, ibid., p. 120; Kelburn: William Drennan to William Bruce, ?May 1783 (D 533/44); Witherow, *Memorials*, II, pp. 243–6 and Kernohan, *Rosemary Street Presbyterian Church*, p. 32.
18 Barkley , *A Short History of the Presbyterian Church in Ireland*, p. 37.
19 Fitzhenry, *Henry Joy McCracken*, pp. 51–2.
20 Elliott, op. cit., p. 138.
21 WD to SM, 21 May 1791 (D 591/300).
22 ibid.
23 SM to WD, 2 July 1791 (D 591/302).
24 WD to SM, 3 July 1791 (D 591/303).
25 SM to WD, 9 July 1791 (D 591/304).
26 WD to SM, 11 July 1791 (D 591/305).
27 *Report from the Committee of Secrecy of the House of Commons* (1798), Appendix IV, pp. 86–92.

28 List of toasts in SM's handwriting on letter D 591/303.

29 ibid.

30 For the history of the Catholic Committee see McDowell, op. cit., pp. 186–8.

31 Lecky, III, p. 10.

32 Jacob, *Rise of the United Irishmen*, p. 62.

33 WD to SM, undated but after January 1792 (D 591/312).

34 WD to SM, 10 November 1791 (D 591/311).

35 WD to SM, also 10 November 1791 (D 591/313).

36 In D 591/312 Drennan expresses surprise that 'the societies do not multiply more'; McSkimmin, *Annals of Ulster*, p. 9; MacDermot, op. cit., p. 87.

## 18 THE COMPANY AND THE LODGE

1 *BNL*, 5 February 1896; [Joy] HC, p. 233; Falkiner, *Studies in Irish History*, pp. 1–2.

2 ibid., pp. 3–4.

3 See Benn, *History of Belfast*, p. 349: 'But Orangeism had a different meaning in 1784 from that which has been attached to it in more recent years'. (Benn's *History* was published in 1877.)

4 *BNL*, 29 April 1783.

5 McClelland, 'Orange Lodge No. 257, Belfast', a paper read at Dublin on 13 February 1965. Sketches of individual members.

6 *BNL*, 28 June 1782.

7 McClelland, 'Amyas Griffith', p. 16.

8 For Griffith's career, McClelland, art. cit.

9 ibid., p. 13.

10 A comedy by Susannah Centlivre first published in 1714. McClelland, art. cit., p. 15.

11 ibid., p. 17.

12 Leighton, *History of Freemasonry in Antrim*, pp. 30–2.

13 ibid. p. 32.

14 *UJA*, second series, vol. 9 (1903), pp. 151–6; vol. 10 (1904), pp. 21–5; 69–72; 138–41; 187–91.

15 ibid. St John the Evangelist is celebrated on 27 December, called 'St John's Day in Winter' by Masons to distinguish it from the Festival of St John the Baptist (24 June).

16 Baigent and Leigh, *The Temple and the Lodge*, pp. 339–40.

17 McLynn, *Charles Edward Stuart*, pp. 532–4.

18 Lepper and Crossle, *History of the Grand Lodge*, I, pp. 53–4.

19 Scott, *Francis Hutcheson*, pp. 15, 18; Francis Hutcheson to Thomas Drennan, 5 March 1739: 'I have got on my hands almost the whole paternal care of my old pupil, Lord Kilmarnock's three sons here' (Mic. 39/B); Robbins, 'When it is that colonies may turn independent', opposite p. 224.

20 Jacob, *Newtonians and the English Revolution*, pp. 219–22. And see Sullivan, *Toland and the Deist Controversy*, pp. 301–4.

21 Rogers, *Irish Volunteers and Catholic Emancipation*, pp. 61–2, 288–9.

22 McClelland, 'Freemasonry', p. 18; Black, 'Volunteer Portraits', plate 17, facing p. 181.

23 Waite (ed.), *A New Encyclopedia of Freemasonry*, I, p. 113.
24 Paterson, 'The Volunteer Companies of Ulster', *IS*, nos. 28, 29, 30, 31, 32, *passim*.
25 Millin, *Sidelights on Belfast History*, p. 171; Benjamin Franklin to William Franklin, 30 January 1772 (*Franklin Papers*, vol. 19, p. 49).
26 Baigent and Leigh, op. cit., pp. 315–16.
27 Curran, W. H., *Life of J. P. Curran*, I, pp. 121–5.
28 Fortescue, J., *Correspondence of George III*, V, p. 24. Martha Harris Johnson (*sic*) was actually Franklin's niece.
29 Baigent and Leigh, op. cit., p. 319.
30 See, for example, the last line of 'The Walk on the Bason at Newry': 'And prove all your rules by the LINE and the SQUARE' (*Fugitive Pieces*, p. 59).
31 Roberts, *Mythology of the Secret Societies*, pp. 133–49.
32 Tone, *Autobiography*, I, p. 113.

19 THE LAST CONVENTION

1 *BNL*, 31 January 1792; *NS*, 26 and 29 January 1792; [Joy] HC, pp. 363–6; [Joy and Bruce], *Belfast Politics*, pp. 6–22.
2 WD to SM, 7 December 1791 (D 591/316).
3 Tone, *Autobiography*, I, pp. 97–8; Elliott, *Wolfe Tone*, pp. 172–7. Mr Hutton was Russell's nickname for Tone.
4 Tone, op. cit., p. 98.
5 ibid., p. 99.
6 Elliott, op. cit., p. 176.
7 ibid.
8 [Joy] HC, p. 383; MM to WD, 1 November 1792: 'I have been all this day singing *Over the Hills and Far Away*, and Prussia and Brunswick skipping before my eyes' (D 591/347A).
9 *BNL*, 14 December 1792.
10 McDowell, *Ireland*, pp. 431–4; WD to MM, 25 November 1792 (D 531/351). For the uniform of the National Guard see Black, 'Volunteer Portraits', opposite p. 183.
11 *BNL*, 28 December 1792; [Joy and Bruce], op. cit., p. 104.
12 WD to SM, 31 January 1793 (D 591/381); MM to WD, 28 October 1791 (D 591/345); MM to WD, 5 January 1793 (D 591/371).
13 'The Church of the Volunteers, Dungannon', *UJA* (second series), I (1894), pp. 48–50; *NS*, 20 February 1793.
14 Samuel Neilson to William Drennan, 17 February 1793 (D 591/390A).
15 *BNL*, 11 December 1792; McSkimmin, *Annals of Ulster*, p. 24.
16 McClelland, 'Freemasonry', pp. 21–2; McSkimmin, op. cit., p. 24.
17 McClelland, art. cit., p. 22.
18 MM to WD, 5 January 1793 (D 531/371).

AFTERWORD

1 Hazlitt, W., 'On Coffee-House Politicians', *Table Talk* (Everyman Library), p. 191, n. 1; Hazlitt's father, see Jones, *Hazlitt*, pp. 3–4; for an interesting extended

treatment of Hazlitt's relationship with his father, see Kinnaird, *William Hazlitt*, chapter 1, 'Puritan fathers, Unitarian sons', pp. 1–36.

2 Chart (ed.), *Introduction to the Drennan Letters*, p. viii.

3 Craig, *The Volunteer Earl*, p. 243.

4 Strain, *Belfast and its Charitable Society*, p. 252.

5 MM to WD, 3 June 1795 (D 531/557).

6 Richard Aldington to Lawrence Durrell, 1 February 1959 (MacNiven and Moore (eds.), *Literary Lifelines*, p. 78). A poem by one of William Drennan's sons, 'The Battle of Beal-an-ath Buidh', surfaces incongruously in Durrell's novel *Balthazar* (pp. 136–7) as part of Scobie's repertoire of ballads. Aldington was able to identify the source.

# Sources and Bibliography

A. Unpublished

*Public Record Office of Northern Ireland*

| | |
|---|---|
| Black correspondence | D 719 |
| Bruce papers | T 1072 |
| Caldwell MSS | D 1518 |
| Drennan correspondence | D 591 |
| | T 765 (typescript) |
| Drennan-Bruce correspondence | D 553 |
| Drennan papers (miscellaneous) | D 531 |
| Presbytery of Antrim minutes | T 1053 |
| Stewart MSS (transcriptions of letters made by the Rev. J. D. Stewart) | D 1759 |
| Transcripts of State papers, Ireland | T 659 |
| Transcripts of wills | T 403 |

*The Linen Hall Library, Belfast*

| | |
|---|---|
| Joy MSS | TD 2777 |

*The Queen's University Library, Belfast*

| | |
|---|---|
| Letters of Francis Hutcheson to Thomas Drennan | Mic.B/29 |

*Edinburgh University Library, Edinburgh*

| | |
|---|---|
| Ane Apology for the Northern Prebyterians in Ireland (1722) by C. M. [Rev. Charles Masterton] | La III 263 |
| Black MSS | Gen. 874/IV/V |
| Class cards, etc., of William Drennan as an undergraduate | Dc 4.95/10 (1–15) |
| Minute Book of the Speculative Society, vol. 2 (microfilm) | Mic M 1076–7 |

B. Published

PUBLISHED COLLECTIONS OF CORRESPONDENCE

*Beresford correspondence* (2 vols.) Letters of John Beresford, London, 1854

*Castlereagh correspondence*, Memoirs and correspondence of Viscount Castlereagh (ed. C. Stewart, 2nd Marquis of Londonderry), London, 1849

*Charlemont correspondence* (Historical Manuscripts Commission, XIIth Report, part X, and XIIIth Report, part VIII), London, 1891 and 1894

*Drennan Letters, 1776–1819* (ed. D. A. Chart), Belfast, 1931

Manuscripts of M. L. S. Clements (Molesworth papers) (Historical Manuscripts Commission, VIIIth Report), London, 1913
*Rutland correspondence* (Historical Manuscripts Commission, XIVth Report, part I), London, 1894
Wesley, J., *The Journal of the Rev. John Wesley, A.M.* (ed. N. Curnock), 8 vols., London, n.d.
– *The Letters of the Rev. John Wesley, A.M.* (ed. J. Telford), 8 vols., London, 1931

WORKS OF REFERENCE
*The Dictionary of American Biography*
*The Dictionary of National Biography*
*Fasti of the Irish Presbyterian Church in Ireland, 1613–1840* (ed. S. J. McConnell and J. McConnell), Belfast, 1951
*History of Congregations of the Presbyterian Church in Ireland, 1610–1982* (ed. W. D. Bailie), Belfast, 1982
*History of Congregations of the Presbyterian Church in Ireland and Biographical Notes of Eminent Presbyterian Ministers and Laymen* (ed. W. D. Killen), Belfast, 1886
*Irish Historical Documents, 1172–1922* (ed. E. Curtis and R. B. McDowell,), London, 1943
*Irish Oil Paintings*. A Catalogue of the Permanent Collection in the Ulster Museum (compiled by Eileen Black),          Belfast, 1991
*A New Encyclopedia of Freemasonry*, (ed. A. E. Waite) (2 vols.), London, n.d.
*Records of the General Synod of Ulster, 1691–1820*, (3 vols.), Belfast, 1890–8

CONTEMPORARY WORKS
Adair, P., *A True Narrative of the Rise and Progress of the Presbyterian Government in the North of Ireland*, Belfast and Edinburgh, 1866
Crombie, J., *A Sermon preached before the United Company of Belfast Volunteers*, Belfast, 1779
Dickson, W. S., *A Narrative of the Confinement and Exile of the Rev. William Steel Dickson, D.D.*, Belfast, 1812
Drennan, W., *Letters of Orellana, an Irish Helot, to the seven northern counties not represented in the National Assembly of delegates held at Dublin, October 1785*, Dublin, 1785
Duchal, J., *Sermon on the death of the late Rev John Abernethy*, Belfast, 1741
Haliday, S., *Reasons against the imposition of Subscription to the Westminster Confession of Faith*, Belfast, 1724
[Joy, H.], *Historical Collections relative to the town of Belfast*, Belfast, 1817
[Joy, H. and Bruce, W.], *Belfast Politics*, Belfast, 1794
Molyneux, W., *The Case of Ireland's being bound by Acts of Parliament in England, stated*, Dublin, 1698
[Smith, J. and Arbuckle, J.], *A Short Account of the Late Treatment of the Students of the University of G . . . w.*, Dublin, 1722
Tone, T. W., *An Argument on Behalf of the Catholics of Ireland*, Dublin, 1791
– *Autobiography* (ed. R. B. O'Brien) (2 vols.), Dublin, 1913

NEWSPAPERS AND PERIODICALS
*Belfast Mercury*
*Belfast Monthly Magazine*
*Belfast Newsletter*
*Belfast Telegraph*
*Northern Star*


SECONDARY AUTHORITIES
Akenson, D. H., *Between Two Revolutions: Islandmagee, Co. Antrim, 1798–1920*, Ontario, 1979
Baigent, M. and Leigh, M., *The Temple and the Lodge*, London, 1989
Baker, H., *William Hazlitt*, Cambridge, Mass. and London, 1961
Bardon, J., *Belfast: An Illustrated History*, Belfast, 1982
Barkley, J. M., *A Short History of the Presbyterian Church in Ireland*, Belfast, 1959
Bartlett, T. and Hayton, D. W., *Penal Era and Golden Age: Essays in Irish History, 1690–1800*, Belfast, 1979
Beckett, J. C., *Protestant Dissent in Ireland, 1687–1780*, London, 1948
– *The Making of Modern Ireland*, London, 1965
– *Confrontations*, London, 1972
– *The Anglo-Irish Tradition*, London, 1976
Beckett, J. C. and Glasscock, R. E., *Belfast: The Origin and Growth of an Industrial City*, London, 1967
*Belfast Literary Society, 1801–1901* (centennial volume), Belfast, 1902
Benn, G., *A History of the Town of Belfast*, Belfast, 1877
Bigger, J. F. J., *The Two Abernethyes*, Belfast, 1919
Bolton, C. K., *Scotch-Irish Pioneers in Ulster and America*, Boston, Mass., 1910
Bossy, J. and Jupp, P. J. (eds.), *Essays presented to Michael Roberts*, Belfast, 1986
Brett, R. L., *The Third Earl of Shaftesbury*, London, 1951
Childe-Pemberton, W. S., *The Earl-Bishop. The Life of Frederick Hervey, Bishop of Derry and Earl of Bristol* (3 vols.), London, 1924
Colles, R., *The History of Ulster from the Earliest Times to the Present Day* (4 vols.), London, 1919–20
Coughlin, R. J., *Napper Tandy*, London, 1976
Cousin, V., *La Philosophie Ecossaise*
Coutts, J., *A History of the University of Glasgow*, Glasgow, 1909
Craig, M. J., *The Volunteer Earl*, London, 1948
Curran, W. H., *The Life of John Philpot Curran* (2 vols.), London, 1819
Dickson, C., *Revolt in the North: Antrim and Down in 1798*, Dublin, 1960
Dickson, R. J., *Ulster Emigration to Colonial America, 1718–1775*, London, 1966
D'Israeli, I., *Calamities of Authors* (2 vols.), London, 1812
Dobrée, B., *English Literature in the Early Eighteenth Century*, Oxford, 1959
Doyle, D. N., *Ireland, Irishmen and Revolutionary America*, Dublin and Cork, 1981
Elliott, M., *Partners in Revolution: The United Irishmen and France*, New Haven, Conn., and London, 1982
– *Wolfe Tone: Prophet of Irish Independence*, New Haven, Conn., and London, 1989
Falkiner, C. L., *Essays Relating to Ireland*, London, 1909
– *Studies in Irish History and Biography*, London, 1902
Fisher, J. R., *The End of the Irish Parliament*, London, 1911

Fitzhenry, E. C., *Henry Joy McCracken*, Dublin and London, 1936
Fitzpatrick, R., *God's Frontiersmen: The Scots-Irish Epic*, London, 1989
Fowler, T., *Shaftesbury and Hutcheson*, London, 1882
Frey, J. (ed.), *Lecale: A Study of Local History*, Belfast, 1970
Gebbie, J. H., *Ardstraw: The Historical Survey of a Parish, 1600–1900*, Omagh, 1968
Gilbert, J., *A History of Dublin* (3 vols.), London, 1874
Goodwin, A., *The Friends of Liberty*, London, 1979
Green, E. R. R. (ed.), *Essays in Scotch-Irish History*, London, 1969
Gwynn, S., *Henry Grattan and His Times*, Dublin, 1939
Hardy, F., *Memoirs of the Political and Private Life of James Caulfeild, Earl of Charlemont* (2 vols.), London, 1812
Holmes, F., *Our Presbyterian Heritage*, Belfast, 1985
Houpt, C. T., *Mark Akenside: A Biographical and Critical Study*, New York, 1944
Huddleston, F. G., *Gentleman Johnny Burgoyne*, London, 1928
Hutchison, W. R., *Tyrone Precinct: A History of the Plantation Settlement of Dungannon and Mountjoy to Modern Times*, Belfast, 1951
Hyde, H. M., *The Rise of Castlereagh*, London, 1933
– *The Londonderrys*, London, 1979
Irwin, C. H., *A History of Presbyterianism in Dublin and the South and West of Ireland*, London, 1890
Jacob, M. C., *The Radical Enlightenment*, London, 1981
– *The Newtonians and the English Revolution*, Hassocks, 1976
Jacob, R., *The Rise of the United Irishmen*, Dublin, 1936
Johnston, E. M., *Great Britain and Ireland, 1760–1800. A Study in Political Administration*, Edinburgh, 1963
– *Eighteenth-Century Ireland*, Dublin, 1974.
Jones, S., *Hazlitt: A Life*, Oxford, 1989
Jupp, P., *Lord Grenville, 1759–1834*, Oxford, 1985
Kernohan, J. W., *Rosemary Street Presbyterian Church*, Belfast, 1923
Killen, J., *A History of the Linen Hall Library, 1788–1988*, Belfast, 1990
Killen, W. D., *History of Congregations of the Presbyterian Church in Ireland*, Belfast and Edinburgh, 1886
Kinnaird, J., *William Hazlitt, Critic of Power*, New York, 1978
Knoop, D. and Jones, G. P., *The Genesis of Freemasonry*, Manchester, 1947
Latimer, W. T. *A History of the Irish Presbyterians*, Belfast and Edinburgh, 1893
Lecky, W. E. H., *A History of Ireland in the Eighteenth Century* (5 vols.), London, 1892
Leighton, S., *A History of Freemasonry in the Province of Antrim*, Belfast, 1938
Lepper, J. H. and Crossle, P., *A History of the Grand Lodge of Free and Accepted Masons of Ireland* (2 vols.), Dublin, 1925
McCreery, A., *The Presbyterian Ministers of Killyleagh*, Belfast, 1875.
MacDermot, F., *Theobald Wolfe Tone: A Biographical Study*, London, 1939
McDowell, R. B., *Irish Public Opinion, 1750–1800*, London, 1944
– *Ireland in the Age of Imperialism and Revolution*, Oxford, 1979
Mackie, J. D., *The University of Glasgow: A Short History, 1451–1951*, Glasgow, 1954
McLynn, F., *Charles Edward Stuart*, London and New York, 1988
McNeice, J. F., *Carrickfergus and its Contacts*, London and Belfast, 1928

McNeill, M., *The Life and Times of Mary Ann McCracken, 1770–1866: A Belfast Panorama*, Dublin, 1960

MacNevin, T., *The History of the Volunteers of 1782*, Dublin, 1845

McNiven, I. S., and Moore, H. T., *Literary Lifelines: The Richard Aldington–Lawrence Durrell Correspondence*, New York, 1981

McSkimmin, J., *Annals of Ulster, or Ireland Fifty Years Ago*, Belfast, 1849

– *A History of Carrickfergus*, Belfast, 1811

Madden, R. R., *The United Irishmen* (3 series, 7 vols.), London, 1842–5

Millin, S. S., *Sidelights on Belfast History*, London and Belfast, 1932

– *Additional Sidelights on Belfast History*, London and Belfast, 1938

– *A History of the Second Congregation of Protestant Dissenters in Belfast*, Belfast, 1900

Moody, T. W. and Vaughan, W. E. (eds.), *A New History of Ireland*, vol. IV: *Eighteenth-Century Ireland 1691–1800*, Oxford, 1986

Moore, T., *A History of the First Belfast Presbyterian Church, 1644–1983*, Belfast, 1983

Morison, S. E., *John Paul Jones: A Sailor's Biography*, London, 1959

Mullin, J. E., *The Presbytery of Coleraine*, Belfast, 1979

Murray, D., *Memories of the Old College of Glasgow*, Glasgow, 1927

Nicolson, H., *The Desire to Please*, London, 1943

O'Byrne, C., *As I Roved Out: A Book of the North*, Belfast, 1946

Owen, D. J., *A History of Belfast*, Belfast, 1921

Pollard, M., *Dublin's Trade in Books, 1550–1800*, Oxford, 1989

Porter, C., *The Seven Bruces*, Belfast, 1885

Reid, J. S., *A History of the Presbyterian Church in Ireland* (3 vols.), London, 1867

Robbins, C., *The Eighteenth-Century Commonwealthman*, Cambridge, Mass., 1959

Roberts, J. M., *The Mythology of the Secret Societies*, London, 1972

Rogers, P., *The Irish Volunteers and Catholic Emancipation, 1778–93*, London, 1934

Scott, W. R., *Francis Hutcheson: His Life, Teaching and Position in the History of Philosophy*, Cambridge, 1900

Sibbett, R. M., *On the Shining Bann: Records of an Ulster Manor*, Belfast, 1928

Simms, J. G., *William Molyneux*, London, 1982

Smithers, P., *Life of Joseph Addison*, Oxford, 1968

Sprague, W. B., *Annals of the American Pulpit* (3 vols.), New York, 1868

Stevenson, J., *Two Centuries of Life in Down*, Belfast, 1920

Stewart, A. T. Q., *Belfast Royal Academy: The First Century 1785–1885*, Belfast, 1985

Stewart, D., *The Seceders in Ireland*, Belfast, 1950

Stuart, J., *Historical Memoirs of the City of Armagh*, Newry, 1819

Strain, R. W. M., *Belfast and its Charitable Society*, Oxford, 1961

Sullivan, R. E., *John Toland and the Deist Controversy*, Cambridge, Mass. and London.

Van Doren, C., *Benjamin Franklin*, London, 1938

Venturi, F., *Utopia and Reform in the Enlightenment*, Cambridge, 1971

Voitle, R., *The Third Earl of Shaftesbury, 1671–1713*, Baton Rouge, Louisiana, and London, 1984

Wall, M., *The Penal Laws, 1691–1760*, Dublin, 1961

Wilbur, E. M., *A History of Unitarianism*, Cambridge, Mass., 1952

Williams, T. D., *Secret Societies in Ireland*, Dublin and New York, 1973

Wilton-Ely, J., *The Mind and Art of Piranesi*, London, 1978

Witherow, T., *Historical and Literary Memorials of Presbyterianism in Ireland* (2 vols.), London and Belfast, 1879

Worden, A. B., *Edmund Ludlow's 'Voyce from the Watchtower'* Part Five (Camden Society, series 4, vol. 21), Cambridge, 1985

Young, R. M., *Historical Notices of Old Belfast and its Vicinity*, Belfast, 1896

ARTICLES

Bailie, W. D., 'William Steel Dickson, D.D. (1774–1824)', *Irish Booklore*, vol. 2, no. 2 (1976), pp. 239–67.

Beresford, M., 'François Thurot and the French Attack on Carrickfergus, 1759–60,' *IS*, vol. 10, no. 41 (1972), pp. 255–74.

Bigger, F. J., 'The Northern Star', *UJA*, 2nd series, vol. 1 (1895), pp. 33–5.
'The French Prisoners in Belfast, 1759–1763'. Notes by Isaac W. Ward, *UJA*, 2nd series, vol. 9 (1903), pp. 151–6; vol. 10 (1904): pp. 21–5, 69–72, 138–41, 187–91.

Black, E., 'Volunteer Portraits in the Ulster Museum, Belfast', *IS*, vol. 13, no. 52 (1991), pp. 181–4.

Elliott, M., 'The Origin and Transformation of Early Irish Republicanism', *International Review of Social History*, XXIII (1978), pp. 405–28.

Ferguson, K. P., 'The Volunteer Movement and the Government, 1778–1793', *IS*, vol. 13, no. 52 (1978 and 1979), pp. 208–16.

Gibbon, P., 'The Origins of the Orange Order and the United Irishmen', *Economy and Society*, I (1972), pp. 135–63.

Jupp, P. J., 'Earl Temple's Viceroyalty and the Renunciation Question, 1782–3', *IHS*, vol. 17, no. 68 (1971), pp. 499–520.

Kennedy, D., 'Thurot's Landing at Carrickfergus', *IS*, vol. 6, no. 24, pp. 149–53.

MacCarthy Mor, The, 'The Fergusons of Belfast', *Familia*, vol. 2, no. 2 (1989), pp. 15–21.

McClelland, A., 'Thomas Ledlie Birch, United Irishman', *Proceedings of the Belfast Natural History and Philosophical Society*, 7 (1965), pp. 24–35.

– 'Amyas Griffith', *Irish Booklore*, vol. 2, no. 1 (1972), pp. 7–21.
'A History of Saintfield and District' (Anderson Trust lecture), 1981.

– 'Some Aspects of Freemasonry in the late 18th and early 19th Century', (September 1958) and 'Orange Lodge No. 257, Belfast' (February 1965) [Copies of papers read to the Lodge of Research].

Maguire, W. A., 'Lord Donegall and the Hearts of Steel', *IHS*, vol. 21, no. 84 (1979), pp. 371–6.

Morrow, A., 'The Rev. Samuel Barber, A.M., and the Rathfriland Volunteers', *UJA* 2nd series, vol. 14 (1908), pp. 105–19

Norton, D. F., 'Francis Hutcheson in America', *Studies in Voltaire and the Eighteenth Century*, 154 (1976), pp. 1547–68

O'Snodaigh, P., 'Some Police and Military Aspects of the Irish Volunteers', *IS*, vol. 13, no. 52 (1978 and 1979), pp. 217–29.

Paterson, T. G. F., 'The Volunteer Companies of Ulster, 1778–1793', *IS*, vol. 7, no. 27 (1965), pp. 90–116, no. 28 (1966), pp. 204–30, no. 29 (1966), pp. 308–12; vol. 8, no. 30 (1967), pp. 23–32, no. 31 (1967), pp. 92–7, no. 32 (1968), pp. 210–17.

Robbins, C., 'When it is that colonies may turn independent', *William and Mary Quarterly*, 3rd series, 11 (1954), pp. 214–51.

Scott, W. F., 'James Arbuckle and his relation to the Molesworth-Shaftesbury School', *Mind* (new series) vol. 8 (1899), pp. 194–215.

Simms, J. G., 'The Making of a Penal Law, 1703–4', *IHS*, vol. 12, no. 3, pp. 105–18.

'John Toland – a Donegal Heretic', *IHS*, vol. 16, no. 63 (1969), pp. 304–20.

Smyth, P. D. H., ' "Our Cloud-Cap't Grenadiers": The Volunteers as a military force', *IS*, vol. 13, no. 52 (1978 and 1979) pp. 185–207.

— 'The Volunteers and Parliament, 1779–84', in *Penal Era and Golden Age* (ed. Bartlett, T. and Hayton, D. W.), pp. 113–36.

Stewart A. T. Q., ' "A Stable Unseen Power": Dr William Drennan and the Origins of the United Irishmen', in *Essays presented to Michael Roberts* (ed. Bossy, J. and Jupp, P.), pp. 80–92.

Stewart, M. A., 'John Smith and the Molesworth Circle', *Eighteenth-century Ireland*, vol. 2 (1987), pp. 89–102.

Van Brock, F. W., 'A Proposed Irish Regiment and Standard, 1796', *IS*, vol. 11, no. 45 (1974), pp. 226–33.

Wall, M., 'The United Irish Movement', *Historical Studies*, 5 (1965), pp. 122–40.

# THE DRENNAN FAMILY

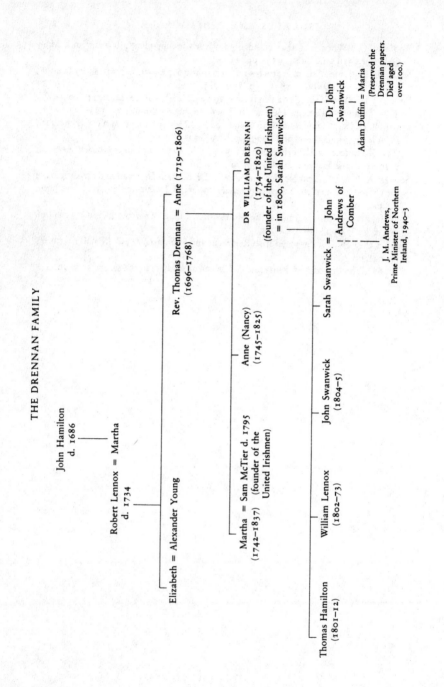

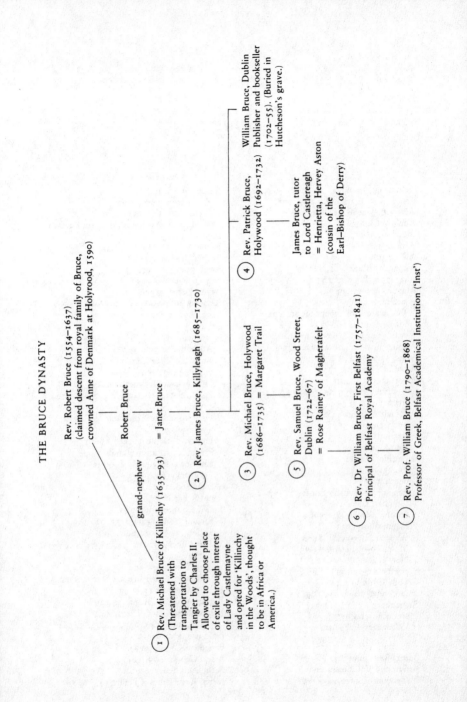

THE BRUCE DYNASTY

Rev. Robert Bruce (1554–1637)
(claimed descent from royal family of Bruce,
crowned Anne of Denmark at Holyrood, 1590)

Robert Bruce
= Janet Bruce

grand-nephew

① Rev. Michael Bruce of Killinchy (1635–93)
(Threatened with transportation to Tangier by Charles II. Allowed to choose place of exile through interest of Lady Castlemayne and opted for 'Killinchy in the Woods', thought to be in Africa or America.)

② Rev. James Bruce, Killyleagh (1685–1730)

③ Rev. Michael Bruce, Holywood (1686–1735) = Margaret Trail

④ Rev. Patrick Bruce, Holywood (1692–1732)

William Bruce, Dublin Publisher and bookseller (1702–55). (Buried in Hutcheson's grave.)

James Bruce, tutor to Lord Castlereagh = Henrietta, Hervey Aston (cousin of the Earl-Bishop of Derry)

⑤ Rev. Samuel Bruce, Wood Street, Dublin (1722–67) = Rose Rainey of Magherafelt

⑥ Rev. Dr William Bruce, First Belfast (1757–1841) Principal of Belfast Royal Academy

⑦ Rev. Prof. William Bruce (1790–1868) Professor of Greek, Belfast Academical Institution ('Inst')

# Index